A GROOM WITH A VIEW

What I Learned Helping My Wife Plan Our Wedding

Sam Ofman

Copyright © 2021 Samuel Ofman

All rights reserved

Some of the names in this book have been altered to protect the privacy of individuals.

No part of this book may be reproduced, or stored in a retrieval system, or transmitted in any form or by any means, electronic, mechanical, photocopying, recording, or otherwise, without express written permission of the publisher.

ISBN-13: 9798519781459
ISBN-10: 1477123456

Cover design by: Sam_designs1
Library of Congress Control Number: 2018675309
Printed in the United States of America

To Heine

*I hope you'll still love me even if
you don't love this book*

CONTENTS

Title Page

Copyright

Dedication

We Are Gathered Here Today ... 1

A Short Story[3]

Yellow Diamonds are a Girl's Best Friend ... 7

When Heine Met Sammy ... 16

Love is a Burning Thing, and it Makes an Engagement Ring ... 22

And on That Farm There Was a Ring, H-E-I-N-E ... 49

The (Available) Venue of Our Dreams ... 73

You Don't Even Like Him: The Unwritten Rules of the Invite List ... 113

The Best Man and the Most Mediocre Tacos ... 121

On the Art of Bachelor Parties in the Age of Airbnb ... 127

Clothes Make the Youth Large Man ... 133

Other People's Weddings ... 143

Wedding Planning is Bigger in Texas ... 149

My Dream Wedding	174
Buying a Suit: Act Two	175
A 45 Minute Commute on the Information Superhighway	183
You Are Cordially Invited to Read This Chapter	193
Submitted for Your Approval	207
A Picture's Worth a Thousand Words (and Dollars)	212
Lights, Camera, Distraction	215
A Groom with a View	219
Shuttles, Not Space Shuttles	227
Cha Cha Real Smooth	233
No Pastor in our Pasture	243
But Wait, There's More!	257
Texas Wedding!	280
Practice Makes Perfect for Each Other	285
Dinner and Revelry to Follow	305
Happily Ever Afterword	312
Acknowledgements	329
About The Author	331

WE ARE GATHERED HERE TODAY

I never wanted to *get* married. I wanted to *be* married.

What a dream, to *be* married. I'd picture being married and conjure images of my girlfriend, Alex, and I sinking into the center cushion of an old couch, shoulder to shoulder with our feet propped on the coffee table, steam rising from mugs of cocoa clutched in our ringed fingers.

Being married, it turns out, isn't anything like that. A cozy evening on the couch as a married couple features my wife in Position A, lying perpendicular to the television, the dog staking claim to as much surface area as she can reach, and me making do with any unoccupied corner of the upholstery. We never drink hot cocoa.

Still, my dream of being married translated to reality in that, besides a lack of hot beverages and shoulder adjacency, being married meant being loved. It meant being home.

What a nightmare, to *get* married. Back in its nascent stages, when the idea of marriage was just a twinkle in my eye (reflected by the diamond in Alex's imagination), I had no idea what I was in for. If being married is a cozy night on the couch, getting married is moving the couch up four flights of stairs.

I'm not the first guy to joke about eloping or skipping the wedding in favor of an appointment at the courthouse. Those methods are just as effective and far more efficient than planning a big wedding, but getting married isn't about finding the least expensive, most cash-flow friendly means to tie the knot. Getting married is about researching a variety of twine, rope, and yarn, sniffing out scams from shoelace vendors, and ensuring that the knot you tie matches the accent color of the bridesmaid accessories. It's about making your wife happy, even when she insists on hiring a costumed chauffeur to drive you from the reception to the hotel in a 1949 Plymouth at a cost of $27 per minute.[1][2]

So I didn't want to *get* married. That doesn't make me a soulless monster, void of emotion and romance; I just couldn't trick myself into thinking the wedding planning process would be worth the time, effort, and money it demanded. If that makes me the bad guy, so be it. My wife and I both sleep well knowing I'm in the doghouse for pinching pennies rather than waitresses.

It turns out you don't need to be married to subscribe to the "happy wife, happy life" mentality. When Alex is happy, I'm happy, so when she wanted to get married I was with her every step of the way. The endgame was to be happily married, and the only way to get there was to marry happily.

This is the story of how we did it.

Full disclosure: I'm not an expert on weddings and marriage. The existence of such people is a paradox. Expertise requires experience, and to gain experience with weddings requires marrying more than once. Ergo, wedding experts stink at marriage. Luckily, I'm a novice. I've had one wedding and, like a newborn, I express my marriage's age in months.

So why read this book? For one, you've already started, and you aren't a quitter. If you picked this up as the first step on the path to overcoming a fear of commitment, I implore you to get through more than two pages.

This isn't a How to Get Married book. It's a How Two Got Married book. Think of this less as a guide to planning a wedding and more as a glimpse into the strange, schmaltzy, and expensive industry that our society constructed to profit from two peoples' love. I'll tell you how I proposed and what insights I gained from the experience, but I didn't interview any professional proposal planners. I'll make fun of Wedding Wire's stamp of approval but, in retrospect, I never went to their website to find out what it means. I didn't undergo painstaking research. I took notes during my painstaking experiences.

Whether you're thinking of buying a ring, stuck on which cliché to include in your vows, celebrating your diamond anniversary, or happen to be a member of my immediate family, there's something here for you. If you aren't in any of those groups, I still recommend giving this book a shot. After all, even muggles find value in the Harry Potter franchise.

I now pronounce you reader and book.
You may turn the page.

A SHORT STORY[3]

The flash lasted no more than ten seconds. White light filled my bedroom. I woke, scrambled into a sitting position and shielded my eyes in the crook of my elbow until the sensation passed. Alex, my girlfriend, was in Miami on a work trip that night, leaving me with only the dog to turn to in the immediate aftermath to ensure my sanity.

"Did you see that?" I asked. I look back and imagine that if our English springer spaniel had said, "No, go back to sleep," I'd have listened and thought nothing of it. That's the danger of losing your mind. Instead, Mona remained motionless on the foot of bed. Too motionless.

I rolled across the blankets and switched on the lamp, conceding to the adrenaline in my bloodstream that sleep had been eighty-sixed from the night's menu. I discovered a man sitting on the pink upholstered stool in front of Alex's vanity. A naked man with four legs, a pot belly, and arms so thin and cylindrical they could have been cardboard paper towel rolls. He had a pleasant face, round and handsome in an ordinary, symmetrical way. He wore his dark hair in a short bowl cut, like a helmet. I say a man, but he lacked certain defining equipment of manhood.

"Who is this?" He said, staring at a photograph of Alex and I from a trip we took to the Dominican Republic.

"My girlfriend." I couldn't believe I spoke at all, let alone answered him as though none of the preceding 30 seconds had transpired.

"Girl...friend..." He sounded out the word, staring down at the 4x6 framed image of us in our swimsuits, glistening blue water behind us, sunglasses hiding our faces.

I stared at his legs, eerily calm considering the flash, the intruder, and the fact that my dog appeared paralyzed. I thought of the first night in the dorm with my old college roommate, only this guy wasn't half as strange.

"Girlfriend," he repeated.

"Well, sort of." I took stock of the room. Nothing had changed in my world other than the frozen dog and the unusual visitor examining my beach trip souvenir. "We're sort of past that stage. We'll get married in the next couple years."

"Married?" He extended his interior legs and crossed them at the ankles on the floor, positioning the outer pair atop them in a cross-legged position. Alex's makeup brushes, hair pins, and various gels and creams littered the vanity behind him.

"Yeah, we'll get married. We'll have a wedding."

"Wed...ding." Whatever this guy was, he struggled with polysyllabic words.

"Who are you?" I asked, but he only stared at the photograph. Mona's eyes darted back and forth, but her body remained fixed on the foot of the bed. "Do you mind lifting the curse from my dog?"

He snapped his fingers and Mona leapt from the bed and scurried out the door.

"I am Brad. I have been sent here to learn of Earth's idiosyncrasies, its eccentricities, and the customs that separate men from other intelligent beings." He released the photograph and it floated back to its home above the dresser. "You will harbor me and teach me these unfamiliar ways. You can start with this 'wedding' you speak of."

"Brad, my man," I told him. "If you're still here when I wake up and it turns out I'm not crazy, you got a deal. Hell, if you stick around long enough I can *show* you what it means to get married."

I flipped the lamp off and closed my eyes. Brad didn't move an inch.

YELLOW DIAMONDS ARE A GIRL'S BEST FRIEND

Brad took up residence in our guest room. The morning after the flash I found him on the couch engaged in a staring contest with Mona. She has a tendency to hold a human's gaze as though paralyzed by alien forces, even when she's not. They'd been at it for hours. I later learned that Brad doesn't sleep.

At first, harboring a four-legged alien and sitting with it each night explaining concepts like pet ownership, exercise, empty calories, and other basic tenets of being a human wore me out. But after the first couple of weeks it became the new normal. Brad was a quick learner, and sometimes I'd forget how little he understood about society. He'd impress me with his immediate grasp of heliocentrism and humanity's struggle to discover our place in the world, then two minutes later he'd interrupt to ask, "What do you mean by 'iced cream'?"

Keeping him a secret didn't pose as much of a challenge as you'd expect. Brad has the ability to stop time and make himself invisible. It's entirely possible that I'm crazy. Nobody can validate Brad's existence. When Alex goes into the guest room she sees it as the underutilized, needlessly clean room where we store the type of crap that humans store. You'd be amazed how much of your stuff you'd throw away if you had to justify its existence to an alien.[4] Brad loves the idea of garbage and the process of putting it out for someone to remove. I'm yet to get into the details of landfills and environmental concerns. I told him how my big brother would tease me growing up and Brad asked why I hadn't simply put my brother in the garbage and had him removed. Aliens say the darndest things.

In the first six weeks after the flash, Brad and I developed a nice routine. He passed his day in the guest room, I spent my day in the carousel of work, chores, meals, and spending time with Alex. Everything was normal, except when Brad froze my surroundings and I presented an intergalactic night school lecture.

His world didn't have relationships the way ours does. His species had no families, no friends, and no lifelong mates. As a result, he found marriage, and especially weddings, endlessly fascinating. Maybe that was because it was the first concept I mentioned after the flash. Maybe it was because no other alien culture or species he'd encountered had a ritual resembling a human wedding. Maybe it was because each time we'd talk about it, we'd discover that even though I was experiencing the phenomenon in real time, I was every bit as mystified as he was.

People give me a hard time about my phone. It's an iPhone 5[5] and it's lived in my pants pocket for longer than Alex and I have been together. Like the steady and imperceptible force of continental drift on the surface of the Earth, I've witnessed the gradual power of planned obsolescence play out on the surface of my palm. My phone is in the same life stage as my father. Watching the Internet search bar crawl across the screen or waiting for an app to reinstall is no different than waiting on my dad as he racks his brain to recall the name of my childhood next door neighbor. "I know this...God damnit, my mind is a sieve." He'll get there eventually, and so will my search results. Both my father and my phone have taught me a lot in life and hold substantial sentimental value, so I'm happy to extend them the patience they deserve.

It was my old phone, still vibrating like a phone half its age, that alerted me to my impending nuptials. The night Brad arrived I received a text from Alex with a link to a custom jeweler's website.

With this subtle hint, our odyssey began.

Alex's coworker referred her to the jeweler, and the jeweler happened to have a studio in the same building where Alex took pottery classes. "What are the odds?" she asked, as I watched the wheels spinning behind her eyes. *Fate*, she thought. *Fate is telling me that this is the time to get that ring.*

Meanwhile, my own wheels spun on a different axis. Here's what I didn't say: The odds are actually pretty good. You work with art conservators and the jeweler works with several other artists in the building where you take art classes. I'm sure many of your coworkers have personal and professional relationships with people in the pottery building.

Here's what I did say: I know! I'll set up an appointment while the stars are aligned!

I don't act fast when it comes to making decisions. If I decide to get a haircut it takes me three weeks to get off my ass and move it into a barber's chair, so you shouldn't be surprised to hear that a month went by before I visited the jeweler's website. I finally got around to it one afternoon while lounging on the couch. Something spurred me to action; some outside force acted as a catalyst, the same outside force that motivates me to take action three weeks after making my intentions known regarding haircuts. That outside force is Alex's voice. She turned her laptop to face me, exposing a Google image search for "yellow diamonds."

Hint taken. Subtlety, you'll find, doesn't work with me.

An hour later I had a mental checklist of Alex's desired design elements.

Yellow diamond for the main stone
White gold for the band
Possibly ruby or emerald for exterior stones
Thin band
Nothing too busy
Empty space
Asymmetrical design
Possibly raised
"Vintagey"

If you're like me, your initial reaction to this list is to repeat each item and add a question mark. Yellow diamond? Exterior stones? Empty space? I felt stupid, at first, for knowing so little about all this. Then I realized that I shared the same reaction as a hyper-intelligent being with powers beyond any human mind. Still, vintagey?

If not for Earth, Brad would've been an all-time know it all. He could see the entire universe, but Earth hung out in his brain's blindspot. Despite his superior mental capacity, he behaved like a toddler, often entering an unending loop of asking why.

"What's a diamond?" he asked.

"A shiny rock that humans place enormous value on."

That answer may satisfy a toddler, but not Brad.

"Why?"

"Because it's worth a lot of money and it's rare."

Again, probably enough for a toddler.

"Why?"

"It just is." Throttle a little menace into your tone and you may succeed in scaring a toddler out of her line of questioning. But not Brad. With Brad, I had to get into the weeds. Where does it come from? I can tell my niece that we find them underground. Brad wants to hear words like "metastable allotrope." Underground isn't enough. He needs to know about Sierra Leone, tectonic plates, and volcanic pressure. Then, and only then, can I move on to the sociological aspects of why we value diamonds.

Unfortunately, while I can expound on the hidden location of every power star in *Mario 64* and recite the entire screenplay of *Happy Gilmore* from memory, I failed to reserve brain space for the basic scientific principles that govern most of my life. I don't know anything about metastable allotropes. I don't know the details of how volcanic pressure, tectonic plates, and human rights violations in Sierra Leone play a role in my marriage proposal. I blame the schools. Fortunately, I live in an age that only requires me to know one thing to know all things: the Wi-Fi password. The night I introduced Brad to Wikipedia acted as a major turning point in our relationship.

Unlike myself and the millions of high school students around the country racing to finish their term papers, Brad agreed with the academic community's insistence that Wikipedia is not a credible primary source. He needed to hear it straight from the human's mouth. And I was the only human he knew, so I kept him apprised of my experiences navigating the diamond industry.

The afternoon following Alex's first mention of "vintagey," I found myself sitting in the guest room as Brad messed around with her Rubik's cube collection. I sat on the edge of the bed, slumped forward, twitchy, scratching at my sweaty palms, no longer impressed by Brad's telekinetic tricks. His ability to dismantle the Rubik's Cube into 27 individual cubes with his mind didn't compare to the million little cubes of my dismantled brain. Why was I so stressed? I woke up in love, ready to commit to Alex for the rest of my life. By the end of the day, that commitment began to take a tangible shape[6]. I thought about the time I went bungee jumping. I knew all week that I had it scheduled. I kept telling myself I'd be ready. Next thing I knew, the guide outfitted me with a harness. *Holy shit*, I thought. *I have to jump*. Buying the engagement ring is like suiting up in the bungee harness, only you wear it for months, until you change into the Men's Warehouse rental.

"I guess I know why they call it 'taking the plunge,'" I said.

"Why?" Brad echoed his typical refrain.

I ignored his question and told him about the ring details. *Yellow diamond? Asymmetrical?* Brad took it all in and nodded his understanding.

"So these diamonds," he said, "they are of value?"

"Yes."

"They come out of the ground, like a tree?"

"Sort of."

"Why not give her a tree? It is much larger. A tree is more majestic. More beautiful."

"That's not how it works, Brad."

"Men have always given women diamonds?"

"Not really."

"And you must exchange Mona for diamonds?"

"What?"

"Mona, the currency used in exchange for goods and services."

"Money, Brad. Money is currency. Mona is the dog you stare at while we sleep. But yes, diamonds cost money. Thousands of money."

"Thousands? But you have shown me your bank statement. Surely you understand how impractical it would be for you to spend thousands of money on a small rock. Alex must understand this, given her existence in this capitalist society and her intelligence, sufficient enough to conquer the Cube of Rubik without aid of my advanced biology."

"Brad, you just don't understand women."

At this point we neared the celebration of our third arbitrarily chosen dating anniversary. We had lived together for about 18 months, her dog had become my dog, and we recently bought a car together, which our friends viewed as a far more impressive symbol of our commitment than anything I could find on a jeweler's website. It's true, the thing that makes a Subaru a Subaru is love, but the car only comes with four years of 0% APR. Getting married would serve as a lifetime warranty on our relationship.

Every big step we've taken as a couple has felt natural and obvious. I didn't stress over whether it was too soon to take a trip together or meet her family. She didn't balk when I started openly farting in her presence. Everyone warned us that things would change once we moved in together. The only thing that changed was the amount of Ellen DeGeneres content on my DVR.

We asked the big questions: Do you want kids? Where do you want to live? How much money will we need to live the lifestyle we want? Can you still love me if I never stop biting my fingernails?[7]

Our love outweighed any minor incongruencies in our answers to those questions. We're a great couple. Our differences complement one another and I try to stay on top of complimenting her for the things that make her different. She's as perfect as a person can be, in that the only thing that's perfect about her is the percentage of perfection she embodies. Who wants to be with someone who's perfect all the time? Alex is perfect 78 percent of the time. The other 22 percent keeps me on my toes and reminds me that we're human. I love that about her. About us.

I have three older brothers. As such, my upbringing lacked a certain refinement. I don't have style. I don't have taste. I turned 29 a few weeks prior to visiting the custom jeweler's workshop and I still had a closet filled with childhood hand-me-downs. Last night I wore my 8th grade basketball jersey and a pair of jeans that, if they were human, would be treated for incontinence due to the frequency with which pocketed possessions unexpectedly slip through a hole.

An old girlfriend of mine once asked me if my brothers had taught me about girls growing up. I had a good laugh. I think between the three of them they've had three total girlfriends. Suffice to say, I don't know much about women, and I certainly don't know much about engagement rings. An advertising course I took in college taught me that DeBeers cooked up the idea of engagement diamonds in the 1920s. A century later and the campaign is still paying off. I sat in that lecture[8] as my female classmates and I were introduced to Blue Nile, a website that sells a surprisingly high percentage of engagement rings in America. The girls didn't like that one bit. They didn't want an engagement ring purchased on the Internet. There's no romance in that.

The consensus among the girls, mostly seniors, which put them at about 21 or 22 years old, was that their future husband should put the time in. He should visit jewelers, shop around, and do his research. That's the right way to do it.

For some reason I registered for this course as a sophomore, a naive youngster amidst the world-weary wisdom of the upperclassmen. I rarely spoke up, silently taking notes in the back row, wearing my alpaca wool beanie as college students sometimes do. I broke my silence that afternoon, as I thought I'd developed a solution that would work for everyone. "What if your boyfriend goes to all the jewelers, does all the homework, puts in the time and finds the perfect ring, then goes online and buys the exact same ring for half the price?"

Seems logical, right? Prudent? Fair?

They replied, "No. I don't want my future husband to buy a diamond on the internet."

A few years later, many of these women would swipe left to find their soulmate.

I'm not coming across as romantic, am I? That's not accurate. I'm great with the little things. I put together small surprises, unexpected flowers, a treasure hunt through the apartment, foot rubs, and on birthdays and special occasions I perform Disney songs with parody lyrics about our lives.[9] I'm a real-life romantic, not a romantic-comedy romantic.

Still, our origin story isn't exactly a MeetCute.

WHEN HEINE MET SAMMY

Alex grew up in Austin, TX. She went to college with some friends of mine at the University of Colorado in Boulder, where she graduated a semester early, proving that being chill as fuck and on the ball aren't mutually exclusive. After school, she moved home and got a job at an art gallery. A lifelong friend of mine, who went to school in Urbana, Illinois, and graduated on time (proving that benefiting from in-state tuition and maintaining a normal class schedule aren't mutually exclusive) moved to Austin and needed a roommate. They got a place together. By the time Alex moved to Chicago, she'd already developed close friendships with two of my best childhood friends.

Years before Alex and I first met, she'd been described to me as a female version of myself. It turns out that just meant she was small and cute. I was driving from Boulder to Las Vegas with two high school buddies. She wasn't on the trip, but they couldn't stop cutting jokes about her. Nothing overly crass, but enough for me to realize they were both probably in love with her. From that trip onward, this mystery woman owned a chunk of my mental real estate.

I haven't been with many women. At the time of that car ride, I think I'd only been with two. I sat in the backseat watching the Rockies roll by, wondering if I'd ever meet Alex Heine, and if I did, whether I'd have a shot at sleeping with her.

I'm not coming across as romantic, am I?

We didn't get off to a romantic start. We saw each other a handful of times in group settings without any love connection. My first memory of meeting Alex takes place outside of the Rainbo Club on Damen Avenue in Chicago. She approached as I regaled my friend Eric with stories about, of all things, a wedding I had recently attended. Alex interrupted to let us know that my story bored her because she didn't even know the couple. It was not love at first sight.

When she moved to Chicago she had a boyfriend. A handsome, tall, all-around great guy who went to the University of Madison and had become friends with some of my Badger pals. I knew him, but not well enough that anybody thought it was inappropriate for Alex and I to get together after they split up. We're the type of friends who don't have one another's phone number. Alex and I see him at parties sometimes and he and I always shake hands a little too demonstratively.

Back then, I waited tables and tended bar at an upscale bistro just outside of the city and Alex worked for an advertising agency in the Loop. One Saturday night[10] Alex and I wound up at the same party. My weekend routine involved racing home from work to find my roommates on the couch underneath blankets, sometimes drunk, sometimes high, sometimes stained with deep dish pizza. But now and then, fate stepped in and spurred them to life. March 1, 2014, was one such fateful night. I found them sitting upright, clad in relatively unstained apparel preparing for a night out.

I grabbed my best jeans[11] and my best shirt[12] and mixed myself a quick cocktail to catch up with the gang. Back in those days I could drink more than two beers without falling asleep.

More often than not, if our group of friends got together it happened at our place. We had a fraternity vibe and a four-bedroom apartment with room for beer pong tournaments. Alex hated staying over because at any hour of the night there could be a raucous miniature golf challenge outside the bedroom door.

Oh, to be in my blissful mid-twenties again, a time in one's life where nothing is certain and nobody knows what matters. There's an onomatopoeia to age ranges. The word "teen" sounds like underage drinking and fender benders. Any emotionally stable, angst-free 17-year-old resents being labeled a teen. Then you wind up a "twentysomething," which aptly describes the existence of most twentysomethings. Their relationships, careers, and dreams float in the air as they grab for them like children catching snowflakes. Everything is just something, so nothing is really anything, yet. That is, until the sobering moment you realize you are "in your thirties." It sounds awful. It is. The realization that the problems you're facing are only phase one of the long, debilitating slog through "middle age," when your children grow up and your body grows out and eventually you realize 25 years went by. Middle age, much like the Middle Ages, is a time for toiling. Before you know it, you've become a septuagenarian, or even an octogenarian. They used to say age is just a number, then one day age becomes a long word that sounds like a medical condition. It's not an age to be, but an age you come down with.

When I met Alex, we were twentysomethings, and it was glorious. I walked into an apartment rented by a trio of twentysomething males, complete with tacky Guinness beer advertisements hanging on the walls, an abused IKEA showroom of water damaged tabletops and skeletal chairs coated with dust, counters littered with half-filled bottles of brown liquor, and, in this particular instance, a gorgeous short-haired bespectacled twentysomething woman named Alexandria Heine.

As I stared, a friend commented on my chest hair, on full display with a top button unfastened and no undershirt. "I can't contain it," I said. And I couldn't. It rose like untamed Saharan grasslands fighting for exposure to the sun. "I'm feeling extra virile tonight." This was the type of comment I hoped would woo Ms. Heine. Oh, to be twentysomething.

The night progressed and I did my best to hit on her. She seemed distracted, but not disinterested. Our herd migrated to a local watering hole, and late in the night our friend suggested everyone return to his apartment for the after-party. Here's where I unleashed my smooth-talking charm.

"So, uh, I, um, do you want to go to the after-party?" I said, though "said" seems like a generous word.

"Not really."

"Me neither, but, uh, I'd go somewhere else, um, with you, if you, er, uh, wanted to do that? With me?"

"Ok."

If you aren't a drunk twentysomething male reading this, these unenthused monosyllabic replies should tip you off to how Alex wasn't really into it. As a drunk twentysomething male, I continued my pursuit unimpeded.

This wasn't a run-of-the-mill, passionate hookup. We weren't handsy at the bar, we didn't make out in the cab, and we didn't race to strip down once we got to her place. In fact, we didn't make any physical contact in the bar, we argued about the difference between Abigail Adams and Betsy Ross in the cab, and by the time we got back to her place, we mostly joked about my personal hygiene routine. She put on a Billy Joel record and eventually one thing led to another.

I'm not coming across as romantic, am I?

Just wait.

I planned to wait three days to text her, but I wound up sending her a brief note confirming her advice regarding loofahs.[13] The joke was well-received and my willpower held for the next 72 hours. Get this: *she* texted *me*.

I'm not a ladies' man. I'm not really a man's man either. I'm more of an old ladies' man. Moms love me. I never got into the drunken hookup culture in college. I picked up women the way deep ocean fish attract prey. I'd play dead, utilizing well-honed evolutionary patience, until they approached me, lured by my mysterious inability to pursue. Then, once they made their intentions clear, I'd strike, releasing years of platonic charm in a bioluminescent cloud of romantic energy.

The few girlfriends I've had all began as friends. As such, I've never really been on a first date, so Alex and I don't have that story to tell our future children. We did have a last date, though. After a few months of seeing each other, Alex invited me downtown for lunch. I worked nights tending bar so it didn't raise any red flags that she suddenly wanted to hang out on a Wednesday afternoon during her break from the office. We picked up sandwiches from Snarfs and, sitting in Millennium Park, she broke it off.

Don't worry, two months later she came crawling back.

Four years passed before Alex had another Snarfs sandwich. Not in Millennium Park, but in her bridal suite on our wedding day. Bring this book to any Snarfs location in the contiguous United States for 30% off your order.

Reunited, we picked up our relationship with all the momentum we'd built in the initial dating period. Again, no first date was necessary, and we skipped ahead to the inseparable phase. I'd take the Blue Line toward O'Hare to get home after work, grab a change of clothes, then take the Blue Line toward Forest Park, past the office, and into Little Italy to spend every second I could with Alex Heine. I'd stop at Walgreens to buy her flowers. I'd stop at the liquor store to bring her Wild Turkey 101. We'd get drunk and play Mario Kart on a Tuesday. What more could a guy want?

I stayed at her place five nights a week. She gave me a key so I could take Mona for walks before she got home. We were living together without living together. I had more space in her closet then than I do now. When our leases ran out, we found an apartment and never looked back. Eventually we'd get married.

The end.

LOVE IS A BURNING THING, AND IT MAKES AN ENGAGEMENT RING

October in Chicago comes in like a lamb and goes out like a slightly perturbed lamb, which, weather-wise, is still a metaphor for not quite winter. Alex and I hopped into our co-owned Subaru Forester, the most expensive and concrete symbol of our love and commitment, and met with the custom jeweler, Regina. The sun shone through clear skies, elderly couples walked hand-in-hand down the sidewalks, and Alex played Beyoncé tunes through our bluetooth sound system, yet another practical function of the Subaru that no ring could duplicate. Following Queen Bey's instructions, I set out to put a ring on it.

Regina worked in a tucked-away corner office on the third floor of the urban artist compound. Hallways and vestibules served as makeshift galleries, with locked display cases showcasing the in-house artists' work, while the less valuable student projects relied on scotch tape and push pins to adhere to the drywall. The best of these, I hoped, went home with their creators, leaving the discards behind as promotional material encouraging us to enroll in a six-week introductory metal-smithing program. Had we visited a different floor maybe we'd have seen a chipped ceramic bowl Heine had deemed unworthy of space in our cupboards.

We knocked on Regina's door and waited. I did not feel nervous. This was a fact-finding trip for Alex. My role was to play the clueless boyfriend, a role I excelled at. We came prepared,[14] but hadn't formed a concrete plan. I expected Regina to read between the lines and pick up on my unspoken expectations. My wardrobe, I hoped, would send the message that I was not a man with style or the cash flow that style demands. I anticipated she'd open the door, give me a quick once-over, register my crummy jeans and 10-year-old sneakers, catch a whiff of the T-shirt that I'd slept in, and infer that I hadn't showered. Thus, subtly, she'd get a feel for my budget.

Regina welcomed us and gestured toward a green loveseat in her shoebox office. That was the first clue. Sitting on a couch is not something you do during a quick pop-in. I missed my own couch. The Bears had a bye week and my fantasy football team hadn't yet proven to be garbage heading into a make-or-break Week 5 showdown. But I love Alex, so I wouldn't check my phone for any football scores during the entire meeting. They say love is never having to say "I'm sorry." I say love is never having to know which Tennessee Titans receiver caught a first quarter touchdown.

Thank God Alex tagged along for the primary visit. She wanted me to take full creative control of the project following this initial meet and greet, the thinking being that once she got the ball rolling in the right direction, even I, the styleless unshowered man, wouldn't be able to knock it off course. But what would I do if Alex got too excited and sent multiple balls rolling in multiple directions?

Regina sat across from us and started into her spiel. She told us about her family, how she started in jewelry, and asked us softball questions about our history so I could provide clueless boyfriend responses.

A box of sample rings, sans diamonds, lay open on the table in front of us. Alex picked them up at random, like a child hoping to avoid coconut in a box of fancy chocolates, examining them quickly and discarding those she didn't like. As uncomfortable as I felt in all aspects of this Sunday afternoon activity—the design, the terminology, the delay of NFL statistics, the idea of spending all the money—I took solace in knowing she was having a good enough time for both of us. Each of Alex's comments was met with an enthusiastic "Yeah, yeah, yeah!" from Regina, who jotted down contradictory notes regarding Alex's preferences as she tasted her way through the box. If Hollywood originality continues to plummet at its current rate and a studio greenlights an adaptation of this book, please cast Molly Shannon as Regina, who was perpetually one cocktail away from being a *Saturday Night Live* spoof of herself.

The poor woman made custom jewelry but had only recently entered into the engagement ring business. Clients came to her with their grandmothers' rings that needed to be reset or touched up, and she'd recognized, as I recognized during this journey, that marriage is big business. So she expanded into a new focus on engagement rings, and hadn't quite mastered the art of blending her sincere desire to help us with her desire to lock in a sale. The result was an awkward enthusiasm, an overbearing wide-eyed desperation that lacked the experience and knowledge to make the whole thing work.

Before sketching Alex's perfect ring, Regina measured our fingers. I am a thin man. My waist is thin, my thighs are thin, my neck is thin, my arms are thin, my dick is average, and my fingers are pretty damn thin. The knuckle of my ring finger is wider than the base of the finger where it meets the palm. My ring will need to be large enough to fit over the knuckle, but will then oscillate over the bony metacarpal expanse.

I don't wear jewelry. I've never worn a watch and I abstained from the hemp necklace fad that several of my hipper friends succumbed to in the 7th grade. I liked the idea of wearing a wedding band far more than the thought of actually having one on my finger, and my experience with the finger sizing contraption, a jeweler's equivalent of a set of measuring spoons, only exacerbated the fear that I'd never be comfortable in one.[15]

To our surprise, Regina hadn't heard of yellow diamonds. That was the first red flag. She's in the engagement ring business, the jewelry business, and has not even *heard of* yellow diamonds? She assured us, with a too big smile and an aggressive forward lean over the table, that she couldn't wait to do some research.

I should have listened to Rick, I thought of my brother and the ring guy he'd recommended. He told me to trust his guy, "a good deal, an Old Jewish Diamond Guy." Everybody has a ring guy. They're all the best. They're all old Jewish guys. Much like fresh sashimi and an honest dentist, everyone I know has a recommendation that they certify as the best. My friends who got married before me have ring guys, and they're the best. "Come out to Colorado, I'll introduce you." Yeah, right. With countless highly touted backup plans in place, Regina didn't have the luxury of too many strikes before getting called out. When we pitched yellow diamonds, she swung and missed. Strike one.

Alex's excitement got the better of her once Regina sketched a few concepts. The bullet points we'd discussed for weeks[16] did justice to their projectile namesake as Alex shot them off like John Wick emptying clip after clip. As her future husband, I should have seen it coming. But as an idiot, it makes sense that I didn't. I learned that day that Alex likes all sorts of jewelry.

Yellow diamonds can be too dark or too bright, so maybe she'd like chocolate diamonds instead? Yep, Alex is into that.

Maybe champagne or cognac to mute the color?
Those look pretty, too.
Tourmaline? Emerald? Ruby? Garrett?
Yes. Sure. Uh-huh. That could work.
Vintagey?
Perfect.

That's the thing about precious stones; they're all just so darned precious.

We planned to get the ball rolling, a metaphor that involves a single-track, linear, constant progression toward the end result. This being the first phase of the wedding process, I was naive enough to believe it may work out that way. After brainstorming with Regina, we'd abandoned the ball on the track and instead took up a dodgeball approach, placing a series of balls on the center line bisecting the gym. I'm not sure if I'm a ball or a player in this metaphor; all I know is that nobody is sure of the rules, somebody's probably cheating, nobody is ever out of the game permanently, and at any moment I could get blindsided by a 100 mph smack in the face.

With our first foray into the marriage process behind us I saw the future with a frightening clarity. I began the day confident that my easygoing sensibilities and level-headed emotional stability would prevail over the horror stories that those who had endured wedding planning were so quick to share. I ended the day confident that no aspect of the ring buying process would be easy[17], that no ring would ever fit my finger, and that a daily grind of tedious decisions and chores lurked behind every shadow. Thank goodness I could vent to the alien in the guestroom.

Two weeks after the initial visit I returned to Regina's office to examine some stones. She'd emailed photos of the diamonds, yellow marquise-cut stones that looked great in the picture but underwhelmed in person. At around $1,500, they just didn't cut it. The biggest one measured about .5 carats, and the color made me think less of shimmering jewelry than dehydrated urine. Getting the right color with a yellow diamond requires a bit of tightrope walking. If it's too dense, you're looking at a pee rock. If it's too pale, the light it reflects drowns out the hue.

I held the pee rock with a set of tweezers and studied it through a jeweler's loupe. I knew it wasn't the stone for me, but I didn't want to be rude and dismiss her efforts without humoring her.

I returned the tweezers to Regina, who promptly fumbled them and sent the diamond skittering across the table onto the floor. I'd soon discover that this is not an uncommon occurrence among jewelers, and that diamonds are durable. I told her the size was a problem. My budget wasn't a hard limit, and getting it right meant more to me than saving a little money. Alex would wear this ring forever, and I figured I'd make the money back by selling the film rights to this best-selling book you're reading.

Remember when Regina said she'd never heard of yellow diamonds and I proclaimed strike one? Here comes the 0-1 delivery.

She gave a fuzzy explanation of how cost per carat

increases as carat increases. Think of it like watching the percentage figure of a Netflix video as it loads. The first 90% zips by, but the last 10 takes just as long. It costs more time the higher it gets. The same is true for diamonds. To increase from a .5 to a .6 carat stone costs far less than increasing from .8 to .9 carats.[18]

With this new information in hand, I had yet another revelation of how this is going to cost me all the money.

Regina, having explained something useful, could sense her success, and was keen to build on it and further establish her expertise. She mentioned a concept called "The Four Cs," and went on to name them. "Cut," she began. "Clarity," she continued. "Carat," she counted on her finger. "And...um....uh..."

"Color," I finished for her.

"Oh," she lit up in astonishment. "You've done your homework!"

"No homework," I said. "I just know the four Cs." That wasn't the nicest way to phrase my reply, so I tacked on, "It's a common clue in crossword puzzles." This way she could go on believing she hadn't lost face, although she was that much closer to losing a client. On the report card, 75% earns students a passing C, but a jeweler who only knows 75% of the four Cs fails in my book. Strike two.

"Where does she get her diamonds?" Brad asked the same question Alex asked earlier that day. He'd crossed the room and discovered my golf clubs in the guest room closet. Rather than explaining how an expensive, time-consuming, and ultimately frustrating sport was a worthwhile hobby, I told him they were designed to help him scratch his ankles without bending over.

"Where does she get the diamonds?" He repeated, now with half a set of irons clutched in his fists, rubbing the club heads against all four of his calves. "Does she mine them and refine them herself?" Alex wanted to know, too. Where did her rocks come from? Were they *blood diamonds*? How much does she pay for them? What does she think of Blue Nile?

I knew nothing and hadn't thought to ask about anything.

All I knew was that making these little decisions made my skin crawl and that it'd cost me a significant percentage of my net worth. At the time, I wished that the ring came later in the process, after I'd been exposed to such a bevy of details and choices for bands and caterers and flowers that taking care of the ring would be second nature. Now that I'm writing this in the past tense, I can assure you there's no need to worry. You get to buy wedding bands later, too!

I returned to Regina's office for the third and final time at the end of October. The day before the visit, I'd played in a golf tournament with my three brothers.[19] I told the eldest what my approximate budget was and his eyes grew as wide and white as the Titleists in his hand. "That's way too high," he insisted. "Though I paid twice as much."

Keep in mind, he makes money and I make rent.

In talks with my brothers, the ones who are married, that is, I'd often been counseled that after three years of marriage, Alex won't care about the ring at all. They assured me that once the reality of life sets in, the silly frivolities and formalities of engagements and weddings look, in hindsight, unnecessary. From where I stood, I couldn't help but think that:

They were probably right
They wouldn't say such things around their wives
Their wives would disagree

If their wives heard such statements, my brothers would return to the jeweler to purchase apology earrings

Like everything else involved in getting married, we need to make the mistakes ourselves in order to learn from them. Some would say this is a lack of wisdom on our part, given the ability to learn from others' mistakes is better than learning from one's own. I think it's healthy for us to make our own mistakes, our own poor decisions. This way, we can learn from them together and recall how we felt, how we reacted, and how we could improve and be more in tune with one another in the future.

In three years, does it really matter if Alex says "We shouldn't have spent so much on rings" or "We didn't spend enough on rings"? Life wouldn't be real life if we looked back and said, "We really spent the perfect amount of money and stress and time on everything."

Back at Regina's, I parked myself in the center of the olive green loveseat and prepared to meet a reasonably sized and unreasonably priced diamond. Would it be too dark, too light, too small, too big? My biggest concern was that the diamond would be just right, but I wouldn't know it because, as I've made clear, I couldn't find a perfect diamond with a geometry textbook and a protractor.[20] Regina fussed in a cabinet in the far corner of the room with her back to me. She turned, smiling with a cartoonish, open-mouthed grin and proclaimed that she had found the solution: sapphires.

Or, as they're known in my native language, "Strike

three."

Yes, they were yellow. And yes, they were much bigger. And dear lord yes, they were affordable. But they don't shine like diamonds. They are, in the most technical term, dull rocks. She placed one of the stones in the crevice between my middle and ring finger, so I can better assess the relative size and color against the skin tone of a finger that will never wear the ring. My face gave away my disinterest, because before I could ask she explained herself.

"I work with an Indian family who supplies my diamonds," she said. "They told me there weren't any other yellow marquise-cut stones in the city. Actually, they may be Israeli. They are definitely a family."

This is exactly the kind of nonsense that umpires hear after they call a batter out on strikes.

"What I love about the sapphires is that they are cheaper...I mean, more inexpensive."

Americans love the minutiae of baseball, the little idiosyncrasies of the game that go hand in hand with being at the ballpark. The call of the hot dog vendor, the hum of the crowd, watching the outfielders mosey about during a pitching change. One of my favorite parts of a baseball game is that each umpire has his own unique way of signalling a strike out. Some go with the full downward punch out, the one that looks like starting a lawnmower. Others opt for the one-handed uppercut. But the best one is the nonchalant, open-handed, single-arm raise, like miming a bocce ball toss, or performing the physical gesticulation of an old Italian man saying "Get outta here." Better yet, tossing a bouquet.

That's the one I'd have made to call Regina out after she showed me those mall kiosk sapphires.

She told me she'd keep looking, but part of me knew that her part of the journey had ended. The time had come for me to embark on my second significant religious rite of passage. First, there was my Bar Mitzvah, the ceremony in which I became a son of the commandment and a man in the eyes of my faith. Next, I would forego the rabbi and instead learn from another sage of the chosen people: the Old Jewish Diamond Guy.

Brad stooped over my shoulder to peer at the email I'd drafted to Regina. I'd introduced him to bathing, and although the hygienic element didn't seem to matter to him he took to the ritual of it. At first, I feared Alex would grow suspicious as our stockpile of candles and bath bombs ran low. After all, when did I have time to take so many baths without pleading for her to join me? But of course, Brad had a solution. A raise of the hand and the burned wax rematerialized into a solid. A shake of his rounded head would do more than send his bowl cut sashaying atop his forehead, but also dim the lights and play "Sounds of Nature" over nonexistent speakers. I worried that he'd been taking multiple dips each day, while all of humanity stalled in unwitting tableaus across the globe. It couldn't be healthy, but it was worth it because he smelled of lavender and eucalyptus.

With all this bathing he'd given up on the hassle of wearing clothes and reverted to his nudist ways, and it's hard to concentrate when an un-nippled chest hovers inches from your eyeball, regardless of any hints of sandalwood.

"What are you saying?" he asked.

I told him what I'd written. It wasn't exactly a Dear John letter, more of a Dear Jewel. Our relationship didn't warrant a breakup, but I thought I owed it to her to inform her of my intentions, that I'd be seeing someone else. I even asked if it was a faux pas in the industry to see more than one jeweler at the same time. She understood. Just thinking about cheating on my jeweler represents my closest brush with adultery.

I never heard from her again. I'm guessing she moved on.

I then emailed the Old Jewish Diamond Guy that my brother Rick endorsed as "the best." I introduced myself, told him how I got his contact info, assured him that Rick had assured me that he was "the best," and gave a brief synopsis of what I was looking for: the elusive yellow marquise-cut diamond. For those who don't know their cuts, think of a geometric diamond like you'd see on a playing card, then, pull the top and bottom apart and add twenty pounds. It's a diamond that's gone a little soft around the middle. It's a diamond in its third trimester.

We chose the marquise because it's elegant and unusual.[21] Heine can't stand having the same thing as everyone else. She'd rather eat off the floor than buy a kitchen table from IKEA. She's an individual with her own style. Why should her engagement ring be any different?[22]

OJDG called me the next morning. We exchanged pleasantries while I stepped out of the office and headed to a small park across the street. Yes, he remembered Rick, and was disappointed that my brother had given up on teaching. And yes, of course he'd be able to help me find a yellow marquise, and from my three sentence email he'd deduced that I needed a fancy yellow, not a vivid or intense yellow. In two minutes he'd established a plan, assured me that the diamonds were certified, and answered several questions that I didn't even know to ask.

Attempting to describe Alex's bullet points over the phone proved somewhat challenging on account of my inexperience with the language and, well, *vintagey?* I'd have to drop by and walk him through it. I gave him a rough budget and told him about our plan to include small emeralds around the exterior. He invited me to meet the next day. Regina could find three yellow marquise diamonds in the entire city. OJDG could find whatever I needed by tomorrow.

"Really?" he said. "She'd never even heard of yellow diamonds." I provided a quick summary of my experience with Regina, and asked if he'd be willing to sell us the stones and have her produce the design and metalwork.

"Yes, I could do that." He paused, or came as close as a fast talking, all-business Old Jewish Diamond Guy can come to pausing. "It sounds like you'd be better off keeping it all in-house. We use computer imaging to produce a 3D printed model of the design so you know exactly what you're getting and how it fits."

I know what you're thinking. It's probably the same thing that I thought. *I doubt Regina has 2D printing capabilities.*

OJDG rattled off some budget numbers that met or beat Regina's estimates, and I agreed to meet him in the Loop later that week. By this point, we'd entered the fringes of the endless gray expanse of a Chicago winter. A brief history of winter in Chicago: at the beginning of time, God sat down and sharpened His pencil. He held the lead tip to His tongue as He pondered what sort of clime would best fit the region and, feeling a divine inspiration, sketched out a plan for the city. Unsatisfied, He turned His pencil around and tried to erase what He'd drawn. But alas, even the almighty can't get a pencil eraser to work properly, and after furiously grating the rubbery nub across the page and blowing away the pink detritus, a bleak, blurred, horrible gray visage stared up at Him. "Oh well," He thought, "they'll deal with it for seven or eight months and I'll give them a great summer." He filed away the plans and thumbed through the North American landscape for His next project. "Now, let's see if I can get it right in San Diego."

The end of October serves as the battleground between seasons. By this phase of the war the sun's armies run thin, their supplies exhausted, their morale low. I approached the building as Winter's forces laid siege to the landscape. Gray train cars rumbled beneath an overcast sky, and below them the gray, overcast faces of urban drones shuffled along the great gray pavement of the city. Set against this backdrop, I thought, a shimmering yellow diamond would really do the trick.

I entered the building and made my way to the 16th floor, where OJDG's office loomed in one of the great gray edifices of the Loop. The hallway to Regina's office featured amateur artwork, but there was nothing amateur about this place. I rang and was buzzed through the first of what would turn out to be three locked doors. I sat down and hastily smoothed out my hat hair while the receptionist phoned OJDG. I arrived two minutes late, and hated myself for it.

Two minutes late to meet OJDG is a travesty in my eyes. Where did I miscalculate? I must have missed a train and waited on the platform. I hoped he'd forgive me. He must be busy, given how fast he talks. A moment later, I buzzed through another set of doors and emerged into the office, a fluorescent box in the sky. OJDG waved me over to his desk and shook my hand.

"You look just like your brother," he said. That's a half-truth. People can tell that we're brothers, but we have different color hair and eyes, so as far as brothers go, we're not exactly twins.

He looked me up and down and asked, "Are you working today?" I guess most would-be husbands follow a stricter dress code than my office enforces. They can probably afford bigger diamonds, too. Before we got into the standard rundown of questions, he commended my punctuality. Besides the absurdity of the wedding industry, society's next biggest problem is its lackadaisical attitude toward being on time.

How long have you been together?
How did you meet?
You live in the city?
Will the wedding be in town?

"Showroom" isn't the right word for OJDG's office. Hidden away on the 16th floor behind several locked doors, it felt more like a secret heroin processing lab than a venue for wealthy dowagers to window shop. His desk had a cozy quality, given that it lived in the center of an open office workspace with no privacy and an endless cascade of ringing phones and muffled voices. I credit the lamp for providing a sense of intimacy, as it shone brightly onto an oversized pad of tear-away sketching sheets. Each sheet's border featured informative charts on diamond cuts and weight conversions, with plenty of room for brainstorming designs. Under the lamp's spotlight, the clean white paper emanated possibility and cried out to be filled.

OJDG is something of a misnomer. He's not that old. He probably goes to temple twice a year on the high holidays, if that. But the important part is that he's a full-blown Diamond Guy.

After some high-quality small talk he brought out the high-quality small rock. I'd requested something in the .5 carat range, but being an experienced Diamond Guy, he knew a half carat ring wouldn't do the job and skipped straight to the .89 carat stone. He thumbed through a stack of index card–sized manila envelopes, found my name, and dumped the stone out onto the paper. It was perfect. He walked me through the specs, jotting down the length, width, height, and table.[23]

What a power play, I thought. OJDG completely ignored my input and did what he knew was best. A .5 carat stone isn't much of a stone, and he'd worked with enough soon-to-be brides to know that I'd end up opting for something bigger so as not to disappoint mine.

He had me hold my fingers out together and placed the stone in the crevice between them. "This will give you a feel for how it will look against the size of her hand and color of her skin. Is she darker or lighter than you?"

"There aren't many people whiter than me," I said.

In high school biology, while learning about recessive hereditary genes, I discovered that I filled the lower right-hand corner of the Punnet Square for mid-digital hair. Some people don't have a single hair between their middle and top knuckles. If you have even one follicle on one finger, then you carry the gene. My index fingers are bald as a baby's fingers, but the other three sport sprouts in tiny blonde patches. It doesn't make for ideal ring testing conditions.

With a price flirting with $4,000, this stone wouldn't leave a lot of options for fancy metal work or exterior stones, and believe it or not, Alex had some big ideas concerning exterior stones.

"Emeralds," he said, "are easy. They're less expensive than, say, rubies or diamonds."

"Perfect," I leaned back in my chair, happy to catch a break for once, "Alex wants emeralds. I know that. But I still think I'll need a little more wiggle room in the budget. Can you find a marquise around .75 carats or so?"

"Of course," OJDG smiled. He didn't add anything about how, as an actual diamond industry professional, the act of procuring diamonds didn't rely entirely on his connection to a single Indian family. Instead, in his usual brisk demeanor, he asked, "When can you come in to look at it?"

"Emeralds?" Alex said when I told her of my journey. "No, no, no; I never said emeralds." She must have said emeralds. Why else would I think emeralds? It's not like I'm capable of making any decisions about this piece of jewelry on my own. If I were, then she wouldn't even know I was buying it. "No emeralds," she repeated. "I want rubies."

Of course she did.

I visited with OJDG three times in an eight-day period. Looking back, I can't imagine what we discussed couldn't have been accomplished via email. Then again, if we used email then I wouldn't have an authentic OJDG, and who wants to buy anything as austere as an engagement ring from some Punk Millennial Diamond Startup?

Alex feared that OJDG worked for a big-box, corporate diamond pusher. I don't know how she arrived at that theory, but she did. Despite explanations of how we get to design the exact, unique ring we wanted using the CAD (Computer Aided Design) software, she worried she'd wind up wearing the same ring as thousands of other women whose men went to Jared. There could be no worse fate for Alex Heine than a mass-produced product in her home. The exception being Girl Scout Cookies.[24]

I texted Heine pictures of the two stones OJDG and I settled on. The larger of the two came in at a whopping .9 carats and a potentially manageable $3,650. The alternative tipped the scales at .79 carats but featured a longer cut, making it the same length as the big boy while sporting an appealing $2,300 price tag. They were nearly identical to the naked eye.

"I like the big one," she texted back.

"Do you like it 160% more than the other one?" I asked. The $1,300 gap meant the difference between doing whatever she wanted with exterior stones or having a slightly wider diamond. She wavered, but she agreed to come in and meet OJDG, see the setup, see the stones, and hopefully walk away with peace of mind and a plan.

We'd entered November. Alex's beloved Houston Astros had won the World Series and the world had witnessed Carlos Correa propose to his girlfriend on the field following the Game 7 victory.[25] Emotions ran high. Love was in the air. Alas, so was Alex. She'd been dispatched to San Francisco for a brief work trip and planned to meet me at OJDG's office direct from the airport. She arrived tired, frustrated, hungry, and as beautiful as always. World Series MVP George Springer, the only man on the planet I thought of as competition for Alex's affection, was nowhere to be seen, yet still I felt perspiration building under my arms and on my neck. Alex's exhaustion left little room for error. She had no patience for my shtick and I sensed the entire night hinged on the success of this meeting. My plan was to nod and agree and try not to grimace at any cost estimates.

Happy wife, happy life. Right?

Not even Alex's foul mood could take OJDG out of his element. If you're a legitimate diamond guy, then you can handle soon-to-be brides of all types, and one doesn't earn an acronym like OJDG without a track record of happy brides. He got her situated beneath the magic lamp and started sketching. His were the sketches of an architect, more blueprint than ballpoint, compared to the whimsical pictionary plans Regina put on paper. As his pencil glided across the blank canvas he allayed Alex's fears by tossing out new ideas, deftly flipping the eraser into action if she balked and confidently pressing the led into darker lines when she assented.

It wasn't long before the entire design had changed. Our months' worth of plans became a crumpled draft, tossed blindly over his shoulder into the vicinity of a trash can. She found herself taken in by a ballerina cut, which is made with baguette cut stones and, to me, brings to mind one of the crustacean humanoids from the *Pirates of the Caribbean* franchise. It may have been wiser to say *The Little Mermaid*, but instead I doubled down with and expanded, "the swashbuckling damned, the scaly-faced monsters of Davy Jones' Locker."

She stuck with it despite my commentary.

Alex took this one-on-one opportunity (I don't count

myself as part of the discussion) to go over her checklist of unclear terminology. Could OJDG handle designing something raised, vintagey, asymmetrical, and loaded with empty space?

With furrowed brow, he leaned back in his swivel chair for a moment before swinging his body forward and returning to sketching position. He drew a circle (I'm embarrassed to say how long it took me to realize it represented the ring in profile), and beside it, an overhead view of the potential design. He then explained what we were asking for wasn't asymmetrical. It was, in fact, loaded with symmetrical elements. We merely wanted something "unbalanced."

Good. I was hoping to get bogged down in further semantics. Half the time I'd use terms like "shank" or "band" and he'd nod as though he caught my meaning, but when he used those terms they didn't equate in my mind to what they meant when I used them. When Alex and I work on jigsaw puzzles, I create my own lexicon of piece-shape terminology. Grabbers, Fatties, and Fakes could pretty much mean anything. The fact that Alex is fluent in my puzzle pidgin meant we were ready to get married. The fact that OJDG understood what I meant with my garbled ring-speak meant he was the right guy for the job.

Regardless of any unbeknownst misunderstandings, we successfully settled on a design.

After a brief tour of the design department, OJDG took us to the 3D printer, a machine that takes a gorgeous piece of jewelry as input and churns out a grotesque bastardization, a dark brown plastic Frankenstein version of the ring it will be in the future. To stick with my 2000s-era film franchise comparisons, think of the jewelry equivalent of when Saruman breeds orcs in *The Lord of the Rings: The Two Towers.*

The basket of old 3D printed rings looked like something I'd feed my dog, or clean up off the rug after my dog rejected it, but the end products we saw helped Alex warm to the process and to the professional "I get shit done" mentality of OJDG.

We'd move forward with our CAD based on the sketches. *Finally,* I thought, *an actual step of progress, and at long last I can begin paying for something*!

The CAD came out all wrong. The imaging software showed us what the finished ring would look like from various angles, but the proportions felt wonky. The brackets that held the stones in place extended too high, the exterior stones looked bulky, and to Alex's dismay, the band itself lacked the thin, round quality she'd hoped for.

Heine wanted to make changes, but would a new CAD look any better? OJDG warned us that it wasn't an exact science. Besides, what Heine wanted that night wasn't what she'd wanted two weeks earlier, so how could I be confident in what she'd want two weeks later? And it had to be exactly what she wanted. We're talking about engagement rings, not sandwiches. If the guy at the deli forgets to add tomatoes, you let it slide, but if your engagement ring isn't exactly the way you want it, you go back to the start and get it right.

I called OJDG about our concerns, pointing out that he drew the ring with 15 baguette stones in the ballerina cut and 18 round rubies, but the CAD showed nine and eight, respectively. He gave his stock reply, "When can you come in?" but added a few words that altered my perception of the problem. "You should see how small these stones are. If we do 18 rounds, they'll be invisible."

We're talking about millimeters. In Alex's most recent sketch, she had 30 exterior rubies running alongside the center diamond. We may as well put red food coloring on 30 grains of salt.

We were six weeks into the ring design process and we'd barely made any progress. The greatest moment of clarity and understanding, the most profound feeling of accomplishment after a month and half, came when I realized just how small these fancy rocks are. Boy oh boy, what an experience.

After the revelation, I mediated a few rounds of "thinner, rounder" requests between Alex and OJDG. She demanded a band (or shank, I still don't know the lingo) that was thinner and rounder, and OJDG sent CADs that weren't quite thin and round enough. Finally, after sending him an email with an attached drawing of one of Queen Elizabeth I's famous rings as a guide, we settled on a CAD we could move forward with. He told us that it would look both thinner, and rounder, in reality than it did in the digital rendering. Again, we're talking about millimeters.

"When can you come in?" He'd emailed once the time came to pick up our 3D mock up of the ring. Remember, OJDG is my brother's guy for diamonds. During this endless string of *When can you come in?* and *thinner, rounder*, I'd been fortunate enough to use my brother as a sympathetic sounding board. Not only had he gone through the same thing, but he'd done so with the same guy. I told Rick how exasperated I'd become going downtown to accomplish nothing.

"Why go downtown to pick something up?" Rick

said. "He lives a few blocks away from you. When I needed something like that he'd bring it home and I'd stop by after work."

Remember at the end of *Space Jam* when Bugs Bunny explains to Michael Jordan that he can break the laws of physics during the big cartoon basketball game in Looney Tune Land? Michael Jordan looks at the clock and says, "10 seconds to go, now you tell me?" That's how I felt.

The diamond game had been good to OJDG. No surprise there. A grand piano slumbered in the corner of the room like a massive hibernating black bear, framed family photos resting atop it like playful cubs, smiling as they waited for papa bear to wake up. A grandfather clock loomed in the back of the room. I couldn't tell if Alex would love it or hate it, which is why she's involved in the ring buying process in the first place. Better to let her make decisions on furniture, not to mention jewelry. I can't be trusted with those decisions. I don't even know the difference between a shank and a band.

There was no change in OJDG based on his habitat. In the harsh fluorescent light of his office, among the car horns and concrete skyscrapers, he was a fast-talking, vaguely aloof professional who I could tell relished not wearing a suit to work every day. At home, among the grandkids' toys and the stained wood finish of his grandfather clock, he maintained the same bewitching blend of Alice's white rabbit and a spacy Dustin Hoffman character. The result came through in his eyes when he listened to me talk, fixing me in a stare that evoked an image of Gene Wilder as Willy Wonka: attentive, yet miles away in a different world.

Afterward, Alex tried on the model ring, examining

the shape and proportion of its curvature. She had to use her imagination to picture how the stones would look, but the fit felt good and nothing stood out as problematic. Hallelujah.[26]

For weeks I had to remind myself that we were on the same team. We had the same goal. Still, each round of decision-making brought tension. OJDG came off as a little pushy, but only because he liked to work fast, and who can blame him when he's facing a thread of 100 emails for what must have been his lowest-revenue client? Alex felt pressured, and we both worried that we'd rush into a ring we may regret. But we'd made it this far, and we were happy with our design.

The yellow marquise took center stage, glinting with just the right depth of color. To the west, a ballerina cut of diamond baguettes, whose length diminished evenly with each stone as they approached the poles. To the east, a series of circular rubies flanked the marquise. The band would be thinner and rounder than anyone ever thought possible, except for one woman who wouldn't give up on her dream. We'd done it.

With Alex's approval of the 3D printed model and the various stones selected, only one step remained. It was time to make the ring. Scratch that. Two steps remained. It was time to make, and pay for, the ring. OJDG told me he expected the exterior rubies and diamonds to cost, we'll say, four units. The main stone came in around five units, and the design work, metal for the band, and CADs should have totaled another two units. I expected a subtotal of 11 units. During this process I'd transformed from a nervous, stereotypical Jewish miser with an embarrassing salary and a fear of getting ripped off into an exasperated young man who just wanted his girlfriend to get what she wanted, no matter the cost. I'd given up on encouraging smaller or less expensive alternatives and conceded to pay whatever charges we accrued. At one point I expected, and accepted, a cost of as many as 14 units.

OJDG asked for seven.

Seven units! Basic arithmetic called for a price of 11 units. I thought I would be getting a *deal* at 11 units. Somehow he'd asked for seven. This provided me some opportunities:

I'd have a nice, fat budget when it came time to design a wedding band. That's something they don't tell you when you decide to buy an engagement ring. You're signing up to buy two rings. And I had every reason to expect that emeralds wouldn't cut it for that one, either.

All of a sudden, I had some money left over for an elaborate proposal. All I needed was an idea for how to propose, and the desire to do something elaborate.

I could get her some diamond earrings. The last thing I wanted was for Alex's lobes to be jealous of her fingers.

On the downside, I felt cheap. Seven measly units? For the rest of our lives we'll see that ring every day, and I'll always remember that I nudged her toward the smaller rock to save a little money, when in the end I didn't need to. Lucky for me, I knew I'd have the rest of my life to make up for it. Starting with diamond earrings (see option C above).

OJDG emailed me to let me know the ring was ready. "Would you like to come in and see it?"

Hmm, I thought, *another trip to the Loop to nod and say, "Looks great."*

I passed.

I had him send it to my mom in Michigan. You don't have to pay taxes if you ship out of state. Plus, my mom would go nuts when she saw it. "No thanks," I wrote back. And with that simple reply, the journey came to a close.

What began with a trip to Alex's pottery classroom ended with a 3D printer and an out-of-state mailing address. Do I have regrets? Sure I do. I regret that Alex's mom never pulled me aside and told me about a family heirloom that would have rendered this phase of the engagement process unnecessary. But I don't regret going through it with Alex.

I regret not springing for the bigger marquise diamond. It's just money, and one thing I'd learn again and again in the months to follow was that every aspect, and boy do I mean *every aspect*, of getting married costs too much. I'd have been happy to cut costs on almost all of them. The ring is the only one I look back on and wish I hadn't. There will always be more money. There won't be another ring.

Don't worry about me, though. I'm sure I'll get over it.

I regret ever attempting to work with Regina and not going straight to the real industry professional.

I regret beating myself up over every little decision. I don't regret learning not to beat myself up over the billions of little decisions to come. There are simply too many choices to get hung up on, and there's nothing to gain by arguing about them. I'm not advocating for a soon-to-be groom to play the "I don't care" card, but I will suggest that all the would-be grooms out there pick their battles and consider which hills are worth dying on and which are better for sledding down.

I regret voicing my opinion about the ballerina cut looking like the inside of a kraken's mouth. I'm sure Heine didn't appreciate that.

The weekend before the ring arrived at my mother's house, Alex and I threw our annual Hot Food in Bowls potluck. Some people throw ugly sweater Christmas parties, some throw Halloween parties. Alex and I have cornered the market on an Autumn potluck featuring chili, queso dip, gumbo, jambalaya, soups, stews, mac 'n' cheese, and anything else that's hot and served in a bowl. #HFiB is a good time. At the 2017 iteration of HFiB, a friend of ours asked me how things were going with Regina. I told him it hadn't worked out.

"Did you end up finding some Jewish guy?" he asked. "I've got an Old Jewish Diamond Guy and he's the best."[27]

"Yeah," I told him. "I'm way ahead of you."

AND ON THAT FARM THERE WAS A RING, H-E-I-N-E

The ring twisted inches in front of Brad's discerning gaze, turning in lazy, gravity-defying revolutions. Each facet reflected Brad's dome-shaped haircut, like a bee's point-of-view shot in a cartoon. I liked the ring, and I think Brad did, too, based on his clinical examination. As he considered it from different angles, I sat on the edge of the guest bed holding the small mahogany box it arrived in.

"It's lovely," he said, one leg laying flat across its three neighbors. He looked like a skeleton under my University of Illinois sweatshirt, arms and chest lost among the folds of fabric, his round head popping out of the collar, giving him the look of a scarecrow whose hay stuffing had fallen out.

"Why doesn't she have it?" Brad floated the ring back into the box.

"I haven't asked her yet."

"Asked her what?" he said.

"If she'll marry me."

"No need. I've surmised from observing your actions, particularly discussions the two of you have had regarding your plans to get married, that her intentions are genuine. You need not bother. I recommend you give her the ring immediately."

"I still need to propose. It's part of the process"

"Propose what?"

"Tradition calls for me to create a memorable moment to give her the ring. I get on one knee, say something romantic, and present the ring."

Brad fixed his eyes on me. By this time I had learned not to speculate what was going on behind those eyes. He could digest the world in ways I couldn't even fathom. His brain functioned like a supercomputer, processing information at unimaginable speeds, while my brain functioned, comparably, about as effectively as a block of refrigerated mild cheddar. These awed, reverent thoughts swam through my mind as I waited for him to reveal his latest pearl of wisdom. Outside the guest room, I knew that time had frozen, but as he gazed and ruminated the air inside felt stilted, too. Finally, his lips parted and he broke the air of suspense.

"That's silly."

The proposal always appealed to me. It suits my style. Planning something cute, clever, fun, and surprising is right in my wheelhouse.[28] I write funny poems and pick up small bouquets of flowers with relative frequency. Our standard gift-giving and celebratory dates cluster around the holidays, with a November anniversary, then Christmas, and Alex's birthday and Valentine's Day both in February. As such, to avoid a 10-month stretch without gifts, I created the "Summer Six," a six-day series of surprises ranging from a side of french fries to eat in the bathtub while I massage her feet to a homemade key lime pie to a scavenger hunt around the apartment. It would have been a seven-day event, but the inaugural year started on a Tuesday, and who wants to end a week of surprises on a Monday?

Despite my track record, when the time came to put my adorable mind to work on an elaborate proposal, I blanked. Anything like my normal surprises would be a cute touch for a guy who isn't prone to parody *Frozen* lyrics, but for me, it would almost feel less special to perform yet another goofy song. I didn't know what to do, but I knew I'd have to do it soon.

Alex dropped hints that she wanted her family to be there when she got engaged. She dropped them hard, right on my head. Remember when she texted me the name of the jeweler? That's the level of clarity she provided. I had a few options. I could fly in her sister's family, or one or both parents. Alternatively, I could surprise her with a trip to Texas, but to maintain the element of surprise I'd need to book flights that didn't require her to take time off work, blindfold her for the duration of the flight, buy top-of-the-line noise-cancelling headphones, find someone to look after the dog, and essentially kidnap her through TSA. That, or piggyback on the pre-existing plan to visit over Christmas.

When Alex first mentioned her preference to share the excitement with her family, I asked, "Does this mean I have to propose over Christmas?" She said no, but as I've explained in the options above, she may as well have said, "No, but you will."

Still, I didn't give in and maintained an alternate course of action. I planned to use Christmas as an opportunity to ask for her father's blessing and check with her sister about a potential visit to Chicago for Alex's February 1 birthday. Then, on December 17th, the finished ring made it into my hands and I knew I couldn't wait. You can't sit on an engagement ring. The moment you get it you need to use it, like how Alex made homemade hummus the day she got her KitchenAid food processor, or how I feel when I buy Imodium.

So, it'd be a Christmas proposal after all.

Alex's sister loves Christmas more than an adult should love a holiday.[29] Allison hosts Christmas at her house outside San Antonio. We play games, construct Christmas-themed pine cones, and eat Chick-Fil-A for a few days. Unfortunately, construction on a new house hadn't wrapped up in time for the holidays, so they couldn't christen the new abode until the next yule. In the months leading up to Christmas, Alex relayed updates like, "Allison looks at the blueprints and her top concern is, 'Where will the tree go?'"

With the North Pole by the Alamo on hold, the alternative was to hold Christmas at Heine Farms, Alex's dad's small house near the family farm out by the Austin airport. At the time, her father wasn't himself. Dave struggled with depression, had lost weight, couldn't sleep, and suffered from crippling anxiety. It was bad. He'd sold his hundred head of cattle, his tractors, and his horses. He returned his dogs to the shelters where he'd picked them up. Soon, he'd sell most of the land. These were not easy choices to make. The fun-loving, exuberant man I'd met three years earlier became a shell of himself. The family opted to move him to a new house closer to his grandkids to get him up and interacting with people, so this would likely be the last time Alex and I would visit Heine Farms.

Maybe a yellow diamond set against a white gold, reverse-tapered band with ballerina cut baguettes and a handful of circular rubies would lighten the mood. Here's what I was up against as I snuck the ring into my toiletries bag for the drive down to Texas:

The Clock: My decision to propose at Christmas was made in mid-December. This left little time to coordinate with anyone on the ground in Texas. There'd be no friends flying in from out of town, no complex scheme to blow her mind. Whatever I came up with, I'd have to come up with it fast.

The Venue: We stayed at her dad's small ranch home. Close quarters prevented any sneaking around. Every minute would be spent together, which didn't allow for any elaborate, time-consuming projects. Whatever I came up with, I'd have to come up with it under her nose.

The Circumstances: Brave Dave teetered on the brink. The smallest thing could send him into a tailspin of anxiety. The trash bag filled up and the Christmas gifts created too much clutter, both of which led to hours of pacing. Then, the ever-darkening clouds of the big stuff would blow in. He needed to sell his home and move in the next 60 days. Think of that. A man whose depression prevents him from taking out the trash needs to pack up his home and find a new house in a new city in the next two months. Suffice it to say that tensions strained during our visit. Our job was to keep him engaged,[30] to get him up and about and out of his wallowing, to remind him of all the positives in life. Not the most romantic setting. My friends insisted I book a hotel and make a reservation at a nice restaurant in downtown Austin. Circumstances didn't allow us to abandon her father during our stay. Whatever I came up with, I'd have to come up with it on the premises.

My General Idiocy: Why hadn't I planned anything? I knew I wanted to propose the day after Festivus.[31] When I woke up two days beforehand, I had two ideas. I could drive to town, pick up some chips and queso, come back, kneel before her, and present her melted yellow cheese and a yellow diamond to melt her heart. Or, while working on a jigsaw puzzle (a favorite pastime of ours), I could pretend to pick up a fallen piece, kneel to retrieve it, and tell her she's been my missing piece (a line as cheesy as the queso from option one) as I hold out the ring box. Whatever I came up with, I'd have to come up with it while overcoming my moronic initial plans.

 The outlook, much like the weather, was cloudy. But every cloud has its silver lining, so with each seemingly negative factor working against me, I found reasons to remain cheerful. The chaotic situation and daily stressors distracted Alex, so she wouldn't see it coming. Sure, her dad would move out soon, so wouldn't it be sweet to have one last joyful memory on the property? And most of all, it was Christmas, for Christ's sake! A tailor-made, pre-packaged theme for an adorable proposal. With 48 hours to go I still didn't have a plan, but I finally had confidence that I could pull it off.

Two of my best friends had gotten hitched in the previous five months, but I didn't want to be the guy who asks for advice on how to propose. One of them took the new-school approach, an over-the-top night on the town featuring a helicopter ride and a reservation at Chez Cliché, the restaurant on the top floor of the Hancock Building. Very nice, but not something I felt too keen to imitate. The other, while certainly not new-school, took an approach better described as drop-out than old-school. While camping in the Colorado wilderness with his girlfriend of many years, my friend slipped on the rain-slicked terrain and tumbled about 100 feet down a hill of thorny bramble bushes. Laying motionless in the mud, he had an epiphany regarding the fragility of life. Minutes later, when his girlfriend had descended the hill and knelt beside him, he propped himself up on his elbows and told her he wanted to spend the rest of his life with her. To this day I think he's piling up interest on that engagement ring he owes her.

The old-school, which lacked accreditation in the eyes of my close friends, conjures simple images in my mind, usually in the form of a man kneeling on the sand during a brisk stroll along the beach or a homemade picnic in the shade of a majestic willow tree. That's what I aimed for, a healthy balance of the spontaneous wilderness epiphany proposal and the elaborate helicopter champagne experience. Something thoughtful, tender, and personal. I worried that given my constraints, my efforts would come across thoughtless, hurried, and generic.

In a moment of utmost shame, I googled "proposal ideas." Disclaimer: if you are the type of person who rolls his or her eyes at Millennials and shakes his or her head at the type of behavior that simply wouldn't be possible or tolerated prior to the Internet Age, now would be a good time to stretch those eyeballs and loosen up your head-shaking muscles.

Remember the good old days when an elaborate public proposal meant orchestrating a message on the Jumbotron? Well, this ain't your mama's marriage proposal. These days, there are people who make a living as proposal planners. Think about that for a moment. That means there are people who, as autonomous individuals with brains and agency over how they spend their hard-earned income, choose to exchange money for the service of planning proposals. Not only that, but there are enough of these people to provide enough business to maintain the proposal planner industry.

Listicles littered the search results page. *11 Things to*

Do For the Perfect Proposal. 7 Dos and Don'ts to Ensure She Says Yes. These lists are, and this is the *mot juste*, stupid. Essentially, they suggest that if your girlfriend is a vegetarian, you should avoid hiding the ring in a porterhouse. I'll save you some time and whittle it down to a single Do and and a single Don't:

Do avoid these lists.
Don't read these lists.

I love the word goober. I don't know exactly what a goober is, but I know a goober when I see one. Any man who willingly posts on howheasked.com is a goober.

Tucked among the inanity of the listicles, I happened upon the bewildering subculture of the wedding and proposal fanatics[32] who contribute to howheasked.com. I assume other sites exist that serve the same purpose, but since I'm not a goober I couldn't stomach searching them out.

Before I get carried away poking fun at these goobers for writing thousand word essays on their proposals, I'll point out that I'm aware of the hypocrisy of writing this book and mocking those essays. At least I'm not posting mine to the internet and shouting out my love story into the endless void of the information superhighway. I'm making you pay for it.

The couples on this site, to whom I wish nothing but the best, have a different worldview than mine. I don't use Instagram, Facebook, or Snapchat. I don't tweet. It's not that I don't feel that what I have to say is worthwhile, it's that I don't feel that what I have to say is worthwhile to everyone. I don't need a picture of me and Alex plastered on the monitor of all of my acquaintances' devices. I don't need their congratulations. When is it enough? The featured couples on this site share the stories of how they met, with professional photographs of the proposal and videos capturing the reaction. That's all well and good, I suppose. It's nice to have the memento. Where is the value of sharing it with me, a stranger?

Maybe I'm just a salty curmudgeon who doesn't understand modern social society. If it doesn't cause me any harm, I should leave well enough alone and let Marco and Angelica get on with their happy wedding planning. But this type of oversharing, attention-hogging commercialization of love harms us all. This is the world that young girls live in. These are the expectations they hold for their own love stories. Will my nieces be disappointed if their future groom proposes on the shores of Lake Michigan with nothing but a plain old, run-of-the-mill, 10,000 Bitcoin diamond? I can see them looking over their shoulder, expecting the flash mob to jump out, the hot air balloon with all of their robot friends to descend from the sky. All you need is love, but you should also consider hiring a videographer.

The website of the proposal planner links to a proposal flash mob company. It's a brave new world. One of the recent posts offers "9 Reasons to Hire a Proposal Photographer." One of these reasons is to avoid photobombs. Another good way to avoid photobombs is to recall that Instagram hearts aren't more valuable than your own hearts. Keep the cameras away for a minute and hug each other. I promise you'll remember if you're present in the moment, not worrying about whether the stranger in the bushes is capturing your good side.

Can't this moment be about her? About us? I'd prefer

to keep this moment, one of the most personal and intimate moments of my life, in which I'm emotionally vulnerable and focused so much on the woman I love, free of any concerns regarding what other people will think when they see it.

The proposal planners, god bless 'em, are brilliant. They saw an opportunity to create a need and fill it. A man who doesn't know the pitfalls of his wife-to-be's tastes probably shouldn't be proposing. A man who needs someone to ask him if she likes being the center of attention or if she dreads having all the eyes on her hasn't taken the time to think about what he's doing.

Tell her you love her. Be sincere. Give her the ring.[33] That's all there is to it. Now, let's discuss my fee.

My brother proposed to his wife while walking on the beach.

My other brother proposed to his wife at the driving range.

There are no photographs of either event. No flash mobs. No helicopters.

They are both happily married and at the time of writing I picture them smiling, holding a small wad of cash, laughing about the prospect of giving that money to a person who would have presumably planned their proposals. I imagine both of my sisters-in-law would describe the proposals they received as perfect, since they are emotionally stable human beings who understand that value is better measured in self-worth than selfie-worth.

However, you aren't me, so do what you want. That's the whole point of weddings. If livestreaming your proposal makes you and your partner happy, you should do it. I'll even like it if I see it.

Feeling the pressure of the new normal in the proposal world, I began to feel an internal panic welling up inside my chest. I didn't want to disappoint Alex. This is an important event in our lives, and there's a thin line between understated and underwhelming. I had fewer than 48 hours. I pondered my predicament while strolling around Alex's father's property with the dog. The land offered enough space and seclusion to let Mona off leash to prowl about on her own, and I accompanied her through the dew-coated fields mainly to keep her from munching on patches of tall grass. She bounded about beneath an overcast sky, sticking her nose up into the breeze, turning back to me from time to time with her tongue out the side of her mouth, radiating unabashed joy.

On our way in, Mona zagged when it came time to zig, and before I knew it I found myself rushing toward the trout pond, where the threat of a wet dog and a serious canine bathing experience hung ominously over my morning schedule. Once before, at my mom's house in southwest Michigan, Mona leapt into a small pond, forcing Alex and me to give her an unexpected bath. The bathing isn't too bad, but drying a long-haired springer spaniel is no fun. Not for the person holding the hairdryer and the brush, not for the person holding the dog in place, and by no means for the dog herself. Afterwards, I'll find dog hair on the ceiling, inside the cupboards, everywhere. Even after a tedious sweep, vacuum, mop, and wipe-down, it's everywhere. I once found two strands of dog hair under the cap of our Neosporin.

While chasing Mona away from the pond, it dawned on me that I had found my venue. A short flight of stairs led to a landing, about 8' x 8', above the water and beneath the cover of knuckling tree branches. The cars in the driveway acted as a sight barrier between the house and the deck, giving me a hint of privacy in which to operate. I figured if I could get Dave to take his daughter on an errand, all I'd need was an hour to clean up and set the stage. Sometime between then and now, I'd need an excuse to sneak out of the house to pick up supplies. Luckily for me, three weeks earlier I'd mentioned that I could use a haircut.

Beside the black waters of the unused and unkempt pond, the deck looked out over a less than picturesque landscape. It wasn't a vista you'd see at a fishing resort in the Yucatan, but it had a homespun beauty to it. Later, when I asked Dave if there were functional outlets by the deck, he told me he'd built the whole thing himself.

A short pier extended into the water among the twigs and debris. During my first visit to Texas, I'd stood on that pier and fired a gun for the first time in my life. Dave tossed a chunk of wood into the air and I blasted it to pieces with a shotgun. "You're a real maverick, kid," he said. No, wait, that's not how it happened. I missed every shot, possibly clipping a floating Coors Light on my fifth attempt. My right ear is still ringing all these years later. I figured the pier would be a good place to take another, figurative shot by asking Alex to be my wife.

With my plan taking shape, I checked with Alex to see when, if ever, she'd be out of the house. I didn't need much time, but it'd be hard to sneak out during daylight hours without being caught or at least arousing suspicions. She'd see the decorations if I put them up in advance, so my only chance was dusk on Christmas Eve. I asked what the plan was for that evening.

"I got tickets for *Star Wars* at 3:30," she said.

Well, shit.

"Then we can make burgers when we get home."

Under normal circumstances, that's a pretty great night. Given the situation I faced, it caused some problems. Alex had no intention of leaving me alone at the house, and she'd essentially winterized any window I had for set up time. Thanks to *Star Wars*, I'd have to force it.[34]

The day before the proposal, I took off in the afternoon to get a haircut, an experience I typically despise. I opted for the closest discount chain, in this case a SuperCuts conveniently situated between a Home Depot and Walmart. This being Texas, the fastest route to the nearest SuperCuts had me taking three different highways and paying three separate tolls. The state is simply too large.

The haircut went as expected, a brief living nightmare that lingers with me until the next one. I didn't have to wait and went straight to the chair, a blessing that turned out to be a curse. Within five minutes, the place looked like a rose ceremony for a realistic version of *The Bachelorette*, as a handful of single men sat staring in suspense at the hairdressers, hoping to hear their names called. Noticing the line, my stylist accelerated the tempo. I was halfway through a 20-minute haircut, and she managed to get through the last 10 minutes in about 40 seconds.

Freshly shorn, I opted to get my proposal supplies at Walmart. That way, I could drop my car at the auto center for an oil change, thus killing two birds with one stone and creating an excuse in case the Christmas supply shopping ran long. A certain percentage of readers groaned when they read that last sentence. They've been to the Walmart auto center. Walmart is a great place to grab Christmas lights or cheap novelty T-shirts. It's not a great place to have work done on your car. I dropped my keys into the mechanic's upturned palm as he cackled an evil laugh, like Jafar when he took hold of the magic lamp. They quoted me 40 minutes. Plenty of time to find what I needed and make it back for *Star Wars*.

I found the remnants of the Christmas area, a post-apocalyptic scene with frenzied shoppers eager to grab whatever mismatched goods they could snatch from the strewn about remains of ransacked shelves. I knew I needed lights, but beyond that my Christmas list would be entirely impulse buys. Did I need 3' tall candy canes? Fake snow? Garlands? Alex's dad spent most of his day complaining about how there's too much shit in his house. Meanwhile, people kept stopping by to drop off more presents and food, only adding to his anxiety. The last thing he needed was a handful of plastic candy canes in the garage.

I had enough lights to line the top and bottom of the railing around the deck, with ample slack to trace a circle in the center where we could stand. When I started my shopping spree I thought, *If only they made a small Christmas area rug.* Maybe there was a Christmas beach towel. Before leaving for the Home & Bath section I stumbled upon a shelf of Santa hats. Among them, I found what looked like a small sleeping bag, rolled tight and made of the same material as the hats, complete with matching white trim. I unravelled it, thinking perhaps my Christmas towel prayers had been answered. They had. I discovered a Christmas tree skirt, a device with an intended use that, as a Jew, eludes me to this day. It would serve as a red carpet for the proposal. With several hundred feet of lights, a tree skirt, and a youth-sized Santa hat, I checked out and returned to the auto services counter.

My triumphant smile dissipated as the 40 minute window passed, turned to a frown when the hour mark drifted by, transformed into a scowl 10 minutes later, and had mutated into a contorted lockjaw expression by the time they returned my keys. Alex called, urging me to get back to avoid being late. This restricted my options for squirreling away the bag of Christmas supplies, as she'd be watching for the car in the driveway. More importantly, this is still Texas, and three highways stretched between me and my destination.

Star Wars: Episode 8: The Last Jedi. For some reason, these new *Star Wars* movies are viewed as culturally significant. I like them. They're fun and familiar, but at this stage in the *Star Wars* lifecycle they aren't special the way they were in the '70s and '80s. Whether I liked it or not, Alex's determination to get her dad out of the house meant we were all going to the movies. We wouldn't be back until after dark, and when we returned I'd have to create an excuse to disappear, then hurriedly clear the deck's landing and assemble my Christmas scene. If I made it that far without arousing suspicions, I'd sneak back into the house, wash my hands, grab the ring from the toiletries bag, sneak back out of the house, and somehow have Alex follow me outside a minute later.

Spoiler alert: I was a little nervous during the movie.

As usual, Mona played a pivotal role in my plans. The dark side grew stronger, on the big screen and in the big Texas sky, and by the time we got back I had to work with only the moonlight, muted behind cloud cover, and the soft glow of a yellow floodlight light from the driveway grasping at the edges of the deck. Alex and Dave went inside and I grabbed Mona, announcing that she'd enjoy a long walk after spending the afternoon pent up.

I snatched my supply bag from the garage and jogged down to the landing. There, wind whipping at my fingers, I got to work. The night provided an unexpected benefit. Thanks to the cover of darkness, I didn't need to clear the debris as thoroughly from the deck.

The toppled, water-stained plastic folding chairs went first. Next, the rusted, inexplicable 12-pound metal dumbbells. I tossed the larger tree branches over the side wall into the tall grass; meanwhile, smaller twigs went unseen. Like blemishes on a regrettable one night stand in a dimly lit singles bar, these small imperfections would go unnoticed until the harsh light of day the morning after the deed was done.

While all of this happened, Mona barked and whined, restless and confused. A few strongly voiced reprimands got her to quiet down before she blew my cover. Besides the chill from the wind, things were going well to this point. I opened the first box of Christmas lights and dumped the contents on the deck. Four tightly wound strings of lights scattered onto the wood. I held one inches from my face to examine the binding in the darkness. *Twist ties*, I prayed, *for the love of god, let it be twist ties.*

It was zip ties.[35] Luckily, I'd found a rusty blade on

the deck while clearing debris. Dave Heine would later refer to it as his fish knife. I'll forever find joy knowing I couldn't have proposed without my father-in-law's trusty fish knife.

Careful not to turn this romantic evening into a trip to the ER for a tetanus shot, I squeezed the tip of the blade under the plastic binding and, with a shameful amount of effort, managed to snap the lights free. Only seven more strings to unbind. The process added crucial minutes to my scheme, but it needed to be done. I coiled the lights around the perimeter of the railing and used the excess to create a ring of lights on the baseboards. The tree-sleeve fit perfectly within the ring of lights and would function as a centerpiece for me to kneel on. Things looked...fine. The candy canes and snowmen and garlands would have made it look like a lot more effort went into it, and they wouldn't have cost much effort at all, but I liked the cleanliness of it. I liked that she'd be the focus of the moment.

Out of breath, pink-cheeked, and shaking with nerves, I breezed through the living room and shut myself in the bathroom. Alex barely acknowledged me as she sat on a recliner watching TV. I worried that she'd be halfway through making cheeseburgers on the stovetop, but the moment I went inside I remembered a key component to our cooking process: if it involves getting your hands dirty, it's a Sam job. When a recipe calls for removing something from the inside of something that was once alive, or a drain catcher needs to be cleaned, I'll be there. I'm not so much a sous chef as an ew chef. Mixing spices into the hamburger meat and rolling out patties are Sam jobs, so before I got my hands dirty, I'd get to ask Alex for hers.

With the ring box in my pocket, I sidled up behind her and whispered in her ear to meet me by the pond in 60 seconds.

Things got real very quickly. I had some idea of what I'd say, but as I raced to my Christmas tableau I realized I hadn't practiced out loud. I caught myself forming the words with my mouth to an oversized, two-dimensional Mark Hamill a few times just hours before, but that did more harm than good. What if I accidentally asked her to marry Luke Skywalker?

Here are the options available to me leading up to this moment:

The Standard:
Alex, I love you. I will love you for the rest of my life and I can't envision living that life without you by my side.

The Hollywood:
Alex, you complete me. You had me at "y'all."

The Nintendo:
Alex, you are the Princess Peach to my Mario. I will rescue you from Bowser's claws as many times as it takes to keep you safe.

Available in SAP:
Alejándria, eres la mujer más bonita del mundo. Tienes mi corazón por siempre.

The Seuss:
Do you like yellow diamonds and ham? Would you like to marry Sam? Will you marry me with a grin? Will you marry me in Austin?

The Family Feud:

We asked 100 single women, top two answers on the board: Will you marry me?

The one that evokes an inside joke about our eventual marriage involving her dad, whose property I'm utilizing as a meaningful stage:[36]

Someone once asked me what I am and when I'm going to be it. In many respects, I'm not sure how to answer those questions. But in the one part of life that matters most, I am. What I am is in love with you, and when I'm going to be it is forever. Will you marry me?

A little convoluted, but I liked it.

The Santa hat hung lazily over my left ear. Behind me, the spindly bare branches of the overhanging tree obscured the dark pond water. I stood atop the tree skirt taking quick breaths as I watched for Alex's approach from the house. All was well in the temple of my body and mind.

But what if she said no?

An unlikely outcome, but a potential outcome nonetheless. These things do happen. A good friend of mine had been with his girlfriend for nine years, beginning their sophomore year of college. They were engaged for a year until they broke it off only a few weeks prior to Christmas. Maybe Alex is worried. Me marrying her is one thing, that's a no-brainer. But for her to marry me? Me? The scrawny guy with the dead-end job? Am I good enough? If I have doubts, then surely she does, too. Maybe she needs more time. She loves me, but thinks we're in a good place right now. She doesn't like yellow diamonds and ham.

These are the types of nonsensical fears that run through one's head prior to the big moment. Depending on what stage you're at in your relationship and whether or not your girlfriend designed the ring herself, you're either feeling a brave, risky man's vulnerability, or, in my case, a Woody Allen–type neurosis.

Before I had a chance to panic, Mona bolted from the house and jumped into the tall grass, grazing with all the ferocity of her animal ancestors and the efficiency of a John Deere mower. I kept cool, rooted in the circle of lights, as Alex appeared around the side of the Subaru. Part of me felt a pang of brand loyalty as I acknowledged our car would be present for the big moment. Alex wore her purple slippers over thick, white socks decorated with green and pink flowers. Her black leggings disappeared under the lower hem of her original "sleepy shirt," a term we use for select items in both of our wardrobes, which peeked out from her penguin suit, a snug teal jacket that resembles Super Mario when he has special wintry powers in the Wii edition. We have cute names for our clothes.

"Merry Christmas, Alex," I said as she reached the stairs.

"Merry Christmas, Sam," the words passed through a beaming smile.

"Step into my Christmas ring." My first adlib of the evening. She approached and joined me on the tree skirt, where I took her hands and delivered my line. "Someone once asked me what I am and when am I going to be it."

"Mona get down!" Alex snapped at our idiot pet as the dog went through her usual routine of jealous behavior.

"The only way I know how to answer that question is this. What I am is in love with you." Mona jumped again, landing her front paws on our forearms, either to join our slight embrace or, more likely, to hog our affection. I swatted her away and took Alex's hand again. "And when I'm going to be it is forever." I dropped down to one knee, removed the ring box from my pocket, dismissed Mona's inquiring schnozz, opened the box, and held it up in the intoxicating haze of the shimmering Christmas lights. "Will you marry me?"

The next minute flashed by in a flurry of snapshot memories. She said yes, as I'm sure you've gathered based on the remaining pages of this account. I don't recall if I slid the ring onto her finger. I don't think I did. She snatched the box and held it aloft with the driveway light behind her to get a better look at the ring. She knew exactly what it looked like, but it was a thrill to see it in the flesh for the first time. We kissed. We embraced. We gave Mona a little attention and told her she'd no longer be a pet out of wedlock.

Alex wiped her face and announced, "I'm going to cry."

I asked if she liked the Christmas scene and told her about my various struggles and pitfalls over the previous two days as we stood wrapped in each other's arms. We let it sink in for a moment before heading back inside. Looking back, the whole thing benefitted from its imperfection. That's how real life goes. The winds were too high, the temperature a bit too low. Our dog got in the way. Later on, Alex admitted that while she knew it was a familiar reference, the source material for my perfect line didn't land for her. What I said confused her, but that didn't matter, because I was the one saying it and it ended with, "will you marry me?"

Thank god there's no professional quality video. We both looked terrible and I'd look like a fool if anybody ever took the time to watch it. We went back outside with her dad and had him take some pictures. He knew what I was up to, but with his anxiety peaked, I thought it better to act independently than enlist his help in any misdirection. The fewer things I could do to complicate things for him, the better.

He didn't say much during the trip, outside of remarking on the amount of shit in his house and how bad he felt, but he did make it clear that he liked knowing that we shared the moment at his home, on the deck he'd built himself. He's a talented man. Unfortunately, operating the flash and other settings on an iPhone aren't part of his repertoire of talents. We got a couple of usable shots for posterity, and we didn't resort to inviting a stranger to lurk in the shadows of the pond.

We didn't tell her family right away. They'd be over in the morning for Christmas, and it'd be more exciting to tell them in person. Instead, we returned to the house and got started on our celebratory engagement burgers. Engagement or no engagement, homemade burgers are our jam.

Thirty minutes after the big moment, we settled into our life of happy small moments. I mixed the ground beef with the spices, rolling out patties between my palms. Afterwards, I approached the sink and said, "Heine." Without looking up, Alex started the faucet and squirted a dollop of dish soap onto my grease-coated mitts so I wouldn't need to touch anything. If that's not love, I don't know what is.

If any professional proposal planner is reading this, I'm sorry. I know we did everything wrong.

The moment my hands were rid of the slick, delicious burger residue, I called my mom. I'd promised her repeatedly for the last year that I would let her know as soon as this occasion arose.

"Hi Sammy, how are you?"

"I'm well, how are you?"

"Good, good, we're just playing Scrabble, how are things in Texas?"

She ended each sentence with a suggestive lilt.

"Things are good. How's the Scrabble game going?"

"I've got a seven-letter word on my board but I can't use it."

"Seven letters, huh? Is it *engaged*?"

"No! But are you?"

"I think my fiancée would say I am."

I don't understand women. That should be clear by now. My mom cried. She knew I would be proposing to Alex that night. Yet, even with the advance scouting report, she cried.

She wanted to talk to her future daughter-in-law, so I strolled to the kitchen and held the phone out to Alex while my mom rambled on. Alex switched the spatula to her left hand and took the phone, picking up the conversation en-media-nonsense. Within seconds, tears sprung from Alex's eyes.

"I'll toast the buns," I mouthed to her, holding the bag up and indicating the toaster with a nod.

We all experience bizarre moments in life. For Alex and me, this will surely be one of them. When the call ended, we ate burgers at the kitchen table, probably talking about *Star Wars*. I called my dad with the news and nobody cried. With our lives set for a merger and our bellies full of burgers, we nestled together on a recliner designed for one, going as far as to bring all 59 pounds of Mona up there with us. I can't think of a more appropriate way for our family-to-be to begin our betrothal than cozied up on the couch, emanating an aromatic medley of meat, dog, and love.

THE (AVAILABLE) VENUE OF OUR DREAMS

How was "Christ-miss?" Brad asked, not fully grasping the idea behind the yuletide holiday. Any religious topic catches his attention. His home planet doesn't deal much with mythology or religion, and the lengths we humans go to in the name of our gods and our faiths tickles him right behind three of his four knees.

He lay on the bed, those four knees like nodes on wheel spokes as he splayed his legs out in a fan formation. Meanwhile, I stuffed our suitcases together like matryoshka dolls to fit them all in the crawlspace. Our landlord converted the attic of the building into our apartment, creating a myriad of oddly shaped storage cavities and angled ceilings. The refrigerator and the laundry machines are both raised two feet off the ground, sitting atop covered ventilation for the floor below us. I need to get on my toes to reach the dryer knobs, but if I stood one inch taller I wouldn't fit comfortably in the shower or on the couch. The shower has an angled wall, too. Alex and I are just big enough and just small enough to live here. We fit. We're on the fourth floor, surrounded by three-story buildings, giving us plenty of light from all sides. When the wind blows, our apartment sways like a tween slow dancing at the Spring Fling. Most apartments in the city consist of rectangular rooms. Ours is a little funky. It's the perfect venue for us.

Brad rose from the bed and paced beside it, using the point when his head hit the gabled ceiling as an indicator to turn around, like Forrest Gump when he encountered an ocean on his cross country run. I don't think

Brad experienced pain the way humans do. He didn't flinch on impact. That cranial dome of his made a deep, resonant tone each time he hit the wall. "So now that she has agreed to wed you," *doong*, he turned, "When will you have the wedding? I would like to attend. Perhaps" *doong*, turn, "this weekend? I have a good feeling that it will not precipitate on your public street festivity." *Doong*, the sound of the collision echoed through the hollow space behind the drywall.

"Good try," I said, citing his continued effort to master English expressions. "Rain on your parade."

Doong.

The first questions people ask when you tell them you got engaged, regardless of how well they know you or how soon after the actual proposal you run into them, are "when is the wedding?" and "Do you have a date yet?"

Before I got engaged, I thought this was a polite way of expressing interest and demonstrating excitement. In reality, of course, my focus revolved around myself and planning my schedule in advance. Now that I've had people ask me this question I realize that I was wrong. Moving forward, I will only ask about setting a date two months after an engagement, when they've had a chance to pick one. I'll stick with the alternative question, "How did he propose?" In my experience, retelling this story again and again grew stale and tiresome. Trying to orally convey the significance of being at Heine Farms got uncomfortable, as nobody wants to hear about Alex's dad's mental health when they ask how I proposed. Regardless of my personal exception, other fiances will likely have more easily tweetable responses.

"The question isn't when we'll get married," I said, reclining my chair onto its back legs. "It's where."

"Austin," Brad replied mid-*doong*. "The capital city of the Lone Star State, Texas, largest of the contiguous United States."

"Yes, Brad, very good. I see you've done your homework."

"Then it's settled."

"If only things were that easy."[37]

A year before the flash, when Alex and I were excited about having a guest room and I didn't harbor any intergalactic guests, she nonchalantly mentioned that she'd found the perfect wedding venue: The Montesino Ranch. This predates any discussion of her and I getting hitched. She just happened to have come upon it one day, the same way I just happen to know where the nearest golf course is when we're on vacation.[38]

With the proposal behind us and her new jewelry firmly in place, we loaded up the Subaru with all of the goods that necessitated that we drive instead of fly. The largest box contained Alex's childhood playset, "The Castle," and the endless figurines that accompany it. This way, in the event that we have a daughter, once she's old enough to play with it, we'll be ready. In the meantime, we'll store an enormous box in our tiny apartment and move it to our future apartments until lil' Alex Jr. qualifies for the suggested age range. I'm sure by then technology will be out of style and girls will be into analog toys from the late 1980s.

We packed up The Castle, an old armchair, three pairs of cowboy boots, all of our Christmas gifts, and still made room for Mona. We started north with everything except a view through the rearview mirror. We were engaged, and as we sat in traffic outside Dallas, we engaged in our first wedding planning task: calling Alex's dream venue.

I don't remember much of the speakerphone conversation, probably because I exhausted my focus checking my side mirrors. More likely, a wave of anxiety washed over me and didn't recede until halfway through the call. The first thing I remember is Alex asking about available dates. I thought we'd get married in March or April of the following year, giving us 15 or 16 months until a beautiful spring wedding in Texas.

Alex suggested Fall…or even Winter.

Fall dates, the Montesino Ranch director told us, would be hard to come by less than a year in advance. Even spring of the following year looked substantially booked up.

I sat at the wheel counting months in my head. The good news is we were days away from January 1, so the math was easy. The bad news was that we'd have less than a year to get everything done, and it sounded like we were already well behind where we needed to be.

I thought about every wedding I'd ever been to. They have certain things in common, including the slew of "thank you" speeches during which the groom and the parents all thank whoever it was who "put this whole thing together" or "made this all possible." They say, "You don't realize how much work goes into a night like this." I've always dismissed these comments as overly gratuitous nonsense.

Within 10 minutes of our first phone call I realized that I truly didn't realize how much work goes into a night like this.

The director of the ranch recognized we were a

couple of wedding planning n00bs, nothing but a pair of naive greenhorns, and mercifully gave us her spiel on what we'd need to know to get started. The engagement honeymoon was over.

We needed a headcount. And not just a total number of invites, but a good idea of who's from out of town. And not just who's from out of town but who's from out of town but close enough to us that they'd want to stay in on-site lodging. She said a lot of couples choose Texas as a middle ground because they are in "bicoastal" relationships. I guess that's the politically correct way to say long distance. I'm not an omnivore, I'm bi-hungry.

We needed a coordinator, at the very least a day-of planner. All of the venues will require this in one way or another.

We needed an approved caterer.

We needed to know if we'd have a band or a DJ, and what equipment they'd provide and what sort of emcee responsibilities they'd take on.

Oh, and what's our budget?

None of this came as a shock. The venue administrator didn't blow our minds telling us we'd need a photographer. Even hearing it all at once wasn't so bad. The overwhelming part was that it seemed like we'd need details from all of them in order to book any individual one of them, like a wedding planning catch-22. Jane Austen meets Joseph Heller. We can't book our caterer until we have our venue, but we can't book our venue until we know the headcount, and we won't know the headcount until we secure a date, and we can't secure a date until we have the venue. We didn't know anything but needed to move forward with everything in order to get started at all. And Major Major just increased the number of missions I have to fly.

You'd have to be crazy to get married, but nobody will marry you if you're crazy.

Google "wedding planning checklist" and the big three components you'll see listed at the top of the flowchart are finding a venue, setting a budget, and establishing a wedding mission statement. As you can imagine, I'm not big on that last one. The idea behind a wedding mission statement is to make sure Alex and I are on the same page in terms of the big questions. Do we want a large wedding or an intimate wedding? Do we want something formal? Traditional? It makes sense to ask these questions, but I detest the idea of writing them down and calling it a mission statement. It reeks of human resources. Like so much else I encountered throughout the planning process, the mission statement made me view a celebration of Alex and my love through a corporate lens, turning the wedding into a series of business decisions, a project to be managed. My wedding was a commodity and Alex and I were nothing but interchangeable widgets about to be plugged into the machine.

There's an excellent book on writing from Anne Lamott called *Bird by Bird*. Anne, as a young girl, watched her brother struggle to complete a school assignment on birds. The scope of the project felt so large that he didn't know where to begin. It was hopeless. There were just too many birds. Her father sat down, settled her brother's nerves, and gave some incredible advice. "Let's just take it bird by bird."

It worked for the bird report, it works when you're one-eighth of the way through the rough draft of a novel, and it works when you plan a wedding.

Our first bird was researching venues.

They say you share everything once you become engaged, and that includes spreadsheets. Cruising into Oklahoma in our weighted down Subaru, we opened our first shared Google Doc, a spreadsheet that would grow from a list of friends and family into an ever-expanding world of details and deposit due dates. The "Wedding!!" spreadsheet developed into a Pynchon novel of planning details. We intended each entry, each new sheet, and each detail to bring us closer to a resolution, but somehow the more we planned the deeper we sank into chaos.

But let's not get ahead of ourselves. Bird by bird, remember? The first sheet in the shared document contained venue research.

Waiting for me in my inbox I discovered a string of unread messages. Alex had been busy. She'd scoured the Central Texas Hill Country and come up with a robust list of venues. They all looked the same to me, as did the forwarded replies from their representatives.

They congratulated us. They warned us that dates were filling up fast. They loved exclamation points and asking us for more information. They copied and pasted form letters with our names swapped into placeholders for BRIDE and GROOM, and often overlooked the resulting inconsistencies in font.

Not all of them shared their prices up front. This, I'd find, would be a common source of frustration when working with vendors.

From Alex's emails I explored each venue's website. I had a hard time keeping them straight. After a quick browsing session I knew three things:

The wedding would be beautiful no matter where we

got married

We'd kiss under a Texas live oak

Our guests would get a photo op next to a rusted 1950s pickup truck parked in the grass

Picking one of the six venues Alex selected seemed easy.[39] Like any other consumer decision we'd opt for the best combination of price, quality, and location.

Yeah, right.

This wasn't like buying a pizza from one of six nearby restaurants. Unless some of the pizza joints in your neighborhood need you to provide your own crust, and another is only open Monday mornings, and the best one requires customers to stay overnight in Wimberley, Texas. The trickiest part of selecting a venue is keeping track of which one provides X, Y, and Z and which one requires X but doesn't provide Y and asks that you use their in-house Z at a non-negotiable rate. It's wild how Alex and I could fall in love with one place but never give it a chance because they don't provide tablecloths and demand we use their DJ. The venue sheet in the shared doc was starting to look like *The Crying of Lot 49*, and we hadn't even seen a single venue in person.

Alex put me in charge of scheduling the tours during out next Texas trip. We'd help her dad move on Friday, check out three venues Saturday, and three more before our flight on Sunday night. This is what a vacation sounds like when you're planning a wedding. Just once, I'd like to visit Texas and bring my golf clubs.

I got to work on scheduling, doing an excellent job of gathering details from venues on their availability, the length of the tours, and how far they are from one another. I aimed to set them up as efficiently as possible. I achieved this goal and reported the good news to Alex.

Turns out I'm not so smart, as she preferred to spread them out to give herself time to stick around and ask questions. I thought it more likely that she'd take one look at a venue and want to leave early than stay late, but I obliged and put a new itinerary together.[40]

Two and a half weeks later we landed in Austin. The girl working the midnight shift at the rental car booth impressed me with her energetic demeanor. Smiling, bouncing on her heels, she showed us to a Nissan Rogue. It wasn't the Hyundai Elantra I'd reserved, but it was the closest available car. She didn't press the issue when I turned down the insurance.

Before we knew it, Alex and I were back where it all began for one last night at Heine Farms. The stars above were big and bright, deep in the heart of Texas.

Vista West Ranch

The tires of our uninsured Nissan Rogue sprayed loose asphalt into the undercarriage. I gripped the wheel at 10 and 2, laser-focused on the road. I realized that Alex's car insurance wouldn't cover me since I'd rented the Rogue in my name instead of hers. Each chunk of broken driveway caroming off the car's body grated on my nerves. Maneuvering through the rain-slicked Hill Country roads brought more stress than anything I faced in the wedding planning process.

Central Texas Hill Country is gorgeous. With so many out-of-town guests, Alex wanted to make sure everyone got out of the city to see what her native habitat had to offer. People think of Texas as a desert environment, all oil derricks in vast, hazy plateaus of dirt. Maybe that's true out west in the mesas, but the Lone Star State boasts incredible rolling hills and forests in the south central region, and out east you'll flirt with Louisiana bayou terrain. Having people drive out to the venue through some of those hills made it onto Alex's checklist, and the Vista West Ranch more than checked that box.

Vista West Ranch, like everything else in Texas, is 45 minutes away. Texas is big. Alex claims that the distance from the northern extreme to the southern tip of the state would stretch from Maine to San Diego. That's not true, but she does make less exaggerated but equally surprising claims that probably are true. Whenever I visit Texas, whether it be Austin or San Antonio, I'm amazed at how far away I am from wherever I need to go. We need a gallon of milk? 45 minutes. We're going out to dinner? 45 minutes. Starting to get late? Sunset is 45 minutes away. Need a haircut? Three highways and 45 minutes to the barber.

I love my 45 minutes shtick. I've been using it for years despite mixed reactions. I don't think people find it as funny as I do, probably because they think it's a joke and I know it's a reality. Nevertheless, within minutes of meeting Carl, our guide to Vista West, I'd broken into my routine on how unsurprised I was to find that it took 45 minutes to get to the venue. He didn't seem interested as he stood staring at the parking lot waiting for Alex, the one whose opinion he knew actually mattered. She stayed behind in the car to finish giving her mom directions. Vivian planned to tag along throughout the weekend's slate of tours. Normally, I'd be thrilled to have her join us. One more set of eyes and another head to nod at Alex's suggestions would take the pressure off me and give me the freedom to roam about the grounds from time to time. However, Vivian had suffered some recent health setbacks and walked with the aid of a cane, which made it difficult for her to keep up during two days of Hill Country walking tours.

Being a true embodiment of the state she loves, Vivian was about 45 minutes away, so we started without her.

Carl showed us into the reception hall, a barn designed with so much rustic flair that I expected George and Lennie to walk in after a morning of buckin' grain bags in the fields. Despite the heavy-handed thematic elements, the barn boasted the typical charms. High ceilings, homemade light fixtures floating like celestial bodies, and 60" roundtops that may or may not have been rented for that night's wedding.

Another couple joined us for the tour, a pair of Latino lovebirds who flitted about with their hands in their pockets, stealing occasional shy glances at us. Two older women buzzed between the floral centerpieces for that night's reception, arranging every petal in its place, properly pollinated and positioned as we stood in the center of what would be a dance floor a few hours later, in the exact spot that a couple of newlyweds would cut the cake.[41] If we chose to get married at Vista West, we too would have that memory in the same spot, as would the couple sharing the tour, and hundreds of others.

The wedding industry sells the myth that your wedding is special. Part of getting married is realizing, and accepting, that it isn't. Your wedding is much the same as the '53 Packard sitting in the grass beside the Vista West barn. It's built on an assembly line, sent along piece by piece on the conveyor belt from vendor to vendor, built the same way by the same people again and again. You get to customize a little more than a

Model T, but what we'd do at Vista West wouldn't be all that different from what our tour compadres would do for their Vista West wedding.

Carl guided us outside to the ceremony space, a patch of grass shaded by a trio of mesquite trees, highlighted by a dense trellis at the far end. Vivian, who'd wobbled into the reception hall at some point during Carl's spiel, asked about the trellis's ability to hold flowers. She'd made a point of telling Carl, and the women doing the indoor prep work, that she'd bring in flowers from Flowers by Nancy 2 in Lakeway, a friend's establishment that Carl did an admirable job pretending to have heard of.

To our left, the '53 Packard slowly disintegrated in the grass, and beyond the trellis the landscape treated us to a beautiful view of rolling greenery. Somewhere out there, Carl said, was another old car for photo ops. The grounds offered plenty of space for guests to roam about and find a quiet spot to sneak a joint, take a leak, or do something more appropriate but less likely given the personalities on my side of the invite list. We strolled around the side of the barn and discovered a quiet area with a firepit, where, for a small fee, we could hire an attendant to keep an eye on the flames.

Carl presented the property like an experienced waiter presents the menu, anticipating the common questions, passing along the wisdom of previous guests, and generally making an effort to smile and act as though he doesn't have to do this exact same routine several times a week. For example, we asked how the grass would look pending the season. St. Augustine's in the summer, ryegrass planted in the winter. A robotic reply. As for the weather, "December can be hit-

or-miss," he warned. "But November should be safe."

Alex and I wanted a fall wedding. She liked the aesthetics of it and I heeded the advice of friends and coworkers who encouraged us to get it over with and not wait until spring. "You'll just sit there all winter finding new problems and stuff to stress about," they said. Given that we started touring venues in February, we didn't have the luxury of picking a date. Instead, we were at the mercy of the venues' availability.

To ensure good weather, we aimed for mid-October to early December.

To ensure we weren't overrun by hip young people, we crossed off the weekend of Austin City Limits.

To ensure our guests wouldn't hate us, we eliminated the weekends on either side of Thanksgiving.

At first, Alex argued that it was more important to avoid conflicts with Halloween, citing Thanksgiving as a "wash holiday." Sometimes I just don't understand what goes on in her head. Halloween fell on a Wednesday that year. Oh, and it is a holiday for children that doesn't involve adults travelling and taking time off work. But I digress. The point is, we had a small window for dates and we knew we'd wind up stuck with whatever date our eventual venue could offer.

Next, Carl led us back through the barn and up two flights of stairs to the bridal suite. If you ever lose sight of the fact that weddings are for brides, not grooms, take a look at the quality gap between bridal suites and groom's quarters.[42] The attic of the barn traded in the rustic theme for a touch of elegance. Like our apartment back in Chicago, Vista West converted an attic with a gabled roof ceiling into a finished space. The suite shared an eerie resemblance to our home, featuring a long, narrow hall with large rooms on either end and plenty of windows to flood inhabitants with natural light. If it was anything like our place, it baked in the sun all summer and couldn't be kept cool. If I'd learned anything from wedding planning, somehow I'd wind up paying for Vista West's air conditioning.

Alex loved it. Alex loved most of the bridal suites. It's hard not to love them if you're a bride, picturing yourself surrounded by your closest friends and family, professional beauticians fussing over every lash and pore, revelling in the abundance of throw pillows. Carl said something about mimosas while Alex and I wandered past the bathroom (thankfully not rustic) to check out the overhead view of the ceremony area, a nice perk for gauging the crowd in those final minutes before heading downstairs.

Most of the venues we looked at have a lot in common. As such, they find interesting ways to distinguish themselves. Vista West Ranch did so through the Bunkhouse. Again, after hearing the word *bunkhouse*, I checked over my shoulder to make sure Curley's wife wasn't sneaking around looking for trouble. But the Vista West Bunkhouse skewed a bit more upscale than its cousin in *Of Mice and Men*. This one was for groomsmen, an oasis in a desert of wedding day stress, where my trusted brothers and friends could take care of any issues and ensure my comfort and relaxation. The ideal setting for *Of Mice and Mensch*.

Somehow, the one-story, four-room structure could sleep up to 20 people.   Or so said Carl. It was the best groom's quarters we'd see on the trip, and possibly in our lives, stocked with a big-screen TV, yard games, plenty of couches, and a full kitchen. It would more than do the job on the big day.

But the Bunkhouse was also Vista West's option for on-site lodging, and the venue had strict liability policies regarding who could stay and who could leave. Anyone who went into the Bunkhouse for a drink after the reception wouldn't be permitted to leave the premises. That way, the venue isn't liable for any after-hours drunk driving. If my eldest brother and his wife wanted to stop in to celebrate for 15 minutes, they'd be forced to crash on the couch within projectile vomiting range of my drunken idiot buddy who'd be screaming at the top of his lungs for the ensuing few hours. Meanwhile, my brother's small children would be on their own, presumably taking shelter in a '53 Packard.

The Bunkhouse would have been the ideal spot for an afterparty if we got married as 22-year-olds. But I'd be 30 on the big day, and I don't imagine anyone I know would want to be trapped in that frat house overnight.

We left Vista West scrambling to find a way to make the Bunkhouse work. Before we made it to the car we developed a list of potential Bunkhouse residents. We acted as though it were the X factor for the entire wedding. We'd go on to leave each tour feverishly tackling some unique challenge the venue posed. Even while it happened we recognized how insane it was to think that way. We hadn't seen the next five venues, nor did we fall in love with Vista West. In fact, the barn was too dark and too rustic and we already knew we wouldn't get married there. Still, we addressed the Bunkhouse issue as though we'd paid the deposit and only then realized we had a problem. We focused on the strange negative, and none of the positives. Next time it'd be the food, or the location, or whatever it may be that wasn't just right, and we'd go through the same exercise all over again.

By the time we arrived at the next venue I'd decided to keep it simple. Why stay on-site with liability issues, limited space for guests, and transportation problems when we can just stay at a hotel with all of our friends and family?

Boy oh boy would that idea cost me.

Pecan Springs

After a scratch- and accident-free rental car commute, our trio of brave wedding planners arrived at their second destination. We approached the main building of Pecan Springs, a 6,000-square-foot air conditioned behemoth, wary of its generic facade. Being at Vista West felt like walking through the pages of *Magnolia Magazine*, entering a world of faux southwestern barn flair. Stepping through the door of Pecan Springs and its prefab, build-by-number architecture felt like entering an Olive Garden.

A scene of utter chaos awaited us inside. No fewer than 20 people pinballed into one another, scurrying about in the cavernous space. An overcast sky poured homogenous gray light through large, window-paned doors lining the opposite wall, turning the contrast down and sapping the room of color. Beyond the doors we saw the open fields of the property, green and dreary beneath a mashed potato sky. Inside, caterers and staff hustled about with the practiced efficiency and indifference known only to veterans of the service industry. We stood in the foyer taking it all in, waiting for someone to acknowledge our arrival. Vivian took a seat on a couch as Alex and I picked up some of the literature sprinkled atop the hall table.

Pecan Springs had earned its share of distinctions. The Knot, Wedding Wire, and Brides Austin had all bestowed their seal of approval, assuring us that the venue was up to their standards, though I don't think the criteria will ever be made public. Another framed certificate informed us that Pecan Springs was an "Official Austin Wedding Venue." The governing body that made the determination remains unknown, so I'll take their word for it.

These awards and accolades rub me the wrong way. Maybe I'm being unfair, since just about every consumer product has a star rating and some sort of institution in place to offer a distinction of record. If I trust Michelin stars and Zagat reviews, why not Best of the Knot?

I'll tell you a story that explains why I don't trust Wedding Wire's rankings. My friend works for a food packaging, manufacturing, and distribution company. They make crackers, bagel dogs, and cheesecake on a stick. He often works with grocery store chains, and once visited a smaller franchise and fell in love with their selection, quality, and price. It was far better than the experience he had shopping at major chains, and he told his boss that he thought this place would grow to become a huge success. The only problem was that the smaller shop was situated on a difficult-to-access corner of a large intersection, requiring would-be customers to make an extra turn to find the entry point. Meanwhile, the major chain sat across the street with ideal access to two main roads. My friend said that if the two had wound up switching places, the smaller shop would have thrived. His boss then explained that it was not by chance that the major chain wound up where it did. The major chains have deals with cities for first rights in selecting any new property for development, so the smaller, better shop will always have a worse location.

I think about this story often, as it reminds me that we don't make as many decisions as we think we do. Even when it comes to weddings, we're subject to the dealings of a few high-powered people who determine our options. The city and the grocery store have arranged for me not to discover the boutique shop, and I'm not so naive as to believe that Pecan Springs and a sales associate at Brides Austin haven't worked out a mutually beneficial arrangement that brought us there to begin with. I can't help but think that the only reason we visited Pecan Springs was because of search engine optimization, a few lines of code that determine where I'll spend the most important day of my life.

The wedding industry is big business. They'll dress it up with all the love they can, but at the end of the day, it's still a business, and the more I learned about it the more my stomach churned. Before I could identify the source of my unease, our Pecan Springs contact finally made contact, introducing herself and complimenting Alex's ring. "Gorgeous," she said, looking up from her two-handed grip on Alex's palm. "Sorry for the noise. We have a wedding tonight."

We followed her through the reception hall. I trailed behind with Vivian as Alex asked questions about which dessert tables were provided and which we'd need to rent. I don't know why she bothered. We knew immediately we weren't going to get married there. The room created an echo chamber, with concrete floors amplifying every sound. Chairs scraping, silverware clinking. I could hear everything except the words Alex spoke 10 feet away from my ears.

Our guide, overworked and double-booked, kindly held the door as she let us out back like unwanted dogs, free to sniff out the ceremony sites around the sprawling property. We found everything you'd expect from an Official Austin Wedding Venue, all right there in front of us. We saw the Tree Line site from the Fireplace site, which sat beside the Pavilion, adjacent to the Pergola. We'd stepped into a catalog. It was like a wedding planning wholesale warehouse. Costco for brides.

A few minutes later our host brought us back to the foyer, only to be distracted by a pressing task. While she attended to the matter at hand, Alex's questions fell to her assistant. First of all, I don't blame our host for taking care of the imminent problems for the clients who had already booked and paid for her services. She could probably read our faces and see we weren't taking the bait, regardless of how many glowing testimonials the Knot offered. However, I do blame her for foisting her assistant on us. Within seconds I knew we were dealing with a special breed of idiot. To be fair, she was a new hire still getting the hang of things. To be unfair, she may as well have been inflatable. Not only did she have zero grasp on anything related to her business, but we could have acted overtly condescending and rude and she wouldn't have had the capacity to realize we were mocking her. Of course, Alex and I are wonderful people who would never do that until we were out of earshot. Though given the acoustics in that room, earshot was tough to gauge.

The Waters Point

About an hour southwest of Austin, halfway to San Antonio, there's a place called Wimberley, a vacation town with a population a smidge below 3,000 and an economy based on river tubing. They import cityfolk and export smiles.[43] Wimberley, like Tom Cruise and roly poly bugs, is exactly what you'd expect it to be based on its name. At least, that's what I can tell from the brief stops I've had there over the years. If you like fun facts that aren't fun, you'll love this about Wimberley: it's where Leon Jaworski, special prosecutor in the Watergate case, died while chopping wood.

#Wikipedia.

Unfortunately, we didn't travel to whimsical Wimberley to float down the river with a six pack of Lonestars or prepare for a long winter with minor figures from 20th century American history. We were there for business. We needed to tour The Waters Point. The venue checked several boxes for us, featuring onsite lodging, a Hill Country experience, and a vibe that suited Alex's tastes. Still, we had an ulterior motive for including it on our itinerary. We knew we had an early start with the next day's venues, and with Alex's family no longer living in Austin we needed a place to stay that didn't put us all the way in San Antonio with a two-hour drive to start our day. Lucky for us, The Waters Point encourages overnight tours.

At first, I felt guilty taking advantage of their generosity. Guilt soon gave way to apprehension, as the threat of an inescapable hard sell loomed over the night. By the time we left, I realized that they offer the overnight experience at no charge because they have to. They have confidence in their product and know the more we're exposed, the more likely we are to book. It almost worked, too.

After a brief chat with the hostess—a lovely woman who, believe it or not, thought Alex's ring was "gorgeous"—we strolled about the idyllic Hill Country scenery. When I say idyllic, I mean straight-out-of-a-fairy-tale idyllic. Deer frolicked through the grass beneath a setting sun, trees smiled at us and tipped their caps as we passed, and birds sang out in melodic choruses.

The southern border of the property runs along the Blanco River, just yards from the point where it intersects with Cypress Creek.[44] We descended a grassy hill to reach the riverbank, where a rocky outcropping served as a picturesque, though logistically challenging ceremony site. While visually stunning, the river produced a lot of ambient noise, attracted insects, and wasn't the type of flat surface that ensures nobody faceplants. Besides, of all the senses, memory is most closely tied to smell, and I'd prefer to remember the most important day of my life without phantom river odors.

Instead of a lush green slope, the opposite side of the river met with a 60-foot rockface. I stood on the outcrop and admired the striations in the rock, thinking of how ludicrous our lives and traditions are in the face of geologic time. Brad would agree. Meanwhile, Alex and our host paced along the bank and back up the hill towards the cabins.

Our tour wrapped up after scoping out the possible ceremony sites, the small, though adequate dining hall, and the outdoor, covered dance floor. It was a beautiful venue, the best we'd seen on day one, hands down. It had been a long day, especially following a day of moving house and trudging along with the knowledge that we'd be doing it all again the next morning.

I needed a couch. The Waters Point provided.

Cabin isn't the best word for the on-site lodging. *Lodge* seems more appropriate. We weren't exactly roughing it in the cabin. Flat-screen TV, full kitchen, and this being Texas, separate air conditioning units in each room. The deck overlooked the river, and could have functioned as the cocktail reception site given its size and seating capacity. I faced so many comfortable outdoor patio furniture options that I didn't know where to sit when I called my brother to recap the day's events.

I explained our day-one dilemma. The best venue we'd seen was in Wimberley, and a Wimberley wedding isn't an Austin wedding. About a quarter of our guests could stay on-site, but who knew if they'd actually want to? With only one night booked at the Waters Point, where do those guests stay the night before? The rest of our out-of-town guests would be forced to make a trip to Wimberley and miss out on their chance to see Austin.

My brother gave sound advice. "Do whatever you want. People will make it work. I went to a wedding once where every guest was forced to get up to watch the sunrise. It'll be fine."

I pondered this while Vivian and I drove into town to grab dinner and swing by H-E-B. Practicing extreme caution, I inched the uninsured rental car through the narrow gate, clearing the brick pillars on either side, and glided past the familiar souvenir shops, antiques stores, and family-owned cafes of an American vacation town.

Despite a recent heart scare and recent cancer scare, Vivian can't deny her sweet tooth. I stood by the register holding three burgers and a 24 ounce bottle of Heineken until she appeared from a distant aisle toting a couple of six packs. One Coca Cola and the other miniature chocolate eclairs. I forget which one started the day and which ended it.

Given the day we'd had, I couldn't blame her.

Mercury Hall

I drove in from Wimberley on my own, with Alex taking the wheel of her mom's old Cadillac to give Vivian a break from driving. The Caddy is an amazing machine. I can't believe it's still running. Every time we visit I notice the hole in the taillight has grown another inch or that the front bumper has new concave design elements. On an earlier Texas trip, Vivian picked us up from the airport in the Caddy. She emerged from the car looking like Mrs. Claus in an all red sweatsuit. Her sleigh was packed for Christmas Eve, too. We spent 15 minutes rearranging junk from the back seat and trunk —including two 20-gallon bags of tortilla chips and a pungent Cavalier King Charles Spaniel—until we could get our luggage and bodies into the car. Wondering about those giant bags and discovering they were filled with chips will forever be a favorite Texas moment for me.[45]

While Alex conducted the queso car, I rolled along the highways relishing the alone time. I rarely put the lone in the Lonestar State during our visits, so you can imagine how relaxing a quiet drive would be in the midst of a stressful string of venue appointments. That's not to say I could relax. After all, I had to rack my brain to remember everything from Driver's Ed. to avoid damaging my uninsured rental. I pulled out all the old tricks, from the scan technique to the racecar turn. That's it, though, since those are the only two things I remember from Driver's Ed. After 45 minutes, we reached our first venue of the day: Mercury Hall.

Here's what I know about Mercury. It's small, it's too close to the sun, and as a result its orbit takes only 88 days. Mercury Hall wasn't too different. Also small, I needed all of 88 seconds to circumvent the property. Though it wasn't too close to the sun, it did suffer a similar uninhabitable proximity to the highway. The hum of cars zipping past and the occasional bellow of a truck's horn cascaded over the sloping yard. Deal-breakers.

Wondering why the Mercury Hall experience doesn't include a description of a woman complimenting Alex's gorgeous ring? I'll explain. She didn't show. We knocked on the office door. Nobody in. We peered into the reception hall, a white building with stained glass windows that easily could have doubled as a house of God. God only knows why it was empty. We called, but she didn't answer. We emailed, texted, and tried some telepathy but failed to connect. She eventually emailed to apologize, citing that she was under the weather.

That type of service goes hand in hand with the quality of the venue itself. It reminded me of the fine dining establishment I worked for in my early twenties. It looked nice enough, but any close inspection would turn up major flaws. I thought of Austin's movers and shakers, members of the subcultures that attend regular fundraisers, charity galas, or networking mixers. I picture these people opening their invitations and rubbing their temples as they think, "Crap. Mercury Hall again."

Barr Mansion

Four down, two to go. That's not a lot left to go. These six venues were the best we could come up with. If none of them fulfilled Alex's dreams, then we'd have been shit out of luck. The last thing I wanted to do was set up a second venue trip to look at six more out-of-the-way places that, at the end of the day, are pretty much the same. I crossed my fingers as I pulled into the parking lot beside Barr Mansion.

Our self-guided trespassing tour of Mercury Hall flew by. It's amazing how much quicker these things go when you don't have to feign interest and be polite. As such, we were early and had time to kill. I arrived first, ahead of the ladies, who had stopped for gas, and idled in the lot with an uninsured door open to let in a warm Texas winter breeze.

The Mansion did justice to its name. From the car I admired the stately charm of the house, with a wrapped porch extending around three sides of the structure, and a second floor veranda to match. I could see why Southern girls would love it. It speaks to the old money, *Gone With the Wind* sentiment, giving off plantation vibes and reeking of original sin despite construction breaking ground 27 years after the emancipation proclamation.

Foghorn Leghorn would fit right in.

I'd need a white polyester suit.

The owner purchased the property from the descendants of the Barr family in 1981 and thought, *Hey, I bet people would love to get married outside this house!* Now there's a website that pays homage to the cultural significance of the edifice. If you skim over the "About" page you'll catch the words "Christopher Columbus." If you're anything like me, you'll enjoy the mystery of how Columbus and Barr Mansion could possibly have any connective thread more than actually reading the two paragraphs to find out.

After Alex and Vivian showed up, we went inside and made our introductions. Our hostess, a young woman of ambiguous race wearing pink shoes, shirt, and eyeshadow, reminded me of a living emoji. She gushed over Alex's ring[46] and we were on our way.

The hostess gave her spiel as we stepped on creaky floorboards and admired creepy portraits of the Barrs. We learned which family members lived where, which elements were the original 1890 fixtures and which had been repaired or replaced. We moved from room to room, each one like a stage set with props to give depth to a period piece. It's not to say it lacked authenticity or failed to delight, but I couldn't shake the feeling that it was a better venue for an elementary school field trip than our wedding. As usual, the bridal suite blew us away. A bit hoity-toity, sure, but it had elegance coming out the wazoo. Downstairs, I'd be posted up in the library all day with my groomsmen. Normally I enjoy sitting around surrounded by books, but on my wedding day? Nah. I need distraction, stimulation. I need the Golf Channel. Unfortunately, they didn't have television in 1890.

It turned out that the house itself was mainly a prop. The ceremony would be held outside (beneath a sprawling live oak, duh) and the reception area waited beyond the yard, hidden by a row of topiary bushes. Access to the interior of the house was limited to the wedding party, and even we'd have restrictions on when we could come in and which rooms we could use. More like Barred Mansion, am I right?

The aesthetic vibe suffered a dramatic shift between the Mansion-adjacent ceremony and the reception area. We strolled down the path through the bushes and encountered a massive wall of glass. It was a Texas take on the Louvre, shimmering in the sunlight, reflecting our image back at us. Me, hands in pockets, waiting to go home, Vivian leaning on her cane, Alex with arms folded over her chest, her body language indicating that the tour could just as well be over. And not to be overlooked, our hostess, glowing like a Hostess Pink Snowball.

Foghorn Leghorn didn't make as much sense in the shadow of the glass behemoth, but then again, if he'd have been on the property they'd probably have served him for dinner, as the venue offered in-house catering and used its own organic garden.

"Shall we?" Pinky motioned towards the door with an upturned palm. Onward, we pressed into the glass goliath. Inside, I felt as though I'd entered an airplane hangar. Remnants of the previous evening's festivities littered the space. Flowers, mostly. Alex hit Pinky with questions as I snaked my way through the tables. Just beyond the glass hangar, Barr Mansion offered a secondary space, a tented area that could easily hold 300 guests. Should we book a date, Pinky assured us, we'd have full access to both areas.

Perfect! We could have even more space that we don't like and no access to the part of the venue we thought we'd be touring.

The tour didn't really get started until we sat down in the office to go over how Barr Mansion handles rentals and pricing. Barr Mansion allows us to create our own menu for the event from their catering catalogue. They make everything on-site with organic ingredients grown in their own garden. This all sounds wonderful, right? So easy, yeah?[47] Never fear, they've concocted a star pricing system to ensure confusion. Each item corresponds to a number of stars. Certain appetizers are worth one or two stars, while entrees run as high as six stars. Within this system there are hundreds of exceptions and caveats, but the general rule involves adding up the stars you've selected and comparing your star count on the star-to-dollar conversion chart to see what pricing tier your menu correlates to. Then you can add or remove stars within the tier. But be careful, because certain substitutions involve additional stars.

I used to play poker with my brothers and uncles. This was back in the mid-2000s, when Texas Hold 'Em took the nation by storm. We'd all throw in $20 and have a good time acting like we knew what we were doing. One of my uncles insisted that we refer to the chips with absurd denominations. Instead of saying white chips are worth a quarter, red chips 50 cents, and blue chips a dollar, adding up to $20 worth of chips, he preferred saying white chips represent 25,000, reds 50,000, and blues 100,000. He should work at Barr Mansion.

Wouldn't it be easier to put a dollar amount next to those appetizers? I know exactly how much a dollar is worth, and I have plenty of experience adding up dollars to find a total cost. I can't say the same about the star chart.

The longer we sat with the Pink Lady reviewing the details, the more certain we were that we wouldn't choose Barr Mansion. After the star chart pricing fiasco, we moved on to the rental catalogue. Some venues really nickel and dime their customers. Honestly, I think it's a bad look that can't be worth the revenue it generates. Plus, it's extortion. Are your guests the type of humans who enjoy sitting down? Yes? Well then, you'll want to rent this couch for $500 so that three of them can sit. Do your groomsmen enjoy sitting in a library reading books all day? No? Better rent this $35 bocce ball set.

The one-two punch of the star chart and the rental gouging catalog left Alex reeling, unable to lift her metaphorical gloves in the Barr Mansion bout. If there were a ref in the ring, he'd have started counting. Unfortunately, after two days of venue visits and 15 minutes of star count calculations, Alex lost the ability to count to 10. It seemed simple enough when Pinky walked us through the day-of schedule. We get nine hours. But that was just a lie. We get nine hours including X hours set aside for prep work, Y hours for a ceremony and reception, and Z hours for breakdown and clean up. We were allowed to show up halfway through the X hours and had to leave half-way through the Z hours.

Nothing like a little algebraic variables to simplify things on the biggest day of your life.

Alex couldn't do it. She just couldn't.

"Wait, so what time do we get here?"

"How long is the ceremony?"

"Oh, so we get eight hours? Or nine? And we get here at noon? No, 1:00?"

Later on, Vivian told me she remembered the exact moment that my face transitioned from a "this is cute" smile to a "let's get the fuck out of here" grimace.

Eventually, Alex got a handle on the whole thing, which meant we could leave and never worry about it again. But before wrapping up, Alex needed to see one of the local photographer's sample books one more time. As I shifted my weight forward and rose from the couch, she flipped to a picture taken outside the house. In it, a southern belle stood on the second floor balcony flanked by her bridesmaids. Below, her bridegroom and his cronies, dressed to the nines in their coattails, stood at attention. "This is adorable," Alex said. "We have to do this. I really want a picture like this."

Given that there wasn't anything else we loved about the venue, we faced the decision of whether the photo op was worth $40,000, or however many stars that figure equates to.

The Addison Grove

My brother Rick married his high school sweetheart. My brother Andy also married a girl from his graduating class, though they didn't know each other until years later, meeting after college.[48] Their weddings took place close to home, at suburban venues around Chicago. Rick's wife, Jenny, had known her entire life where she'd tie the knot. No out-of-state trips for them, just a pitstop on the way home from Sunday brunch to meet the coordinator and sign the paperwork.

Rick and Jenny hosted me for dinner a few days before I left for the venue expedition. Sitting with an old fashioned in my hand and my feet up on the coffee table —showing off the Costco socks that matched Rick's, almost certainly a Hanukkah gift from our mom—I turned an open laptop to Jenny and had her peruse the websites of each venue on our list.

No.
No.
That's cute but no.
No.
No.
This one is my favorite.

Before she started, I pledged not to share her opinions with Alex. I didn't want any outside influence anchoring Heine's judgment. The good news is Jenny preferred the same venue that Alex liked the most. We saved the best for last, reserving our final tour for the odds on favorite: The Addison Grove.

Tension filled the uninsured rental car as I steered my way to our final venue and our last hope. Five failed trips drifted away in the metaphorical rearview mirror, while I compulsively checked the literal rearview, stressing over every bump and dip of the Hill Country roads. I preferred to follow Vivian instead of having her tail me. The last thing I needed was to get rear-ended by that Cadillac.

They parked in the shade on the gravel lot and exited the car as I trundled in behind them. I stepped out, took one look at the property, and suggested we pay the deposit and head to the airport. We knew right away. It checked all the boxes. To the left, trees rose above a small pond. Beside the pond stood a low rock wall straight out of *Shawshank*. The bridal suite was situated directly in the center of the lush natural scenery, a small yellow cottage among the dense green of the shaded grass and lazy, swaying trees. Past the cottage stood another grove of trees, an area designed for ceremonies, and beyond that, lining the edge of the property, actual Texas longhorns grazed beyond a wooden fence, waiting for that night's wedding guests to feed them delicious pellets and pose for selfies with the local fauna.

To our right, in front of the fence, we took in the majesty of the barn. Heine had described the vibe she wanted as "shabby chic." I didn't know exactly what that meant until I entered a powder blue barn with enormous chandeliers inside. The barn offered enough space for seating and a dance floor without feeling cavernous or cramped, and one side of the structure was outfitted with sliding doors to allow an open-air feel. On the other side of the doors, abutting the longhorns, a patio served as a cocktail hour space with a bar and a handful of high-top tables. They even had a fire pit for good measure.

Not only was the venue itself exactly what we wanted, we'd also somehow found a place that was less than 45 minutes from downtown Austin. At only half an hour, it allowed our guests to experience some Hill Country charm without requiring a trip to Wimberley.

I had one happy Heine on my hands.

Happy Heine=Happy Sam.

Here's how I knew I was ready for marriage. Throughout my life I've made the mistake of going a bit too far, saying something for a laugh that shouldn't have made it through my filter. I've never been good at passing up a joke, and a lot of my jokes are bad,[49] so this trait often leads to regret. That day, I made it through the entire tour of the Addison Grove without making any snarky comments to Alex about how we should have skipped the entire trip and trusted what we saw on the Internet. A bad joke, right? Yet still, it was one that I felt compelled to make. But I held it in because her happiness means more than satisfying my childish, petty sense of humor. There'd be plenty of time for tactless jokes in my vows.

We enjoyed a mostly self-guided tour of the property and ended in the barn. Alex paced the center of the room, measuring an imaginary head table with her stride as I wandered toward the bathroom to do some reconnaissance. I've found that it never hurts to know the toilet situation in advance of a major life event. That's Nervous Pooper 101. Single use? Powerful exhaust? Does the floor appear to be sweating? How well do these stalls lock?

Wendy, who ran the ship over at the Grove, made sure to point out how gorgeous Alex's ring was as she met us in the barn. She showed us to the groom's quarters, a room at the far end of the barn where I was thrilled to discover a private bathroom for VIPs. I'll let your imagination run wild on what the P stands for.[50] As I've discussed, the groom's room doesn't need to be complicated. Give me a couch, a toilet, some yard games, and a television. Meat and potatoes. Once again the Addison Grove checked all the boxes, with a mini fridge to boot.

Wendy walked us through our options for dates. Saturdays, as usual, weren't available until 2055 because people are insane. But Sundays come with perks, like 20 percent off alcohol costs. Does it create problems for your guests because they'll need to take Monday off work? Yes. Is it worth it to save thousands of dollars? You better believe it. Would I be sitting in that groomsman room with my brothers tracking our fantasy football teams hours before the ceremony? The kick is up...and it's good!

Wendy escorted us to the bridal suite to end the tour

and talk details. They know what they're doing. The bridal cottage is the crown jewel of the property. Any bride-to-be who's on the fence about the Addison Grove takes two steps into the cottage and her decision is made. Then she mixes some cement and reinforces the metaphorical fence so that no other bride can ever discover the treasures on the side she chose.

The groom's room was perfect because its furnishings consisted of a simple couch, table, and television. The bridal cottage was perfect because I'd have been laughed at for not knowing the appropriate name or pronounciation of its antique furniture. A settee? Probably had one of those. Chiffarobe? Vanity? Dressing table? Sure, whatever that is.

The spacious interior may as well have been decorated by Alex herself. It was exactly what she wanted. I pictured her in front of the mirror touching up her makeup, her dress hanging behind her on the special wedding dress hanger in the special wedding dress hanging alcove. Knowing we'd book the venue made the images even more real. This was where we'd get married.

We sat chatting for 10 minutes, Alex fielding questions while I happily played the cliché of the clueless fiance. Everything was wonderful. We could finally go home and get some rest. But you've been reading this tale long enough to know that nothing is easy.

Planning a wedding is like attempting to transfer a pile of laundry from the dryer to the folding area. Try to stick with me on this one. Each article of clothing represents a planning task. The duvet cover is the venue; it's big, you grab it first, and there's no way you'll let it drop out of your arms. The duvet cover engulfs smaller clothes, the same way less important tasks get wrapped up in a venue, like an in-house DJ or caterer. Your fiance's sock stands in for something smaller, say, choosing a cute postage stamp for your invitations. You need to complete every planning task, and you need to move every item from point A to B, but in the process you will inevitably drop a sock. No matter how many times this happens, as humans, we reach for the dropped sock. As we bend down, clutching a week's worth of wardrobe to our chests with one arm, we blindly grope for the fallen item with the other. Just as our talons grasp the runaway, another sock, and maybe an undershirt, fall to the ground. It's one step forward, two steps back, and the entire load of laundry is held up that much longer. Gravity makes fools of us all. The same holds true for planning a wedding.

Having selected the venue, Heine and I returned home finally ready to open the dryer and begin gathering our metaphorical laundry. The rental car made it back unscathed and my future looked as bright as the LED light indicating a secure door lock on my washing machine.

Ok, that's enough laundry talk. My point is, there's always more work to be done. Having selected the venue and date, we were far from finished with the Addison Grove. We barely had time to start a load of laundry before we faced our first venue scam.

The Addison Grove offered a 20 percent discount on the primary reservation fee if we could sign and submit our contract within 48 hours. As much as I loved the look and feel of the place, I especially liked their generosity when it came to offering substantial discounts. Unfortunately, they didn't send us a contract until more than 24 hours had passed. And surprise, surprise, we found pages of fine print that didn't come up during our all-smiles chat in the bridal suite. We scheduled a call to address our issues, but of course, there'd be no availability until after the discount deadline had passed. The process is designed to take more than 48 hours.

I was steamed like a patented Skinner burger.

Looking back, I can't help but smile at my younger self. Sure, it's only been a handful of months, but planning a wedding changes a person. The man I was during the Addison Grove call was an idealist. A whippersnapper. A naive kid who still thought he could reason his way out of the lunacy trap of the wedding industry. Now, as a wise, married man I know how exhausting it is to fight all the battles, and that it's much easier to holster the haymakers and roll with the punches instead of throwing them back.

But I didn't know that then, and it'd be a long time before I made peace with the scams and gouging.

Here are some of the unexpected clauses we found in the contract:

A confetti fee: $500 to clean up confetti if we have our guests use those novelty pull-string poppers.

Staff meals: Apparently a standard in the industry, but we'd be responsible for feeding various venue and event staff

The guest and vendor clear-out deadline

The parking attendant. I'm going to take a 23.5 hour break from drafting this part of the book because merely thinking of this memory has my blood boiling. Maybe I haven't made peace with the scams after all.

Before I undo months of therapy and unbottle my

suppressed parking attendant rage, let's tackle some of Heine's concerns. The contract required everyone, guests and vendors, to exit the property by midnight. This meant every decoration, the band's gear, and my drunken idiot friends would need to be packed up and shipped out quickly and efficiently.

This worried my bride-to-be.

Heine couldn't fathom all of that work getting done in such a brief period. We'd have to assign someone to box up our personal items, the caterer would have to pack up all of the silver, rental pieces, and linens, and God forbid the flower petals dropped at the ceremony fell under the confetti clause umbrella. Having spent time in my early twenties working in fine dining, I will never doubt the speed and efficiency of industry folk setting up and knocking down events. When the only thing between you and the end of the work day is moving a bunch of tables and folding some chairs, you sure as hell move those tables and fold those chairs. Rarely in my life have I had the honor to participate in a machine as well-oiled as the staff of that wine bar. Looking back on the post-shift boozing we did, well-oiled is definitely the correct phrasing. We behaved as though the restaurant were a communist utopia. Each staff member worked according to their ability for the greater good. For me, the greater good often meant racing home early enough for a date with Alex Heine.

I tried to explain to Alex that these vendors work events three nights a week, every week. They will be out on time because they are always out on time. But sometimes you need to hear it straight from the day-of planner's mouth.

The Grove assured us that the midnight policy

wouldn't pose any problems and that flower petals didn't count as confetti. Apparently, there's no method for removing confetti from grass more effective than picking it up with human fingers. The tedious process takes a long time and can't be done without the exchange of at least $500. We weren't interested in confetti to begin with. I can't imagine anybody being so determined to have confetti at their wedding that they'd pay a fee of any size to keep it on the itinerary. Then again, I can't imagine hiring a proposal planner either.

Okay. Take a deep breath. Inhale. Exhale. Calm your mind. It's time to discuss the parking attendant.

At first, I scratched my head and thought, *what is a parking attendant?* Surely they don't mean he's a valet. With plenty of spaces and most guests arriving via shuttle, there'd be no need for such an employee. It turns out "parking attendant" is nothing more than a made-up term that sounds better than "deceitful scam."

The parking attendant worked as a full-time employee of the Addison Grove. He's essentially their groundskeeper, and they found a way to line his pockets with gold by demanding all of their clients give him money for no reason. Per the contract, he'd be responsible for enforcing the outside alcohol policy and handling any spot maintenance, like changing light bulbs. His presence was required by the Addison Grove beginning an hour prior to the ceremony and he'd be on the clock until midnight. They wanted us to pay him $45/hour and buy him dinner.

I didn't like the idea of a stranger, presumably armed, patrolling my wedding looking for troublemakers. What would happen when he inevitably found one? Call me a Unioner, but that's just the way I felt.

Here are the concerns I brought up during the call:

What does this guy do? He seems entirely unnecessary.

How do you not mention this until now? This is a $400 scam.

The contract also stipulates that the Addison Grove provides an On-Site Manager who shares many of the same responsibilities, including, verbatim, "changing light bulbs." Couldn't you at least come up with another example of a bullshit chore to veil this scam?

If this guy is required by the venue, shouldn't our venue fee include him? He sounds like an Addison Grove employee, not an additional vendor. Why do I have to pay his salary if I don't want his services?

Congratulations! You've scammed us. What choice do we have? It's not like we are going to bail on the venue over this. I guess we'll feed your parking attendant and then we'll eat the cost.

The call with the Grove went well. Alex and I huddled over the speakerphone and received enthusiastic assurances that everything would be great and we didn't have to worry. It wasn't a video call, but I'm sure the lady on the phone assumed Alex's ring looked gorgeous and complimented her just to be safe. They'd honor the 48 hour discount, the cost per staff meal wouldn't be too bad, all of the vendors operate with soviet efficiency when the time comes to haul ass off the grounds, and, after I tossed a few strongly worded complaints about deceptive practices and unscrupulous scams, they caved and knocked $10 off the hourly rate for the parking attendant.

Small victories.

With a date and venue locked in, we were finally

ready to let the other pieces fall into place. We'd taken a big step forward, and rather than taking two steps back, we'd realized we now needed to take eight more steps in all sorts of directions at the same time. Not even Brad had enough feet for that.

YOU DON'T EVEN LIKE HIM: THE UNWRITTEN RULES OF THE INVITE LIST

Two days had passed since Alex and I returned from Texas and Brad still hadn't pushed the universal pause button. I lost sleep over it. I wasn't concerned that he'd returned home or that he'd been hurt or exposed in the tabloids; I was worried that he'd deemed me an unworthy guide to humanity and my introduction to the world of wedding planning failed to satisfy his supernatural curiosity. It wasn't until the third night, just after Alex, Mona, and I had climbed into bed that I felt a sudden stillness befall my surroundings. Alex's breath ceased to tickle my ear, Mona's snores fell silent, and my self conscious, self-centered fears were put to rest.

My alien friend had been busy during our venue scouting trip, having discovered our collection of jigsaw puzzles while we were away.[51] I slid out from under the covers and joined Brad in the guest room, where he had completed a beautiful seaside landscape, complete with a lighthouse shining into the horizon and a series of hot air balloons hovering over the waves. A jigsaw trifecta. After admiring his handiwork, I showed him what Alex and I had pieced together: the guest list.

"Why is Henry's name written in all capital letters?" Brad asked, peering over my shoulder at an early draft of our list.

"Henry is a special case," I explained.

Of all the wedding tasks, putting together a guest list is relatively painless. There's no real risk involved. Writing down a long list of the people you care about can be a nice boost to your self esteem. Look how many friends we have! In many ways, compiling the invite list is a lot like, you guessed it, working with laundry!

When it's time to clean out your closet you need to assess your wardrobe. You create three piles: the Yes Pile, the Maybe Pile, and the No Pile. Certain items aren't even considered for the pile system. Your favorite jeans are exempt from the piles the same way your parents are understood to be invited to the wedding. Your best friends are your go-to outfits; they're definitely not at risk of missing an invite and you don't bother sorting them. Chances are they're in the dirty clothes hamper anyway because you just hung out with them last night.

Still with me? It only gets more confusing, as this metaphor bleeds worse than Alex's red pajama pants.

You may not see your uncle more than a couple of times a year, but he's definitely in. You aren't going to throw away your favorite Christmas sweater just because it's exclusively for special occasions.

We tallied up the Yes List, rambling off our immediate family members, close friends, and any significant others associated with these groups. Things get tricky with the second-tier friends. The guys you haven't seen since high school and the college buddy who, these days, you only see a handful of times a year for your rec league basketball games.

Say hello to the Maybe Pile.

You want to invite these people for sentimental reasons, the same way you want to hold on to that old T-shirt you've had for 15 years. This is when Heine reminds you that you never wear that faded shirt with holes in the collar and she'd never heard you mention Sean once in her life. Sorry pal, you didn't make the cut.

"Henry is someone I'm obligated to invite," I continue. "Heine doesn't want me to, but I have to. His name is in capital letters because he's a hotly contested invite."

I think we all have a Henry in our lives. I'm fortunate to have a core group of friends who have been very close-knit since childhood. Henry has been our undesirable hanger-on since the 4th grade. In high school, we let his calls go to voicemail because the girls didn't want him to come over.[52] These days, we see him once or twice a year for token gatherings like Super Bowl parties and New Year's Eve. Regardless of how I feel about him, he feels that I am one of his oldest and dearest friends.

I couldn't not invite him to my wedding. It would be too harsh a blow. If Henry is reading this book, it's probably coming as a pretty harsh blow.

If you feel that I'm being unfairly rude to Henry, then perhaps a few examples will help demonstrate why, after 20 years of friendship with him, we've wound up with this relationship. I'll use wedding-specific examples.

Exhibit A: Henry, utterly oblivious of his standing as one of the least welcome invites on our list, requested to bring a plus-one to the wedding. This wouldn't be unreasonable had the potential date been a long-term girlfriend, but he was simply hoping to jump-start things with a girl he'd recently met. He pestered me with text messages for weeks, checking to see if the RSVPs were trending in a favorable direction. Eventually, he stopped, and I assume things fizzled out with the acquaintance he wanted to impose on us.

Exhibit B: About a month before the wedding, Henry texted me asking for information about the venue, hotels, and transportation. These are the types of questions that you just can't ask the bride or groom four weeks in advance. We have enough to worry about without holding our least welcome guest's hand while he books flights and accommodations. Of course, this being 2018, all of the information he needed was available to him in both digital and analog media through our wedding website and the snail mail invitation I felt obligated to send.

Exhibit C: After the wedding, we returned to our hotel for a small after party in the lobby bar. Three friends waved me over to the bar and asked what I'd like to drink. The moment shaped up to be a good one; with the formal aspects of the night behind me, my future featured familiar smiles, a draft beer, and a chance to sit down. But before ass could meet stool, Henry took me by the elbow, panic-stricken, demanding I search through my emails to find a copy of the shuttle company contract so he could call their offices to inquire about his lost sunglasses. I tried to explain the whole, "it's my fucking wedding, they won't be answering the phone at 1 am, and oh, it's my fucking wedding" situation, but he insisted. By the time I got him the number, my stool had been usurped.

Exhibit D: Henry, a man I invited despite my wife's protests, made a point of telling both Heine and me how disappointed his parents were not to have made the guestlist. In fairness, Henry's mom is a sweetheart, and Heine would have preferred her in his place.

"So you will invite your Henry," Brad said, scanning to the names at the bottom of the list, those with red font indicating the No Pile. "But you will not invite Kevin? I have heard you speak highly of Kevin."

"Kevin is a coworker. Heine and I agreed not to invite

work people."

"But you spend 40 hours a week with Kevin. That is more time than you spend with your family." Brad made some keen observations, but I could tell his homeworld had no grasp of a work/life balance.

"Right. I spend a ton of time with Kevin."

"And you do not like Henry."

"Right."

"Why not invite Kevin instead of Henry."

With a heavy sigh I rubbed my temples and leaned back in my chair, tilting my head up to find Brad's spherical noggin staring back at me with an expression so sincere that I couldn't even hate him for it.

"Because nothing makes any sense."

I explained to Brad the numbers game of the guest list. Coworkers are tough, because if you invite one, you probably have to invite another, and another, and then Alex will want to invite one, and another, and before you know it our wedding is a company happy hour. Not only does this drive up the costs, but it leads to the collisions of worlds. Much like Relationship George and Independent George, Work Sam and Normal Sam can't coexist. A Sam divided against itself cannot stand. I don't want my coworkers hearing my embarrassing secrets as my best man roasts me, and I don't want my friends and family to gain insights on exactly how unfulfilling a career path I'm rotting away on.

With the office invite hiring freeze established, Alex and I would have an easier time keeping the numbers in check. We aimed for about 100 to 110 guests, a medium-sized wedding where we knew that anyone in attendance truly belonged.[53] The caterer and the bar package charged by the person, so by the time RSVPs filled our mailbox we were rooting for regrets. The people who mattered most were the ones who wouldn't miss it, so anybody who could feasibly miss the wedding wouldn't be missed at the wedding.

We acted judiciously with our invites, winding up with about 140 potential attendees, but there's another school of thought appealing to the less scrupulous couples out there. The more you invite, the more gifts you receive. Some folks in my life, who will remain nameless, encouraged me to invite everyone I knew, especially the extended family members who I didn't anticipate would make the trip. "Get it while the getting's good," I was told. Part of me considered embracing this philosophy. If every vendor wanted to scam me out of a few extra dollars, why couldn't I pass on the costs to my second cousins? Oh right, because I'm a decent human being who doesn't need to exploit people for personal gain. I'm more than content to take cash and kitchenware from 110 people instead of a 150 while retaining a positive self image.

Compiling an invite list is one of the easier wedding planning tasks, but don't let that fool you.[54] Alex and I jumped into our list mere days after I proposed. We were in traffic outside of Dallas on the drive back to Chicago when she opened a Google Drive spreadsheet and started rattling off names. It's fun. At least, it's fun until you try to explain why three quarters of your mom's book club need to be invited.

In a perfect world, Alex and I would have the same amount of old friends, new friends, and extended family. The bride's side and the groom's side would coexist peacefully, providing a harmonious balance on our special day.

In the real world, I haven't made a new friend in 10 years, and most of my old friends' parents are like family, being a part of my life, and in most cases, a part of my mom's book club for decades. Where, then, do I draw the line on which of these parents receive an invitation?

These are tough calls to make, but it's important to remember that receiving an invitation to a Sunday wedding 1,000 miles from home isn't as coveted as you may think it is. Yes, it's nice to feel wanted, but it's also a huge hassle.

There are plenty of reasons to turn down our wedding invite. We had to consider which of the guests on our list faced significant travel, whether it be from Chicago, other parts of Texas, or anywhere else in the world. Some wouldn't take on the financial burden, some could have prior commitments, some could just say "nah" and skip the whole thing. We ended up with late scratches due to the birth of a grandchild, an unexpected health issue, and a fear of flying.

A trio of family friends, three brothers I'd known my whole life, told me point blank not to bother inviting them. No offense taken.[55]

When it's all said and done, you feel pretty good about the list you've made. I know we did. That feeling lasted until our parents chimed in.

"I must invite the Steins."

"My friend Kim needs to be there."

"Oh, the Millers would be disappointed."

"What about Nancy?"

Here's a tip: make it clear from the outset that you aren't letting your mom invite Nancy. I have seen Nancy one time in the last 12 years, and that was at my brother Rick's wedding. She showed up with a girlfriend (not a romantic girlfriend, just a gal, an insignificant other) as a plus-one and never gave them a gift. When my mom reached out to suggest a few invites, I laid down the law. No Nancy. Still, she managed to squeeze in a few names, as did my father, and Alex's dad, and of course Vivian dropped a few, too. Alex had never heard of Vivian's new "lifelong" friends, but that's besides the point.

The list will change up until the day of the wedding. As long as you make sure your favorite socks and underwear make it, don't stress too much about the old hoodies in the back of the closet.

Fun fact: despite being left out of my wedding, Nancy got us an ice cream maker! In your face, Rick.

THE BEST MAN AND THE MOST MEDIOCRE TACOS

Alex and I moved in together more than two years before our wedding. We knew then that we were serious about our relationship, but we'd never broached the subject of marriage. We'd talked about buying a Subaru together, which carried the same commitment, but even that decision hadn't been finalized. Yet even at this early stage in our union, I had the foresight to take preliminary steps for when the time came to name my best man.

Just weeks after moving in, I journeyed to the Paulina Meat Market for a pound of frozen corned beef hash. The meat market is a must-see for any tourist. You can't find more authentic Chicagoans than the butchers behind the counter at Paulina. While strolling home I came across a Little Free Library on the sidewalk. For the rest of the walk, my frozen beef shared its plastic bag with Scott Turow's *Identical* and a faded paperback so old and so British that I can't find evidence of its existence on the Internet: *The Best Man's Duties*.

A quick search reveals that the best man industry is on par with the proposal industry, boasting countless handbooks and guides to performing your best and understanding the various responsibilities associated with the role. All this despite the fact that the various responsibilities don't really exist. You give a speech, you hold the rings, you do what you can to help the groom relax. I'm tempted to buy one just to see how much filler and repetitive nonsense it took to bulk that baby up from pamphlet to paperback and justify the $3.95 on

Amazon. Ten pages on how to apply studs to a button hole? A chapter on pinning boutonnieres to lapels?[56] A diagram that indicates how to compliment the bride without psychically putting your foot into your mouth? I suppose it's a pretty good scheme; only a moron would ever consider buying one of these books, and you'd have to be a moron to need one. Lucky for me, I got mine for free! Yes, I am aware that I mock these books while writing something extremely similar.

The Best Man's Duties leased property on my bookshelf until the time came to move it to a permanent home.

Selecting a wedding party can be a tricky business. If you need to pick four friends, you better believe your fifth best friend will feel alienated and snubbed. The College Football Playoff has a similar problem. The fifth team wants in, but if you expand to eight groomsmen you'll wind up with too many people standing around and you'll still have your ninth best friend sticking his hands up with an incredulous, *what am I, frozen corned beef hash?* look on his face.

I averted any controversy on the strength of my fraternal relationships. I have lots of brothers. So many, in fact, that I could get away with an all-in-the-family set of groomsmen. Alex auto-filled the matron of honor spot with her sister, tossed in a couple of sisters-in-law as bridesmaids, and only had one decision to make to complete the elite eight.

Some of Alex's closest friends during her adult life have been men. Would she pick one of them as a bridesmaid? We've come a long way since Patrick Dempsey was *Made of Honor* on the silver screen. In today's world of gender fluidity and secular ceremonies, nobody balks at male bridesmaids. I myself once walked a male bridesmaid down the aisle. Tossing a Y chromosome on the brides side of the altar would match the asymmetrical aspects of her ring, too.

In the end, she opted for her best gal pal. This friend has been close since college, and the friend's then fiance, now husband, was part of their still very much intact college gang. We'd planned to include him in the ceremony as an acoustic guitarist. At time of drafting, they'd recently asked me to act as officiant for their upcoming nuptials. Yikes. We'll get to that later.[57]

With the wedding party selected, all that was left was to formally bestow the honor upon them and deliver 1967 Britain's most complete guide to handling the pressures of standing next to me during the ceremony. We'd reached our decision shortly after our venue trip. Alex immediately made plans to visit a bridal shoppe (some product lines warrant the extra letters, though I'll never understand how The Vitamin Shoppe fits the criteria) in Holland, Michigan. We live minutes away from Michigan Avenue and endless high-end big city boutiques, yet Alex decided to buy her dress in a city whose entire population wouldn't sell out Wrigley Field.

She planned to drive up for her first fitting after our Passover seder, held at my mom's house in Southwest Michigan harbor country, a convenient coincidence considering how much of the drive to Holland she'd cut out of the journey. With the exodus to Holland just weeks away we needed to conjure up an excuse to get all the brothers and sisters together to ask them about our wedding party plans. We had to act fast so the girls could clear their schedules for the first major "you look great" bridal task.

Naturally, we invited them out for mediocre Mexican food.

Every family has its restaurant hot spots, the places you know you'll settle for when you see the all-too-familiar and far too indecisive chain of text messages:

Brother: "I'm good with anything"
Uncle: "Whatever works"
Sister In-Law: "You pick"
Fiancée: "I don't care"

For my family, and many other family's from my township, the fallback restaurant is That Little Mexican Cafe in beautiful downtown Evanston, Illinois. It's halfway between the north suburbs where my brothers and I grew up and the northside of Chicago where my brothers and I moved after college. While my mom empty-nested in the burbs, it was a compromise of proximity to meet in Evanston. By the time my mom moved to Michigan my oldest brother had moved to the suburbs, and so the middling quality midwestern Mexican joint remains our go-to family gathering spot, and thus served as the colorful setting for our bridal party announcement.

Going out to dinner with twin toddlers is tough. Fortunately, the chaos they created melded into the general wave of sensory stimuli. Colorful banners of tissue paper cut-outs criss-crossed the ceiling above, mariachi music blared down from the speakers, the smell of fresh guacamole rose from dense, pewter mortars and the cloying aftertaste of margaritas clung to our tongues like chalk.

"We had an ulterior motive in asking you all to have

dinner tonight," I said, hoping to overcome the ambience and hold the table's attention.

"We'd like you all to be in our wedding party!" Alex added, eliciting pleasant smiles and raised margaritas from the audience. Most of the focus remained on corralling my nieces, who seemed more interested in locating the mythical balloon animal man, known to make the rounds at the restaurant on weekends. Participating as ring bearers didn't excite them so much as a giraffe made of rubber and helium that could be used to bop their uncles on the head.

I pulled *The Best Man's Duties* from my coat pocket and handed it across the table to Rick, along with two surprisingly high quality cigars given to me at Christmas by Alex's brother. Rick is a cigar guy. I'm not. I take two puffs and feel light headed and queasy. Whenever I mention these acute symptoms to Rick he reminds me that I'm supposed to feel this way. "Cigars are poison," he says. "They are made of poison." Then he drops his on the grass, hits his drive, picks it up, and puffs his way back to the golf cart. He was pleased with the quality of the cigars I gave him that night, and up until the moment he reads this paragraph he'll believe that I purchased them specifically for him.

I don't think Rick was surprised to be selected as my best man. After all, he chose me for his wedding five years earlier. I've always said of my brothers that Andy is the best one, Dan is my favorite, and I'm closest with Rick. If Dan gets married, he'll pick Andy, and we'll all get a turn to be the best man.[58]

There are no bad seats at my family's dinner outings. Nobody gets stuck next to anybody. However, there are evenings where you're on the wrong end of the table and you wish it were 6th grade again and the boys and girls would follow the laws of chemistry and naturally separate like oil and water. I nodded along to the wedding dress discussion, an island of testosterone in a sea of pre-wedding buzz, longing to be across the table talking about the upcoming 2018 Masters. Alas, we sit where we sit, and I took solace in knowing that I'd be surrounded by my loved ones when I stood at the altar and surrounded by margaritas and guacamole in the present.

ON THE ART OF BACHELOR PARTIES IN THE AGE OF AIRBNB

"There are two types of men on earth," I said to Brad as we strolled down the sidewalk with Mona.

"Good men and evil men?" He asked.

"No," I said. "Some men can be both good and evil. That doesn't separate the two types."

"Old men and young men?"

"Old and young are relative terms."

His four feet slowed to a stop while he sped up his guessing. "Married men and single men? Happy men and sad men? Living men and dead men?"

"Let me finish or I'll show you a dead man."

"Is there a dead man on the street? I'd very much like to examine one."

"No, Brad." I took a slow, deep breath as my alien co-ambulator twisted his spherical head in search of a corpse. "On Earth, there are strip club guys, and there are non–strip club guys. Nobody is indifferent to strip clubs. You're either in, or you're out." Mona tugged at the leash, obeying her instinct to hunt squirrels and, given the temporary suspension of squirrel movement around the globe, she actually had a chance at this one. I corralled her with an authoritative yank. "I am not a strip club guy."

"I see," Brad said, half walking and half floating beside me. He'd reluctantly agreed when I suggested he use his temporal perception skills to make Mona's walks less stressful, but only after I showed him pictures of the venue and made a fuss about his inability to comprehend the beauty of the outdoor ceremony site. He thought he was learning to appreciate the sensation of a slight breeze and the softness of the earth beneath his feet, but really I just wanted the neighborhood to myself.

"These strip clubs," he said, "are they similar to your golf clubs?"

"No, 'club' is a homonym. It has more than one meaning."

"The same way the tea we drank differed from the tee you keep with your golf clubs."

"That's a homophone, but yeah, sure."

I bent down to pick up Mona's dump,[59] utilizing the reverse bag technique. We use the orange poop bags from Amazon. We get 1,000 for $10. It's a great deal. I've often thought of writing a short story titled *1,000 Poop Bags Later*, where a couple meets the day the package arrives and the story ends when the final bag is soiled and thrown away at the dump.[60] I haven't decided if it's a wedding or a break up for the ending.

"So the strip clubs are long, thin, individual clubs?"

"No, that's the noun usage of strip. Think of the verb usage."

"Another homonym?"

"Yes."

"My home language is far simpler."

"A strip club is a place where women take off their clothes for money to entertain men."

"Ah." Brad stopped, looking down at the crack in the sidewalk. "I do not believe I am a strip club guy."

No matter how many responsibilities *The Best Man's Duties* contains, there's only one that matters to the modern best man: the bachelor party. It took all of five minutes before my brainstorming brothers began badgering me with bachelor party possibilities. Luckily, we are a family of non-strip club guys.

I asked Brad whether he'd ever come across the term *bachelor party* during his stint on planet Earth. He must have frozen me before he replied, as his answer reeked of Wikipedia regurgitation.

"They call it a stag party in the UK," he said. "In Germany, a *junggesellenabschied*. Frenchman take part in an *enterrement de vie de garçon* while the Israelis have their מסיבת רווקים. And of course, Tom Hanks is famous for his."

I unclipped Mona from her harness as I opened the door to our building. She wagged her tail, whimpering with excitement and jumping to paw at the doorknob. After brushing her aside I held the door and made way for the two creatures to pass through, shaking my head and grinning at my adorable pets.

If the planning of a wedding warrants an entire book, the planning of a bachelor party could aptly be captured in a tweet:

Rent a house, book golf/dinner, buy 2x as much beer as you'll need #NotAStripClubGuy

That's 83 characters, including a pretty lame hashtag.

It really is that simple. It's the antithesis of a wedding. None of the details matter. All we had to do was pick a city and figure out the rest as we went along. As a freshman in college I took Psychology 101, a great, wide-ranging course for rote learners like myself. I can still remember many of the concepts I memorized for the final exam. One of these is Maslow's hierarchy of needs. Maslow drew up a tiered pyramid, each level representing a step toward human self-actualization.

Toward the top you have things like self-esteem and a sense of belonging. These are not essential to live, but they are essential to live well. Bachelor parties aren't about living well. They require only the base level of Maslow's pyramid. To plan a bachelor party you only have to ensure the psychological and physical necessities to keep a human being alive: food to absorb beer, water in your beer, shelter to pass out beneath after consuming beer. Start with food and shelter and you've got the foundation of an epic bachelor party. Maslow knew how to rage.

My generation has reached marrying age. As such, many of my friends are recently married, engaged, or on the verge of Googling "Old Jewish Diamond Guy." This means bachelor parties take up a lot of my vacation days. Some of them are simple, requiring only a few emails and a clear schedule. Others demand flight itineraries. Both are tons of fun, though the latter becomes more of a financial burden. I've always believed that if one's friends need to fly to attend one's wedding, then one shouldn't require guests to fly to his bachelor party.

My brothers suggested Toronto, which would have been a great choice. I know we'd have had fun in that town because, when I was 19, I spent a weekend chasing my drunk friends around Toronto and it was one of the greatest "you had to be there" weekends of my life. But my friends would have to fly to Austin for the wedding, and damned if I was going to make them renew their passports for a bachelor party.

I picked Milwaukee. Mainly, I chose the city because it's only 90 minutes from Chicago by car. Far enough to be out of town but close enough that my brothers' friends could drive up for a round of golf and get back to their infant children for dinner. Far enough that we'd need to rent a house but close enough that my friend Jack, in training for an Iron Man at the time, could ride his bike 126 miles in 95 degree heat to meet us there.[61] A perfect compromise.

Two weeks before we left we hadn't planned any activities, hadn't booked any golf courses, and hadn't made dinner reservations. With all the decisions needed to plan a wedding, the laissez-faire approach to the weekend offered a much-needed reprieve. As long as you have one type A friend, the kind who is an asshole when he needs to be, you can rest easy. Just leave it to that guy to make a few calls, demand a few discounts, and tell you what the plan is. I have one such friend, and he did just that. Nobody hesitated to remit when this friend sent a group text: "Everyone send me $100 for a slush fund."

I won't get into the details of what happened at the bachelor party. That's not how bachelor parties work. Suffice to say, we had a blast. Mine wasn't the type where we all left carrying a secret to our graves. I've been to bachelor parties like that, and trust me; mine wasn't one of them. I may not be a perfect partner, but Alex doesn't have to worry about me when I'm away with the fellas. I don't stuff my wallet full of condoms; I stuff it full of chewable dairy digestive tablets.

I can't pinpoint the exact time when Airbnbs became the norm. All I know is that it was sometime between when my eldest brother regularly attended bachelor parties and when I started regularly attending bachelor parties. We had about 15 people on our trip, and the house we rented easily accommodated all of us. "I can't believe this place," my brother said. "It's like it was designed for us to stay here."

Yep. Welcome to the Internet Age, big brother.

His Airbnb naivete showed again as we packed up to leave. "Don't we need to clean this up? It's a complete mess."

Oh Andy. Sweet, innocent Andy. We'll let the type A friend, the one whose credit card is on file, worry about that.

CLOTHES MAKE THE YOUTH LARGE MAN

Four times in my life I've patronized a Men's Warehouse, each time thinking the same, sad thought. *How will they botch it this time?*

Sleeves too short.

Waist too wide.

Shirt too long.

Toddler-sized socks.

If you want to know what it's like to be totally powerless (without getting married), try renting a suit or tux at Men's Warehouse. You'll inevitably wind up standing in the middle of the store as an incompetent employee devises new schemes to miscalculate your measurements.

"Are you sure you got that right? My arm was bent."

"Wouldn't it be easier to measure my pant length if I'm not sitting down?"

"When you reviewed the contents of this order, didn't it strike you as odd that every component is for an adult male and the socks are for an infant?"

There's nothing you can say or do to stop them from getting something wrong.

I doubt anybody has ever left a Men's Warehouse with confidence. Male models smile down from the in-store signage, looking confident despite their burgundy cummerbunds and teal pocket squares. But those suits fit. Plus, they're getting paid to wear them. For us normal folk, there isn't much to smile about, besides a hilarious pair of tiny socks, of course.

You probably aren't going to get a suit that fits, at least not the first time. Maybe you'll get it the second time, and there's always a second time, since you can expect to find a bowtie instead of a vest, or a white jacket instead of a black one. Once, the woman behind the counter looked up my order history, scoffed at the jacket size from my previous rental, and told me she'd make some adjustments. I asked if she needed to measure. She said, "No, I can eyeball it."

What could go wrong?

Before you know it you've made two trips to the brick and mortar, you're out $200 and the best you can hope for is something in the correct color scheme and a pair of socks designed for a person with a fully developed sense of object permanence.

I'm lucky. I have a woman in my life who looks out for me. I didn't have to go to the Men's Warehouse. From day one Alex insisted that we take advantage of this whole wedding thing as an excuse to get me a new suit. I'd be on my own for socks.

My wardrobe is not my strong suit.[62] Formalwear is a lost cause. Hell, even business casual is beyond me. I have one pair of slacks that I wear almost exclusively for job interviews and golfing. I never seem to perform as well as I'd like while wearing them.

Take a stroll through my walk-in closet.

Item 1: The Charcoal Jacket

Last seen: Age 22—Photograph of my mother and me standing outside the Sydney Opera House.

Description: Would qualify as a knee-length midi if worn by a woman, and based on the shoulder padding it may actually be designed for a woman.

Item 2: The Corduroy Blazer

Last seen: Age 30—This thing sees an embarrassing

amount of action.

Description: Likely as old as I am—a hand-me-down from my mom's partner. He loves telling me how he used to be thin like me. The blazer may disintegrate at any moment.

Item 3: The Three Piece Suit
Last seen: Age 25—May of 2014 at a family friend's wedding.
Description: Hot damn. Another hand-me-down likely stitched together during the Carter administration, the suit is what the kids call "groovy." This dark blue, pinstriped number includes a vest and has garnered its share of compliments over the years. While it fits me as well it was intended to, stylistically that fit comes off just a tad dated.

Item 4: Agent Smith
Last seen: Age 30—Somewhere in the Matrix
Description: This is the one piece of formalwear I've actually purchased instead of accepting as a used item from a loved one. It's a black suit and it fits me. Once my friends started to have weddings (which is, sadly, how I think of getting married) I realized I couldn't keep showing up in the retro three piece, caved, and shelled out for grown up clothes.

People pick and choose which superstitions to adhere to in life. Alex has no problem opening a Christmas gift a few days early. She'll walk under a ladder, pop open an umbrella in the kitchen, or step on a sideway crack without a second thought. The only time she knocks on wood is while hanging a picture and listening for studs. Suffice to say, she's not superstitious when it comes to bad luck or jinxes. And yet, we rearranged our lives to ensure I'd never know a single fact or catch even the most fleeting glimpse of her wedding dress before the big day.

We took the traditional approach. All I knew was what she'd tell me, and that wasn't much. "It's cool," she'd say after wrapping up a 45-minute description for her mom over the phone. In retrospect, Vivian must have been keeping Alex on the line for company while driving somewhere in Texas. Why else would it take 45 minutes?[63]

During that call I was exiled from the room with a door closed in my face, lest I discover any hints regarding the dress. Little did Alex know that I lack the vocabulary to understand even the first thing about wedding dress details. I know what a train is. I'm not sure what a bustle is. I guess I should look it up:

"A pad or framework expanding and supporting the fullness and drapery of the back of a woman's skirt or dress."

There you have it. I still can't picture one in my head.

I didn't pry. If she wanted to keep the dress a secret then so be it. We'd hang it in the guest bedroom and I wouldn't be allowed to enter that part of the house for a few months.

My wedding wardrobe, I learned from my bride-to-be, would need to match the accent notes of her dress. Much like one can't get the ball rolling with vendors until a date and venue have been booked, one can't get started with groomsmen suits, bridesmaids dresses, or the groom's outfit until the wedding dress comes together. Not a bad metaphor for weddings in general. It all revolves around the bride. In fact, the sample swatches of Alex's dress (which were always concealed from me) were used to make decisions about napkins and other unrelated accoutrements of the wedding. Now that it's over, I can't remember what our napkins looked like. Everyone was right, I don't remember the details.

As a first grade graduate and mostly competent adult I thought I had a strong grasp of colors. I learned three life-changing lessons in the first grade. I can still picture my teacher with her too-small glasses and thinning auburn hair as she pantomimed slicing up the word "together" into three smaller words, "to," "get," and "her." I learned how to spell together. I also learned that putting powdered sugar on my nose and climbing onto a table, while exhilarating, results in disciplinary consequences. Lastly, I mastered the colors of the rainbow thanks to ROY G BIV. It was a good year.

I definitely knew my colors. Sky is blue, grass is green. I even learned the colors in Spanish back in elementary school. Sometime between escuela and adulthood, the colors changed. Our wedding colors weren't red, green, and pink. They were burgundy, sage, and blush. Burgundy? Who wears burgundy formal wear? Would I become a bellhop after the ceremony? Heine told me that my tie would be a creamy beige color. I'd call it cream or beige, and even that made me feel a little pedantic. The new color lingo had me choosing between champagne and oyster.

Oyster?

Empty space?

Vintagey?

After decades of reinforcement, it'll be hard to unlearn ROY G BIV. For those planning a wedding, O is officially for Oyster.

You may think, having avoided the Men's Warehouse of horrors, that buying a suit would be easy. What's that, reader? You say, "Wait, Sam, I thought nothing was easy."

Good job, astute reader.[64] If you've been reading closely you'll also recall that I am not a stylish man. If clothes make the man, then I am a crowdsourced man. I rely on hand-me-downs and have no eye for fashion. I knew I couldn't be trusted to shop on my own, so I put together an All-Star team of personal shoppers.

I had Alex, of course, to make all the decisions. She's the captain, the coach. My mom drove in to offer her two cents, which, because she loves me and loves Alex, I knew would be supportive and full of glowing praise for any decisions made by Coach Heine. Mom is the cheerleader. Finally, the big gun. Uncle Rueben. He's our ringer. A tough guy from the old neighborhood who ran a high-end men's boutique back in the day. HIs store, Sirreal, was a Chicago institution. He'd take trips to Europe to scout out what trends would be popular once they caught on in America. He brags about demanding a personal check from Michael Jordan, who didn't like giving away his signature on checks. He invented an upscale, faux-European clothing line called André Danielle, named after my brothers, Andy and Danny. He once caught a kid shoplifting and had his employees tie the perp to a chair in the basement. My uncle blindfolded the kid and walked down the stairs dragging a police billy club across the newels to scare him. I think the kid peed himself.[65]

Rueben is not someone who gets ripped off. On any given day, regardless of how recently he may have purchased a new car, he is engaged in ongoing negotiations with at least two car dealerships. The haggling goes on for years. He isn't happy unless he's outwitting someone that's trying to screw him. With Rueben on my side, I knew I'd be getting a deal. That is, as long as I was prepared to walk out and play hardball, and assuming I could convince Heine to postpone the wedding until Rueben got the price he wanted.

The June sun shone down on Alex and I as we parked our trusty Subaru outside Nordstrom. Heine, armed with her wedding dress sample swatches, strolled out ahead of me towards the enormous entryway, eager to get started. I lagged behind, slipping my phone out of my pocket to check an incoming text from my boss. His wife works for Nordstrom in the corporate office and I thought if I let him know what I was up to he may pull some strings for a friends and family discount. Instead, I got his standard pithy reply. "Thanks for feeding into our retirement!" With a sigh, I set off towards the megastore, in search of my bride and a suit that actually fit me.

Once inside, we located the other members of my small council and set to work. We arrived shortly after the store opened and the first salesman to greet us may not have woken up yet. Tall, doughy, red-faced, and orange-haired, he radiated ineptitude. His slouching posture and bulging midsection gave him an off-putting, almost vagabond air. I'm certain that he wore a suit that fit; after all, he did work in a men's department store, but my mind chooses to remember him in something baggy and disheveled as it seems more appropriate to match his slovenly aura.

Needless to say, Rueben ate him alive. Within two minutes of browsing the racks, Rueben had seen enough. He pulled me aside and whispered, "This guy doesn't know shit. Let me make some calls."

Rueben had been making calls for weeks, having old acquaintances pull size 36 suits throughout the Chicagoland area. The salesman escaped his one-on-one with Rueben and began showing symptoms of PTSD. He'd faced off against our ringer and he'd been rung. Gathering what strength he had left, he used whatever wind he could muster to ask what we thought of the jacket I had on.

I'm short. I'm not as short as people think I am, though. That's a side effect of being so skinny. Stand me next to a fat guy of the same height and we become a human version of the Müller-Lyer optical illusion. Mine isn't a popular size. They don't make a lot of suits for skinny guys. They have entire stores catering to the giants among us, so the Big and Tall can shop with confidence. But what about the Slim and Small? Where's our store? We're the ones who fought off the temptation to try a KFC Famous Bowl and avoid hydrogenated oils. Shouldn't we be the ones rewarded with a bevy of stylish options for our wedding day? As a nation we claim to be fighting an obesity epidemic, but as long as we supply the obese with easy to find formalwear we're nothing short of enablers. These were the thoughts swimming through my head as Alex and Rueben debated the merits of regular-length and short-length suit jackets.

I liked the short.
Alex liked the short.
My mom liked the short.
The doughy salesman liked the short.
Rueben preferred the regular.

"It makes for a better silhouette," he argued.

The salesman showed me to the fitting rooms and, safely out of earshot, reiterated his opinion. I apologized, assured him that while my loving uncle could be somewhat abrasive, he came from a good place. I filled him in on Rueben's history in the industry and the dough seemed to rise, impressed by the credentials. Still, he pushed for the short. "It's more modern," he said.

We'd been at it for no more than 20 minutes and I'd lost my patience for shopping. Rueben had angered the staff and felt alienated, Alex felt dismissed, my mom wanted everyone to get along, and I still didn't know what color oyster was.[66]

I left the dressing room, slalomed through the circular racks of slacks and discovered the doughboy mid-giggle. Rueben had stalked off, presumably on the phone with one of his grey-haired contemporaries working out the logistics of shipping a 36 Regular in from the Amalfi Coast. "We're leaving," Alex said. "We'll come back in August for the big annual sale. He says they'll have more selection and big discounts."

Sometimes, the gods smile down upon me. One minute I'm trying to explain my uncle's psychological makeup to a red-faced manchild, and the next I'm sitting down at a Jewish deli to a bowl of matzo ball soup, a diced salami and cheese omelet, and a weak cup of bottomless diner coffee. If matzo ball soup is Jewish Penicillin, the crappy coffee that comes with it is a mazel tov cocktail. I ate well knowing I wouldn't have to go suit shopping for two more months.

You know those Corona commercials that suggest consumers "find their beach"? Sitting down at a Jewish deli to a hard salami omelet is my beach. For a few precious moments, I wasn't planning a wedding. I wasn't staring down 600 more tasks. I was just a man on his beach. However, like the Corona ads, the omelet disappeared in a matter of seconds, and the scheduled programming of wedding planning returned to the airwaves.

We had work to do.

OTHER PEOPLE'S WEDDINGS

My friends love golf. Those without a woman in their lives often play twice a weekend, sometimes more than once a day. I'm satisfied with one round every other week. To me, that is not enough golf, but to Alex it is far too much. She has no interest in being a golf widow. That's why she detests the idea of Treetops.

Treetops is a golf resort in Northern Michigan where my friends and I have taken an annual buddies trip the last three years during Memorial Day weekend. As much as we love to play golf, we love to talk about playing golf even more. This trip receives an absurd amount of attention in the months leading up to the action. We draft teams, design overly complicated scoring systems, buy prizes, name captains, and waste hundreds of man hours, costing our respective employers a fortune in lost productivity.

Two years ago I wrote a player prospectus, a color-coded spreadsheet highlighting 30-odd twentysomething men and their eccentricities, skills, and foibles. It's all a part of the Treetops spirit. Not everyone on the trip knows everybody else. There are friends of friends and guys you only see once a year at Treetops. It's one of the best weekends of the year. We all buy into a camaraderie that brings us together and we retain the glow for days after the trip ends. I couldn't wait to go back.

In December, just weeks before I planned to propose, Alex and I went to dinner with a couple who'd recently gotten engaged. "Have you picked a date?" Alex asked.

"Yes! Memorial Day!" Her friend said.

"I guess I'm out for Treetops," I said, aloud.

"What?" The bride-to-be turned to me and furrowed her brow.

"Nothing," I smiled. "Congratulations."

Instead of a trip north to hit the links, Alex and I would hop in the Subaru and drive down to beautiful Champaign, Illinois, to scout out Katie and Alan's wedding.

Champaign, home of my alma mater, the University of Illinois, heats up in the summer. And although Memorial Day may be the ceremonial start of the season, temperature-wise it hasn't quite made up its mind yet. When I look back on my college climate, I think of winter winds, rain-soaked spring days, and archipelagos of broken glass floating in the murky puddles across the campus streets. A lot had changed in the seven years since I'd been to town.

Mother Nature smiled down upon Katie and Alan, blessing their special day in late May with the unforgiving heat of an August scorcher. Since we know that things are never easy with weddings, you're right to assume the ceremony took place outdoors.

Our pores poured sweat as Alex and I pored over the details of their venue and paraphernalia. On the way down I-57, I pictured us huddled together, pointing at floral arrangements or boutonnieres, jotting down mental notes on what ideas to steal and which to avoid. By the time we found back row seats with a modicum of shade, all thoughts of comparison had vanished. I couldn't care less what Katie and Alan's wedding was like.

It didn't matter if the food was bad. (It was.)

What difference did it make to me if the background slideshow broke? (It did.)

Did they offer signature cocktails? Yes. Were they disgusting? Yes, but who cares? (I didn't.)

The ceremony, as I recall it—though to be fair, in 95-degree heat it may have been a mirage—could aptly be described as cookie-cutter. Scratch that. Taking into account the heat, "boilerplate" makes for a more apt description. We heard plenty of "two becoming one" generic nonsense. The bride and groom didn't share their own vows. They simply stood facing one another as a stranger, a woman they had met once or twice in the previous year to hire for this occasion, recounted what little notes she'd written down about the two of them.

Flanking them on either side stood the bridal party. Those poor souls, fighting off their bodies' urgent desire to give in to the heat with a cliché fainting incident. I'm all for the bridesmaid mid-ceremony swoon. It makes the whole day more memorable, introduces an element of danger and, particularly in this case, satisfies the guests' collective need for something interesting to happen. Even if one went down, there's a whole bunch of them left.

People love collective nouns. A murder of crows, an unkindness of ravens. I'm sure there are non-macabre, non-avian examples too, but you get the idea. A quick Wikipedia skim reveals that somebody thought it was necessary to think up a collective noun for the extinct stegosaurus. Sure, it's been 65 million years, but it could be useful. That guy must have had the perfect word to capture the essence of the magnificent dinosaur, why else would he bother? Off the top of my head, I'd have guessed "an avalanche of stegosaurus." Nah. The official term is a "handful." A handful of stegosauruses. Not only does it seem lazy, but we're talking about a massive beast, not gummy bears. You don't grab a handful of dinosaurs. This is a subject I'd struggle to explain to Brad. But I digress.

Staring up at the wedding party beneath the Champaign sun I got to thinking: Why don't we have collective nouns for these people? What would be the best catchall for bridesmaids? Or groomsmen?

Bridesmaids are:
Overly sweet—a Saccharine of Bridesmaids
Often loud—a Cacophony of Bridesmaids
Frantic—a Chaos of Bridesmaids? A Flutter?[67]
Overcome by romance and at risk of fainting—a Swoon of Bridesmaids
Dressed in unflattering pastels—a Cringe of Bridesmaids
At the service of brides as demanding as four-star generals—a Platoon of Bridesmaids

Groomsmen are:
Uninvolved—an Indifference of Groomsmen
Brothers—a Fraternity of Groomsmen
Drunk—an Inebriation of Groomsmen
Hungover, confused, and loitering—a Muddle of Groomsmen
In rented clothes—a Consignment of Groomsmen

At one point during the ceremony, Alex leaned over to whisper in my ear. I expected her to say something about love, or how we had to remember to find a meaningful officiant to perform our ceremony. "Sam," she said. "I'm trying so hard to keep my pits cool." A quick glance down found my resourceful fiancée utilizing a ceremony card to fan herself, discreetly directing stale air to her underarms.

I'm a lucky man.

We didn't know anybody at this wedding besides the bride and groom. It made for a good research opportunity, allowing us to observe and critique without having to socialize with friends or family.

Our table at the reception—numbering in the double digits—was in a separate room, apart from the wedding party and the happy couple's VIP guests. They probably referred to it as a sunroom, or a conservatory. These are only euphemisms for "the back." Much like my office, where we received an email one day announcing the Basement would henceforth be known as the Garden.[68] We couldn't see the first dance from our vantage. We never saw them cut the cake. When forks found glassware, we found ourselves peering around French doors to glimpse non-French kisses.

It wasn't all bad in the annex, though. We shared our space with the bar, and later in the night, the nacho buffet. Besides the mandatory small talk with our tablemates, we really had no reason to speak to any of the guests, and were free to enjoy the evening at our own pace. In the minutes of facetime we shared with Katie and Alan, the conversation transitioned quickly from our congratulations to behind-the-scenes insights on what had gone wrong. Katie had no qualms explaining that the DJ had missed his cue on their entrance. Alan, the groom, had a good laugh when the bartender asked to see his ID.

We learned nothing useful, and exercised enough tact to forego telling them that all of the speeches were completely inaudible to those of us relegated to the auxiliary seating area.

Attending a wedding in which you don't know anybody can be a chore. It's the karmic price one must pay to also experience weddings at which all of your friends or family are in attendance. The latter are so fun that it makes up for the former. Yes, it stings when you are at the former and all of the guests who'd make the latter so great are together at Treetops without you, but that's life.

Alex and I had fun. Not as much fun as we'd had at the weddings of closer friends, but we'd made the most of it. We boarded a half-filled shuttle bus, just as we had on the way to the venue, and rode home holding hands, her head resting on my bony shoulder. We'd learned an important lesson: our wedding would be our wedding. It wouldn't be Katie and Alan's and it didn't need to be. Beginning that night, I stopped praying for too much sun on our wedding day, and made a mental note to look into paper fans.

WEDDING PLANNING IS BIGGER IN TEXAS

A Walkthrough, a Tasting, Some Rented Sleep, and a Quick Stop to Smell the Flowers

There are approximately 200 suns burning in the Milky Way galaxy. The only other place to find that many suns is the monitor of a Samsung Galaxy smartphone displaying the 10 day forecast for Central Texas in June. And yet, despite the UV index and the projected mid-afternoon highs reaching triple digits, Texas is freezing in the summer.

If you can survive the short walk from the car to the front door, then there's really no need to pack shorts. To counter the extreme heat beyond the walls, Texans fight fire with freon, blasting the air conditioning to arctic extremes. Having learned this lesson over the years, I stepped into my favorite sweatpants, pulled on a pair of wool socks and boarded a climate controlled plane bound for the frigid interiors of the Lone Star State.

As always, we had work to do.

We wouldn't be as busy as we'd been during our venue touring itinerary, but we had more than enough on the schedule to make a potential golf outing a ludicrous prospect. There were florists to visit, hors d'oeuvres to sample, and the Addison Grove was just begging for a preliminary walkthrough.

I'll walk you through it.

In truth, there's nothing spiritual about the Addison Grove itself. Sure, the ceremonies that take place there could have a religious bent to them, but the architect designed the space for commercial, functional purposes.

It is a venue, not a shrine. It's home to longhorns, not a house of God. Still, the Grove administrators granted us permission to walk the hallowed earth on the condition that we remain as silent as churchgoers, lest we disturb that evening's bride.

The bride of the day is to be treated with reverence. It was implied that, in the event of a run-in, we were not to make direct eye contact with the bride of the day. God forbid we introduce any uncontrolled variables to the perfect equilibrium she has strove for months to achieve. Luckily, she stayed in the forbidden lair of the bridal suite during our self-guided tour.

I assumed our goal was to select a ceremony site. We knew the available options, and I figured we'd be in and out in no time. Easy-peasy lemon squeezy.[69] We wound up facing a litany of new questions.

Where does the shuttle drop off our guests?
Do we need a sign to direct the guests from the shuttle?
Where do we put the sign?
What should the sign say?
Should we rent a couch for $800?

Those were all actual concerns. Remembering one of my mantras, I avoided stressing over most of them. *They host 100 weddings here each year.* We don't have to decide where the shuttle will drop people. Shuttles drop people off here every weekend. Our guests have brains, and those brains receive intel from their eyes. They'll get off the shuttle and figure out where to go regardless of whether we have a sign and what that sign says.

These are the types of details that married couples warned us about. *They'll drive you crazy*, they said, *and you won't remember them at all*. It's hard to heed these warnings. Learning from the mistakes of others is tough. It's easier to learn from our own mistakes. An $800 couch rental was a mistake I didn't need to make myself. Heine liked the idea of it. "It'd be nice for our guests to have the option," she said.

It wasn't easy, but I found a way to play devil's advocate. "It's $800 to borrow a couch for four hours so that 1-2 percent of our guests can sit down," I said. "And we have no idea if it's even comfortable."

With the support of Alex's sister, we moved on. This was a rare victory for me and the joint bank account.

We strolled across the property vetting the ceremony site candidates. Alex instructed me to "take lots of pictures." Months later, she'd find these photos while scrolling through my phone and ask me why I'd taken so many worthless pics of the Addison Grove. I suspect she made up the assignment to keep me occupied and out of the way.

The morning moved swiftly. A light breeze carried our hushed voices around the grounds as we remained ever-vigilant in our effort not to disturb the bride of the day. We sidled from each ceremony site to the reception area, where a new set of questions arose.

If it rains, where is our plan B?
What about a plan C?
Where will the bar go?
What about the dessert table?
Where will the photo booth go? The guest book? The gift table?
How much space does the band need?
Is there enough space for all of our guests?
Will we rent special chairs for the head table?
Will we rent a head table?
What about a plan D?

While Alex pondered these pressing concerns, I double checked on the dimensions of the groom's quarters. The groom of the day wouldn't arrive for hours, and I can't overstate how important it was for me to be confident and comfortable with the bathroom situation on my wedding day.

We had a plan B for ceremony sites, this much I know. I believe we had a plan C as well, though I can only guess what it was and I can't think of a circumstance that would make plan B obsolete.

"Where does the dessert table go?" is an Alex question. Sometimes when she asks me for an opinion I know that she really wants one. She may ignore it, but I know she still wants me to throw something out there. I didn't bother to venture a guess with the dessert table. Placing furniture is one I'd never get right. When we moved in together, we drew diagrams for how to arrange the apartment. I missed on all counts. I tried to create a sanctuary in the guest room, suggesting that she make all the decisions for the rest of the house, and I maintain creative control of just the one room. I didn't want a man cave. I wanted a room to keep all my junk, all the stuff she'd wind up throwing away. Call it a hoarder's quarters. Wisely, she said no. That way she got all the rooms. A shrewd negotiator, Alex Heine. Glad she's on my side.

The shabby chic space seemed cavernous with no people inside. I stared up at the deep brown wood of the ceiling, worried that our wedding wouldn't be large enough to fill the space. Naturally, Alex worried that we'd be too big a group. Again, I reminded myself that the venue hosts all sizes of weddings, many smaller or larger than ours. We'd be fine.

I assume that Alex and her sister made the important dessert table placement decisions because before I knew it we were walking up the path to the parking lot. The very same lot that, after careful deliberation, we'd decided would be the perfect spot to have the shuttle drop off our guests.

Alex and I threw a housewarming party shortly after we moved in together. That night, I stood on our new balcony with my friend Dan and Alex's former co-worker, whose name escapes me. Let's call her Ruth.

"Phoenix has the best Mexican food," Ruth said.

"Why is that?" I asked.

"There are a lot of Mexicans in Phoenix."

"There are a lot of Mexicans in Chicago, too," Dan said. "Probably more than in Phoenix."

"But they aren't as close to Mexico."

"What about Texas?" I chimed in, standing up for my new roommate's homeland.

"What about Texas?" Ruth replied.

"It's close to Mexico. Plus, it's Texas. The portions are probably bigger. Everything is bigger in Texas."

"Except Alex." Classic Ruth.

It's true. Everything in Texas is way too big, with the exception of Alex and her sister. Allison, like Alex, is a tiny human being. Next to her, everything in Texas seems even bigger, especially her Cadillac Escalade with illegally dark tinted windows. This car has its own ecosystem. Passengers experience different seasons depending on which end of the vehicle they occupy. After leaving the Addison Grove, we entered the gaping abyss of the Escalade and began what was probably a 45-minute drive to our next appointment, the highly anticipated caterer tasting session.

Planning a wedding on our own was often an alienating and disillusioning process. The tasks you expect to be easy become needlessly complex. The people whose job it is to help you wind up complicating things or scamming you. We saw this with the venue and the parking attendant. Trust me, I'll share about 40 more examples once we get to the rapid fire vendor round up. Planning a wedding means you keep trying. You send another email, make another phone call, try and try and try to communicate as clearly as possible. Most of the time you get nothing back.

The caterer tasting session has a reputation for being one of the rare perks of planning a wedding. And it is, but not for the reason you'd expect. It's not about free food or decadent desserts. For one thing, it isn't free; you're paying thousands of dollars for it. What makes the caterer tasting special is that it's the first real return on your investment. When we sat down at our tasting, it was the first time that our decisions and money and emails and aggravation culminated in something concrete.

We booked the band knowing we wouldn't hear them play until the wedding. They didn't offer to have us stop by their practice space to enjoy a brief medley of our requested tunes.

When we booked the shuttles, they didn't offer a ride to our next appointment.

All of our work wouldn't materialize for months. At the caterer tasting, we didn't just sample the food we'd serve; we tasted the fruits of our labor.

The Escalade rolled into the parking lot of a strip mall and Allison found a space with some shade. No redwoods grew in the area, so we couldn't get the whole car out of the sun, but it was better than nothing.

I grabbed a couple of OTC lactase digestive tablets, took a deep breath, and prepared for the harrowing trek from the air conditioned car to the air conditioned building. I treated the day's consumption schedule much like I would a Thanksgiving, striving for the sweet spot where I've eaten light enough to maximize hunger but not so light that my stomach would have shrunk.

I set out to eat my weight in canapes.[70]

I had higher expectations for the sampling than I did for the actual wedding. I've been served some questionable meals at weddings in my lifetime, and I suspect the bride and groom didn't sit down at their own tasting session and give their stamp of approval to an objectively offensive dish. Some caterers can prepare four plates of superb chicken at their facility, but suffer a decline in quality when they have to prepare 200 plates and transport them across town. In our case, we'd be talking about a solid 45-minute Texas transport.[71]

We could rest easy knowing that we'd selected a highly rated, Best of the Knot credentialed, Wedding-Wire official caterer. In fact, our venue suggested our caterer as the number one option on its list of approved vendors. That list included only five caterers, and Heine was rather upset when, through some casual Instagramming, she discovered that the venue regularly worked with vendors outside their approved list. I assume there are mutually beneficial relationships (read: kickbacks) involved for those on the list. You can't spell wedding industry without industry.

Our contact, Tiffany, welcomed us with a smile as wide as the Rio Grande. She was, in every way, exactly as I'd expected her to be, draped in pink, tittering nervously after every sentence, with a pink laptop nestled against her bosom like a newborn babe. Tiffany was the type of administrative worker incapable of responding to an entire email. Here's a typical back-and-forth leading up to the tasting:

Alex: Hi Tiffany, before we come in, can you answer a few questions for us? First, how many passed appetizers can we sample? Second, can we substitute queso for salsa? Lastly, will the arugula salad be in season in early November?

Tiffany: Hi Alex! Thank you so much for reaching out! We're so excited to work with you! Yes, you can sample passed apps on your plan and we do offer queso and salsa.

Alex: Tiffany, that's great. But how many passed apps can we sample? The plan we're looking at doesn't have queso, is it possible to get queso *instead* of salsa? We're happy to pay a fee for the substitution. Will the arugula salad be available in November?

Tiffany: Yes. Sorry. We have the event date down as November 4th.

You'd think that replies like this would frustrate us, but in this example she actually acknowledged various components from our emails, which, regardless of failing to answer our questions, is far above average. After an exhaustive back and forth, Alex managed to arrange the tasting and line up a menu that fit our needs. God bless Alex Heine.

Inside, the kitchen dominated the space. Stainless

steel tabletops, mixing bowls, unlabeled plastic jugs filled with sauces and spices and the friendly camaraderie of hourly employees easing their way into the workday routine. I tried to glimpse the action, but Tiffany quickly herded us into a narrow room with a long oak table. We took our seats on either side as our hostess set down her laptop at the head of the table and handed out freshly printed menus to help us keep track of our tasting notes. Our sampling menu featured several items we knew we wouldn't serve at the wedding, but as Americans it was our duty to take full advantage of what was offered, maximizing consumption and wasting as much food as possible.

I once loved passed appetizers, and I'd gleefully overindulge when the time came. Who doesn't? They're served when you're at your hungriest, span a variety of flavors and cuisines, and often appear from nowhere to save you from small talk with obscure relatives. However, as I grow older, wiser, and more cultured, I've come to see the truth of the passed app. They ruin appetites and show up cold, if they show up at all. They ruin people, too. We all have a friend who forgoes socializing, scouring for footprints and sniffing the air to track the migration patterns of the tray-toting waitstaff. Worst of all, with a drink in one hand and a passed app in the other, you're left vulnerable to countless threats and unable to show acquaintances pictures of your dog or look up the name of that actor from that thing.

We knew we'd skip the passed app, but since it was included in the tasting, we picked a few off the website anyway. Each item is priced per guest, typically at about $2.95. It adds up fast. The one benefit of changing our minds on passed apps would be adding "I once spent more than $300 on crab cakes in a single night" to my Two Truths and a Lie arsenal.

By the time we sat down for our tasting, we'd already hired the caterer and had a good idea of what we'd select for our menu. We'd serve Texas BBQ at our rehearsal dinner and offer a Tex-Mex buffet at the wedding. I told my vegan friend in Los Angeles several months in advance so he'd know what to expect.[72] Given the style of food we'd serve, the buffet would make things much easier and faster for the guests and substantially more affordable for us.

Tiffany got up to retrieve our first dish, a platter of chips, salsa, guacamole, and queso. We decided on the salsa bar instead of passed apps, and crossed our fingers hoping it'd be good. Alex reminded her mom and sister to keep their opinions to themselves. "It's too late to switch caterers, so don't bother saying anything if you don't like it."

Alex and I love watching *Chopped* on the Food Network. In doing so, I've become a master at regurgitating culinary criticisms, and because I'm an arrogant narcissist, I feel that I'm qualified to weigh in on professionals' cooking despite how I'd be less stressed diffusing a bomb than baking a potato. I can't cook, but I could give a TED Talk on how to win a cooking game show.

I picked up the first chip and rotated it in front of my face, getting a feel for its density, rubbing my thumb across its surface to test for loose salt. It checked out. A decent chip. The salsa earned a passing grade, and the guacamole merited a nod of approval. But we didn't touch any of that until after we'd tried the queso.

Alex loves to tell stories about how much queso she ate as a little girl. The family would head to Matt's El

Rancho and instead of enchiladas or tacos she'd order queso for dinner. It remains her favorite food. For those who haven't tried queso, think of a cheese dip. For those who have only tried the queso served in, say, Chicago, that doesn't count. You may think it's the same, but any Texan reading this will call you a lunatic. "You can't find queso up north" is something I hear a lot. It's a point of regional pride. If Alex's dad called me and said "we've got this great new Italian beef sandwich place down here!" I'd hang up the phone and laugh my way through an authentic Chicago beef. Then I'd stop for deep dish on the way home.

Alex will never rate Mexican food in Chicago as highly as what they serve in Austin or San Antonio. It's not as "authentic." I used to argue with her, but If you've ever had a breakfast taco from Mary's in Boerne, Texas, there's no need to have this discussion. We just don't make them like that up here.

Serving Alex Heine queso is like performing a piano concerto for Chopin. To put it lightly, the queso we sampled tasted out of tune. I wrote on my menu, "watery cheese oatmeal." Having just received Alex's warning about not saying anything negative, we all sat in silence. Normally, when a bowl of queso sits on a table, there's a traffic jam of hands jockeying for position to get into their next bite, like cars exiting a crowded parking lot from three directions, all driven by my Uncle George trying to beat the traffic. This time, we all idled in place until Alex mercifully broke the silence. "I don't like this. I can't serve this at my wedding."

The floodgates of criticism flung open and the critiques poured out. "Grainy," "horrible," "tastes like queso from Chicago." We discussed bringing in outside queso, but the thought of introducing yet another vendor was out of the question. Tiffany, once aware of our feelings, agreed to have them change the recipe. Way to go, Tiffany! You saved the day.

We nibbled on a few passed appetizers, just for kicks, until the bell rang for the main event. The clock struck tac-o'clock.

If queso is Alex's culinary best friend, tacos are her celebrity crush. She talks about tacos like they're rock stars. A good taco is a hit song, and the restaurant it came from will become a popular band at our apartment. Some places only have one good menu item, those are the one hit wonders. Others haven't been good since their early stuff and some are just too mainstream.

Chipotle is the Coldplay of tacos.

While Alex lacks any musical talent in real life, in this analogy she is a virtuoso.

Plate by plate, we waited with mouths watering as Tiffany toted in the components of the taco buffet. First, a tray of sauces and toppings, including a pickled watermelon slaw. Within minutes the table became a cornucopia of Tex Mex staples. Creamy orange rice, pinto beans, a seasonal salad, and four enormous bowls of proteins. We had to choose two options from greasy beef picadillo, achiote pork, pulled chicken, and braised short rib. I added the word "greasy" and still don't know what picadillo and achiote mean. Based on the quantities, I'd guess picadillo means "for fifteen" and achiote means "way too much." We could have fed five families with our bowls of Way Too Much Pork and Beef for Fifteen. And we probably did. What better perk of working weekends for a caterer than taking home a leftover sample bowl of greasy Beef for Fifteen? It's a job that literally puts food on the table.

We dug in, and within seconds Vivian forgot the criticism embargo, sharing a rather witty and urbane barb. "I don't like the beef."

"Mom!" Alex snipped. I don't remember if the conversation continued as all outside stimuli ceased to reach me. As I did at the Jewish deli after looking at suits, once more I had found my beach.

We knew we'd pick the chicken because it's a crowd pleaser. Everyone gets down on chicken. Except those fools who decide to ruin chicken for the rest of their lives by being conscientious consumers and watching a documentary on the inner workings of the chicken industry. The Way Too Much Pork went down smooth enough, but fell short of the short rib.

With the main course put away, all that remained was to sample the dessert and watch Tiffany clear the main course. The former service industry professional in me yearned to help clear the table. I'd like to believe the root of my desire was altruism, eager to help Tiffany and be a kind person. In truth, I just wanted the pie sooner.

I can't remember the last time Alex baked a pie, but she's living proof that you don't have to bake pies seriously to take pies seriously. Much like queso, Alex knows what she wants in a pie and is prepared to make a caterer bend to her will to get it. Her first contact with the caterer dealt exclusively with the year-round availability of strawberry rhubarb pie. She was assured that any of the pies on the menu, even those with month-to-month seasonal availability listed in writing, would be available at any time. Tiffany balked when she brought out the rhubarb, pointing out that it may not be on the menu for November. Alex set down her fork, turned her head, and calmly said to Tiffany, "The only reason we are here is because I have it on good authority, from your boss, that you can make any pie on the menu at any time during the year."

God bless Alex Heine.

The gluttony resumed with a dozen slices. That's one and half full pies for the four of us. We started with the strawberry rhubarb, hoping it would be just as good in November as it was in June. Next, the all-American double crust apple. And finally, the wild card: chocolate peanut butter.

Alex prefers fruit-based desserts. She orders black raspberry ice cream instead of cookies and cream. At Sonic, she opts for limeades instead of not going to Sonic. It's the same story with pies. She'd opt for any fruit flavor before French silk or Oreo. But our guests aren't all like her, and I thought it'd be wise to sample something from the chocolate end of the spectrum.[73]

I'm not ashamed to admit that the chocolate peanut butter pie was a mistake. Imagine a store bought graham cracker crust. Now picture Tiffany, clad in a pink apron, dipping a pink ladle into an industrial sized, military grade vat of peanut butter. Toss on a frozen disc of chocolate syrup and you've completed the recipe. Even I found this one to be a bit much, and I'm a 30-year-old man who ate Girl Scout cookies on four separate occasions yesterday. If I can't handle a sweet, it's really, really sweet.

Tiffany cleared our plates and the four of us took a moment to catch our breath. Alex appreciated my feedback and enthusiasm throughout the tasting. Finally, we'd found a component of wedding planning that I could take the lead on and really dig into with gusto.

As we stood up to leave, I reflected on the experience and crunched some numbers in my head. A few months later, I'd be cutting a check for more than five thousand dollars so that my friends and family could eat chips, guacamole, tacos, and pie. I held the door for Alex and my soon-to-be in-laws and stepped out into the hot Texas sun, shaking my head and dreaming of a future career in the wedding industry.

Please enjoy this children's poem, which should help you deal with vegetarians while you plan your wedding.

> I told my friend the vegan,
> That he ought to come prepared,
> Cause when it comes time for eatin',
> His lifestyle won't be shared.
>
> He called me a barbarian,
> But said he'd eat before he came,
> though not all vegetarians,
> Would be so quick to say the same.
>
> Pescatarians are pesky,
> Fishing for a non-meat choice,
> These demands became a pest, see,
> I'd prefer they go unvoiced.
>
> The caterer had salmon,
> For ten extra bucks a head,
> Ten dollars, or their famine?
> I'd prefer they starve instead.
>
> One guest, she made us toil,
> She's allergic to all food,

"Could you ask about the cooking oil?"
Can you believe that attitude?

No olive oil, nothing fried,
Does the salad come with ranch?
If she weren't so scared of tree nuts,
I'd smack her with a branch.

What you're asking is too great,
Adding to our list of chores,
Trust me, there's enough on our plate
Without worrying so much about yours.

I wonder, Do you ever eat out?
Food is supposed to be fun.
The thing I got so mad about?
This girl was just a plus-one.

I feared the rental showroom more than any other stop on the wedding planning tour. Glassware, plates, tablecloths, napkins, silverware. You name it, I'd be asked for my opinion of it. I dreaded it the entire 45-minute ride. Not only would I have to concoct countless commentary, but I'd have to do so while living in the fear of taco aftermath. What if I needed to lie down? What if I ran out of opinions about linens? What if I had to take a big ol' Tex-Mex dump? The atacolypse loomed.[74]

I rode with Vivian, following Alex and Allison's Escalade Biodome. Vivian, eager to befriend me and gain my sympathy, asked if I thought Alex was being too hard on her following her criticism of the taco beef. I demonstrated my trademark tact, not taking sides, defending Alex while showcasing my understanding and counseling patience. Unfortunately, the beef was just the beginning.

I'd been a fish in water at the caterer. At the rental showroom, I was a man in a rented kayak lost at sea, on the verge of losing my life and the deposit on the kayak.

We had the entire showroom to ourselves, accentuating the vastness of the space. In typical Texas fashion they revved the AC to maximum power, producing a climate that would freeze the water in the previous paragraph's metaphor. I shuddered, in part due to the temperature but also as an involuntary reaction to the 9,000 napkins waiting for my thoughtful examination.

To our left, the yellow glow of the fluorescence shown down on the day to day items. Dining rooms were scattered about like prizes up for bid during the Showcase Showdown, complete with place settings and centerpieces. "I love this one," Vivian said as she wandered towards an elegant setup with a smoothly sanded tree branch curving three feet high off the tabletop. If we host a dinner party for the gods of Valhalla, I'll know where to get my decorative accents.

I truly believe that I did a good job of being present and offering thoughtful opinions throughout the wedding planning experience. However, there are exceptions. Choosing which forks we'd rent is such an exception. I can't tell you anything about any piece of silverware I saw that day. In fact, I can't tell you anything about any silverware I've ever used at any wedding I've attended. I'm not entirely sure I could describe the silverware I use at home. If I were using a fork right now, I wouldn't be able to describe anything about it besides the basic characteristics shared by all forks. Rather than provide critical insights like, "I love the one with the tines," I decided to let Alex take the lead.

I loitered about as Alex, Allison, and Vivian examined the available glassware. Hundreds of glasses lined the floor-to-ceiling shelves along the back wall of the room. I stood watching them scrutinize the cups, thinking how impressive it was that Indiana Jones could select the holy grail in less time than we needed to pick a water glass.

"Alex, honey, this one is just like your dress!" Vivian said.

"Mom!"

"What?"

"I can't believe you."

As we've established, Alex's dress was a secret. A carefully guarded secret that kept me out of our guest-room for three months leading up to the ceremony (and forced Brad and me to move our meetings to the living room). The moment Alex got over her beef with her mother's beef critique, Vivian went straight into a wardrobe malfunction, revealing just a little more dress than she should have. Vivian stammered whatever excuses she could cook up while Alex stood stone-faced, arms crossed tightly against her chest.

Thankfully, I was paying so little attention that I honestly didn't know which cup she was talking about, and was able to partially diffuse the situation by claiming ignorance. Sometimes it pays to be totally oblivious and disinterested in what you're doing.

In an effort to change the subject, I directed Alex's attention to a herd of chairs and suggested I take a look. After all, I knew we'd be renting special chairs for our head table. What sort of wedding would it be if we sat in the same chairs as our guests? We aren't animals.

"No, Sam," she shook her head. "We get the chairs at

the next rental place."

Fuck me.

I spent the next 20 minutes asleep on a loveseat. After all, a nap is nothing but rented sleep.[75]

We woke the next morning in Pflugerville, Texas, a city apparently named by Dr. Seuss. I've come across some strange places in Texas. I guess when you have so much space you have to fill it with more places, and it gets tough to come up with names for all of them. Hence, you wind up with towns called Bee Cave, Ding Dong, and Cut and Shoot.

We spent the night as guests in Allison's in-laws' house. So, let's take it one degree of separation at a time. My fiance's sister's husband's parents, Michael and Marsha. Not exactly blood relatives, but don't tell them that. After I proposed, we went by their house to pick up Alex's niece and encountered Michael and Marsha's extended family celebrating Christmas. These are people I will likely never see again in my life, people who weren't even considered for the "No Pile" during the invite list brainstorm. "Are you sure you're ready to join this big crazy family?" Marsha asked me, gesturing to a not-so-crazy collection of strangers.

I smiled politely, as I thought that was a more appropriate response than saying, "I'm not sure I am joining this family."

Michael and Marsha are Texans. They live in a Texas house, one that I'd expect to have a second story and a basement, but like many homes in Texas, is simply one high-ceilinged, foundationless structure. In it, they live with their two enormous dogs and so many decorations with Bible verses scrawled into them that I'm not sure whether they shop at Hobby Lobby or if Hobby Lobby shops at their house. Is the Bible public domain? Does God get a percentage of each framed placard quoting Joshua 24:15?[76]

Marsha is amazing. She would love nothing more than to supply Hobby Lobby with her own line of embroidered ottomans and personalized knick knacks. She makes dope Christmas gifts for the family, the big crazy family that I'm now a part of. She got Alex and me 48-ounce portable drinking vessels with our names on them. Texans love taking their drinks to go. When I told her how much we enjoy using our novelty sized containers around the house, she went out and got me another one to use at the office. It's great to be a part of this big crazy family.

Michael is more the quiet type. He's the sort of man who's satisfied with the knowledge that he's won multiple chili cook-offs and doesn't bother to brag to his son's wife's sister's soon-to-be husband about it. He's happy to spend 90 minutes preparing a breakfast scramble, even if the same recipe could be made in 12 minutes if he were willing to sacrifice 2 percent of the quality. He's a man's man. He keeps old westerns running in his office 24 hours a day. He'd be more than happy not to show up in this account of our trip to Pflugerville, but it'd be a disservice to readers not to share his remarkable story from that very day.

Michael has a beard that extends down to his belt buckle. He looks like a member of ZZ Top. He looks so much like a member of ZZ Top that, earlier that day, a sound engineer working with ZZ Top approached him at the grocery store and invited him to a concert the following night to go on stage and meet ZZ Top. This story, while incredible in its own right, also represents the most Michael has ever said to me in one sitting.

Most folks would pounce on this opportunity, a once-in-a-lifetime chance to share a stage with Rock and Roll Hall of Fame inductees and facial hair icons. But Michael isn't most people. Michael is one of those "up at 4 am for no reason" guys. Going on stage at 10 pm means staying up past 8 pm. He passed on the concert.

Am I part of their big crazy family? I guess I am. They made sure of it. They didn't have to love me like they did, but they did, but they did. And I thanked them. The next morning I put on my cheap sunglasses and we left for the flower shop.[77]

Kudos to our florist. Anyone who understands and can act on the input, "Pink. But not so pink that it's pink," earns my personal Austin Wedding Florist endorsement.

We arrived ahead of Vivian, which I thought would help us save time[78] since she was old friends with the Flower Lady and would inevitably want to catch up. Vivan had even worked part time at the shop for a while. It's still not clear to me at what point in her life this employment took place.

I knew she was the Flower Lady the moment we walked inside. The floral print on her blouse was a dead giveaway.

Flowers by Nancy 2 shares a parking lot with a speedboat dealer's showroom. I sat between Alex and the Flower Lady as they leaned in to inspect a Pinterest gallery on Alex's iPhone. Meanwhile, I stared through the front door and dreamed of fixing up a rundown speedboat on the shores of Zihuatanejo.

I learned all about flowers that morning. Did you know that peonies can't handle the hot Texas climate?

They require a deep freeze and prefer places like Chicago. Believe me, it's worth it to suffer six months of head colds and hat hair when you factor in the affordability of peonies. You can't go anywhere during a Chicago winter without hearing the same old small talk:

"Wind chill is negative fifteen today. Man, my commute is going to be rough on those icy roads. But it's worth it. Just think how pink those peonies will be once my nose hairs thaw out in a few months."

"Not too pink, I hope."

"With 10 inches of snow? No way. Pink, but not so pink they'll be pink. Hey, do me a favor and hand me my long underwear."

I should not have sat between Alex and the Flower Lady. My only contribution during the entire experience was successfully checking in for our flight the next morning.[79] As usual, Alex had put a lot more thought into this aspect of the big day than I knew was possible or required. She rattled off responses to questions that would have left me stupefied. She had a plan for tea candles, had considered the pros and cons of doilies, knew where she'd shop for mismatched three-to-six-inch bud vases, and needed advice on where to put the bouquet after the ceremony.

I planned to throw my jacket over the back of my chair (assuming the chair we rented had a back). Alex's bouquet would rest in a large bowl filled with river rocks on a rented table near the entrance, alongside God knows what else. If you ever catch me claiming to have contributed to planning this wedding, remind me of how much I don't know. God Bless Alex Heine.

I wasn't even involved in selecting "our flower," the

one that featured in the bouquet and boutonniere. I had no input on whether our moms would need corsages. I had no head for our nieces' headbands. As such, I'll forego any details on these decisions and we'll play some floral-themed games.

First, try to identify which of the following are flowers and which are spells from Harry Potter.

Amaranthus
Alohomora
Scabiosa
Protego
Protea
Ranunculus
Agonis
Astilbe
Finestra
EXPECTO PATRONUM!!!

If you guessed that numbers 1, 3, 5, 6, 7, and 8 are flowers, you've demonstrated a mastery of either latin roots or *Hogwarts: a History*. Either way, you are a huge nerd. Also, I snuck in an Easter egg. If you combine those numbers into 135,678, you get the number of dollars it'll cost me to pay my legal team once the Harry Potter folks see that I used "Finestra" without permission.

For our next game, let's pair flowers with a corresponding *Game of Thrones* character![80]

Peonies: We've already discussed their preference for cold climates, so let's call them Wildlings.

Peace Lily: Peace lilies don't require much sunlight to survive, which is one of the main traits of the cave dwelling Three Eyed Raven. Plus, the Three Eyed Raven isn't really a raven, and the peace lily lives a lie too, as my two minutes of research turned up the fact that it's not even a lily.

Impatien: This small, resilient flower survives at all cost. Let's call an imp and imp and match it with Tyrion.

Ranunculus: This is the fancy name for Buttercup flowers. They are beautiful, bitter and poisonous to men and wolves. Sounds like Cersei Lannister to me.

Luminous Pineleaf Beardtongue: Can you believe that's a real thing? It's bright orange, it's a wildflower, and you can't look at it without thinking of a beard. Tormund Giantsbane, the wildling fan-favorite known to Alex as "the orange-haired man," makes a great match.

Globemaster Allium: Holy shit, I never expected to have so much fun looking up the names of flowers. The globemaster flower is an enormous purple orb. It is feminine, yet powerful. It once defeated the Hound in single combat. Gotta call this one Brienne of Tarth.

Agonis: These little guys are white, dirty, and pretty much total bitchasses. We'll call them the Theon Greyjoys of flowers.

Dusty Miller: White as snow, frosty, pale and relegated to playing bit parts in a floral arrangement, the flowers of a Dusty Miller sound a lot like Craster's daughters.

Bachelor Button: Here's a flower that's perfect for Jorah Mormont. Bachelor Buttons represent celibacy, which is right up his alley with the whole unrequited love thing he's got going on. We'll say his particular batch of Bachelor Buttons are riddled with botrytis, better known as gray mold, which is essentially the floral equivalent of grayscale.

Hodor: Hodor Hodor Hodor. Hodor? Hodor Hodor.

Thistle: Skeletal and haunting, thistles seem to appear out of nowhere. Any bouquet that uses thistle will use it in more than one place at the same time. Remember that weirdo warlock who tries to steal Daenerys's dragons in the House of the Undying. He's a thistle. This also works for the army of the dead. Thistle is pretty much the zombie version of a normal flower.

King protea: Robert Baratheon. It's enormous, and it's the king.

Gunni Eucalyptus: Feminine, seemingly sweet, and reeking of too much time in the forest, this breed of euc fits perfectly with Margaery Tyrell, who Bart Simpson would refer to as the Milk Dud Queen.[81] The Internet suggests hanging Gunni Euc in the shower, which is where many adolescent boys took Margaery in their hormonal imaginations.

Gardenia: Elegant and fragile, like Sansa Stark before she becomes a heartless, hardened woman of Westeros.

Alohomora: Wait, that's a Harry Potter spell.

MY DREAM WEDDING

Shortly after our summer trip to Texas, on June 18, I dreamt that I had no pants on during my wedding ceremony. I didn't panic in the dream. Thanks to our foresight, we'd booked a venue with an on-site pants shop in the same room as the cocktail reception. I snatched a pair of khakis off the rack, which, obviously, were several sizes too big. You don't need a technicolor dreamcoat to interpret this dream. An unprepared, emotionally immature boy can't fit into a grown man's pants on the day he takes a wife.

Yikes.

None of the guests cared about my predicament in the dream. They were too busy enjoying themselves.

Only 100 more nights to sleep through before the big day!

BUYING A SUIT: ACT TWO

I was 27 years old the first time I wore a suit that fit. Until that point, donning formal wear made me feel like a boy in men's clothing. The three piece hand-me-down came close. Snug enough in the waist, sleeves about right, but having been tailored two decades prior to the invention of "slim fit," my legs wound up swimming in, of all things, *empty space*.

I'm too thin. Manufacturing suits in my size simply isn't good business. The consumer pool for suits my size is, in more ways than one, too small. When we returned to Nordstrom for the anniversary sale, I strode into the store with my head held high. We had it on good authority from the least authoritative salesman I'd ever met, the doughy, red-faced man, that they'd have a bigger selection of suits in my size during the sale. I didn't notice the salesman this time. I assume Rueben scared him into a new career, or some sort of asylum.

I walked behind Alex and my mom, already checking my phone to make sure I had enough time to get back to the city for an afternoon softball game. I can't recall if Rueben couldn't make it or if we'd intentionally left him off the invite list for round two of suit shopping. Neither would surprise me, but one would make me feel a lot better about myself. I'm pretty sure it's the other one.

We captured the attention of an older, salt and pepper salesman. He gave me a quick once over. I wasn't exactly masking my skinniness, with mesh shorts billowing over a couple of toothpick legs. A decade of diligent laundering had worn out the elastic on my shorts to the point where if I didn't tie the drawstring they'd fall around my ankles.[82]

"This way," he said. A moment later Mr. Salt'n'Pepper held an upturned palm out to indicate a small corner of a single rack. "These five suits are all that we have in your size."

Five suits? *Five suits*? Give me a break. I get it, I'm thinner than the jack of diamonds, but have you seen his outfit?

"You could try another store," the salesman said. Nordstrom really needs to improve their hiring criteria.

We left Nordstrom in the hopes of providing a nice commission to a more competent employee. I checked the time, and sure enough, it was linear, continuing in its steady march forward toward the first pitch of a softball game that I'd almost surely miss. We window shopped for more than an hour before I tried on a single piece of clothing. Macy's had nothing that worked. Bloomingdales showered us with attentive sales personnel, but unfortunately, I can't wear good service at the altar. We were on the verge of conceding the day to the grand demon of wedding planning when we opted to make one last stop and do a little more digging at Nordstrom.

"You know what, Sammy?" My mother took my arm as we strolled past a Cinnabon. "You could probably fit in a youth size." I pretended I didn't hear the suggestion to save my sweet mother from the embarrassment of having said something so ludicrous. Perhaps silence was too subtle, as she elaborated. "You know, a boy's suit?"

I'd be 30 years old on my wedding day. I wasn't about to wear a child's suit.

"Nobody would know," she said.

I would know. Each word that escaped her lips added to the shame. A boy's suit. It's not like I'm that small. I'm a good 5'9" with a decent shoe. Oh, and I'm an adult. No clip-on ties or toddler socks necessary.

Luckily, the boy's suit was moot, as we found many appropriate sized suits designed for grown ups that would fit me just fine. It turned out Mr. Salt'n'Pepper wasn't quite the seasoned employee his two-tone hair suggested. Several designers had their own racks, and on most of them we could find a handful of 36 Shorts.

But this is wedding planning, so having taken a step forward we had to take two steps back.[83]

We'd entered with the plan to find a dark gray suit. Now that we were on the verge of executing that plan, Alex reconsidered. Maybe a light gray, or a dark blue? What if we did a light blue? Rather than try on a suit that fits, we went back to the drawing board. I wound up wearing a variety of jackets and pants in sizes that had me pining for a boy's suit.

To better envision the color scheme, the women in my life required that I borrow a sample shirt. Fittingly, the store loaned me something several sizes too large. I looked like a clown. I wore that shirt like a lab coat. Having returned to the color matching phase of the process, the suits I tried on didn't need to fit just yet; they were merely tools for color wheels. Remember when Tom Hanks' character in *Big* transforms back into a kid at the end? That's what I looked like in the dressing room, clad head-to-toe in the latest from the Zoltan Fall collection.

I stood next to Alex in front of the mirror, a demonstrative frown painted across my face. She asked me to take my hands out of my pockets to better see how the jacket fell. Little did she know my hands were busy keeping the pants from falling around my ankles.

If there's a single moment in the 10 months between the proposal and the ceremony that captures my role in the planning process, it's what happened next in that dressing room. Alex invited my mother in to help her compare colors against the cloth samples of her dress. As the dress was still meant to be a surprise, I had to turn around. There I stood, staring at the corner of the dressing room cubicle with my head down, pantsless, emasculated by a shirt that covered my knees. I'd been put in timeout. Meanwhile, my mother and my fiancée decided what I'd wear on the most important day of my life. Freudians, take your best shot.

I was a pawn. A prop. Somehow, by the time I received permission to turn around, we'd selected my wedding suit.

In the end, I made it back to the city in time for softball. When my teammates asked what the suit looked like, I told them the honest truth: "I'm not sure. You'd have to ask my mom."

"How do I look?"

"Relatively speaking," Brad answered, "not very well. Your ocular organs lack the perceptive capacity to look with even a minute fraction of my own looking abilities."

"I think I look damn good." I'd learned to ignore his more obnoxious statements. Plus, I did look damn good. I posed in front of the living room couch, admiring myself in the window's reflection as Brad and Mona stared up from the upholstery, unimpressed by the pants and jacket Heine and I had worked so hard to obtain, and the skinny man wrapped up inside them.

Heine's dress had arrived, so Brad and I had moved

our classes to the living room.

More than a month had passed since we'd purchased the suit, which arrived in the mail two weeks earlier. Being an idiot, it never occurred to me that suits aren't like shoes. You don't just ask the salesman to check in the back room to see if your size is in stock. You have to come back to the store and have the damn thing tailored.[84]

So we went back to Nordstrom, me armed with an untailored suit and Heine armed with a woman's eye for how clothes should fit her future husband. When we purchased the suit, they assured me that alterations were free on any product purchased during the anniversary sale. As they measured, pinned, and chalked the suit they assured me, yet again, that the alterations would be free of charge. You can imagine my surprise when, after leaving the store with multiple assurances that my alterations would be free, I received a call from Nordstrom alerting me to the alteration they'd made to the cost of the tailoring.

It just isn't a wedding planning task without a last minute scam.

They were asking for a fight and I was ready to give them one, but I wasn't sure how because I've never been in a real fight. I did the next best thing, sending a strongly worded, irrefutably clear email that I believed would result in a timely resolution of my complaint.

The customer care representative got back to me within one business day. She did her colleagues proud, earning her place among the ranks of Dough Face and Salt'n'Pep with an irrefutably inane bit of corporate jargon. Maybe I'd bring Rueben in when I picked up the suit, he could go to bat for me.

Incompetence is a double edged sword.[85] Two weeks after having the alterations drawn up, I barged into Nordstrom and made my way to the Men's Department to pick up the suit and try my best to raise hell over $40. I had my key arguments rehearsed, fully prepared for any rebuttals. I was ready to let them have it. Instead, they let me have it, handing over the suit at no charge because nobody there has any idea what they're doing. Before they could catch their mistake, I turned and walked out, hoping never to buy a piece of clothing again in my life.

"What do you think of the suit?" I tried again, fishing for compliments from a four-legged, noodle-armed creature.

"This is normal clothing for a wedding?" Brad rose from the couch and circled me to inspect the no-cost alterations.

"Not always. Sometimes people wear tuxedos."

"I approve," Brad sat down again and Mona shimmied across the couch to rest her head on his outermost thigh. I hadn't taken my eyes off my reflection. We selected a dark grey suit with subtle purple undertones that gave it a little texture at close range. "Will Alex's suit also require tailoring?"

"We've been over this, Brad. Alex will wear a dress, not a suit."

"May I see it?"

"As long as you don't tell me what it looks like. It's the reason we're out here instead of your room."

"*My* room?" His eyes lit up at the prospect of ownership. His very own box in the sky.

"If you've been here this long, you're no longer a guest. You're a full-time resident."

I did my best DeNiro, demanding the handsome man in the glass tell me exactly who he was talking to. After a Zoolander look and a few very suave finger pistol/winking/clicking sound combinations I noticed Brad speaking again.

"I approve of the dress," he said, presumably after freezing me in time. I don't remember him leaving the room, though it's certainly possible my vanity kept me so occupied with the reflection that he didn't have to bother. "Was it as hard to acquire as your suit?"

I wanted to say no. How could it be? But looking back, it must have required considerably more work. If I had as much trouble with my suit as I did, and I'm a guy who, as he writes this sentence, is wearing a reversible mesh tank top, mesh shorts, and no underpants, then a stylish young woman like Alex must have exhausted herself to ensure her wedding dress would be perfect. But I didn't know any of the details. They were kept from me and I lacked the vocabulary to understand them.

All I knew about Alex's dress prior to the wedding was that its alterations alone cost more than my entire outfit. I told Brad as much.

"I wouldn't worry about it," he put a hand on my shoulder. "I'm sure she'll get plenty of use out of such a beautiful and expensive piece of clothing."

"Uh, actually—"

"It's not like anybody would make such a fuss and go through all that trouble just to wear something for one night! Not even human weddings would justify such insanity."

"Oh, poor, sweet Brad," I gently removed his hand from my shoulder and gave a series of slow, knowing shakes of the head. "Have I taught you nothing of my people?"

Six months after the wedding, Alex took her dress to a specialty dry cleaner to have it cleaned, steamed, and packaged for long-term storage. If you thought spending a few hundred dollars on wedding stuff ended after "I do," well, it don't.

These wedding dress preservation specialists are, unfortunately, tangentially affiliated with wedding planning. As such, they are required to fuck it up. And they did. The dress came back showing no evidence of cleaning and steaming, with significant wrinkles and obvious lipstick and queso stains.[86] Alex got her money back and took it upon herself to spot clean, steam, and box up her wedding dress. This was a win-win-win. Alex won because she enjoyed spending more time with that dress. I won because we got the refund. The dress won because it got to hang out in our guest room for another three weeks.

A 45 MINUTE COMMUTE ON THE INFORMATION SUPERHIGHWAY

As a golf fan, the 2018 Masters was a must-watch tournament. Tiger Woods, the world renowned champion/sex monster, returned to Augusta National after missing eight consecutive major tournaments due to a supposedly unrelated combination of back surgeries and sex addiction. The iconic, once-in-a-generation athlete/adulterer clawed his way back to the golfing community's good graces, and despite his titanium-infused spine and reconstructed Frankenstein knee, he'd managed to make the cut and advance to the weekend.

While I watched Tiger's historic return to relevancy, my fiancée approached with a stack of old wedding invitations, which she placed on the coffee table, directly between my eyeball and Tiger's golf ball. Using my well-honed skill of taking hints, I turned my attention her way. We reviewed each invitation, reading aloud to see how our recently wed friends and relatives chose to invite us to their weddings. After a surprisingly brief summit, Alex scooped up the obsolete recyclables and returned them to wherever it was in our little apartment where those things lived. Meanwhile, I focused my attention back on the television, foolishly thinking I'd gotten off easy.[87]

A short time later I announced that I'd be leaving for my brother's annual Masters party, an event that begins every year at 2 pm on Masters Saturday. Unfortunately, Alex had decided that 2 pm on Masters Saturday would be a good time to begin working on our registry. A premarital argument ensued.

"So you're just going to leave instead of helping me?" she said.

She'd known for weeks that I would be unavailable at 2 pm, and yet there we were. I made a case for beginning the registry tasks any other time except for one year later at 2 pm on Masters Saturday, as we both knew I'd be busy then.

"Well," she countered, "you could have started working on this last week."

It's true. I could have. But I'm not stupid. The last thing Alex wants is me deciding what kitchen utensils we'll have for the rest of our lives. Even if I had an opinion on such matters, I'd still manage to mess it up. I'm wearing socks that I've had for more than seven years.[88] I don't buy new things when I need them, so I shouldn't be in charge of selecting a new baking sheet when I already have more baking sheets than I could ever use.

In short, I'm not wired for registry building.

Alex let me have this one, and we got started on the registry that evening instead of that afternoon.

Because I am a fool and do not learn from past experiences, I went into the registry-building phase expecting it would be easy.[89] I thought we'd scroll through and select the items we needed. A stock pot here. A crystal punch bowl there. The basics. Had I been solely responsible for setting up our registry, it would have totaled eight items and I'd have finished in eight minutes.

But Alex possesses a wonderful quirk. She cares about the aesthetic and quality of the things that comprise her home. I recommend living with someone who shares this trait. It makes life beautiful.

Alex cooks, Alex has taste, and Alex ruminates on

spatial organization. She once told me that her ideal Saturday involved organizing the kitchen of a friend who had moved into a new apartment.

In short, Alex is wired for registry building.

And boy oh boy did she build a registry.

Digital food scale: check.

Multiple cast iron dutch ovens: check.

Three seemingly identical white ceramic serving trays: check, check, check.

"What are you doing?" I asked. "We don't need any of this stuff."

Alex rolled her eyes and explained that registries are not for stuff you need. Instead, they are for stuff you specifically do not need. "Look," I followed the cursor across the monitor to a set of crystal highballs. "We don't need these. We would never buy these ourselves. This is the one chance in our life to get them."

Like every other phase of wedding planning, setting up a registry was a far more involved process than I could have imagined. We hosted our site on Zola, which made it easier with some useful tips to maximize the value we squeezed out of our loved ones' wallets. They don't call it the Information Age for nothing. These days you can't even receive gifts without an anonymous expert pumping you full of do's and don'ts and top ten how-to tips. Somehow, I'm at peace with committing to Alex for the rest of my life, but the idea of diving into the rabbit hole of Zola's how-to pages scares the hell out of me.

Here's a tip! It's important to bolster your registry with an endless array of once-a-year kitchen tools that cost $5–$10. Many of your guests will find a more substantial gift, but feel inclined to tack on smaller items.

If someone plans to spend $100, but the gift they find only costs $75, they can balance it out with a crystal bud vase, an artisanally crafted wooden honey dipper, and some sort of cheese slicing wand.

Did you know that some people are old? Old people don't understand computers, so be sure to have items available at brick and mortar stores so Aunt Edna can show up to the bridal shower with a physical gift instead of a newfangled e-receipt.

Zola does a great job. The platform has an algorithm that tells you how many gifts of each pricing tier you should add based on the number of guests you invite. It recommends X "Dining Essentials," Y "Experiences and Gift Cards," and Z "Cleaning and Organization" items. They boast a healthy catalog of inspired articles, including "The Beginner's Guide to Towels." This one caught my attention. I've never witnessed a human birth, but my understanding is that babies get wrapped up in towels within minutes of entering this world. There is no such thing as a towel beginner. We are all experienced in towels.

Given my lifetime of experience and expertise in towels, it came as no surprise when Alex asked for my opinion on a set of towels she wanted to add to the registry. "While it's difficult to judge any towel without an honest, tactile examination," I began my pontification, "these seem too thin to offer adequate absorption. And besides, the tassels on the end are dryer prohibitive."

"Yeah," she said, "but they're cute!"

We now own these towels. They don't absorb that well and I've been instructed not to dry them. You can find them hanging on the auxiliary towel rack, serving as backups to the towels they were meant to replace. If you ever see them there, please remark on their cuteness.

Thanks to Zola's gift tracker we knew when to expect our gifts to show up at the apartment. That's something they don't warn you about. The gifts don't arrive in one big delivery after the wedding, they arrive piecemeal as they're ordered. These days, when I hear the word "wedding," I don't think of my wife's dress or our vows or even the Old Jewish Diamond Guy. I think of breaking down boxes. Boxes and boxes and boxes. If you aren't an Amazon Prime member, the frequency of box breakdowns represents a serious lifestyle change.

Alex enjoys silly smartphone games. This doesn't bother me, as everybody gets into Temple Run or Candy Crush for a few weeks every now and then. But Alex doesn't jump from trend to trend. She finds a game she likes and she milks it for all its worth. Her relationship with the cartoon chef in Cooking Dash dates back farther than her history with me. I often suggest that she's the longest tenured player in history. "Imagine what you could have accomplished in all that time!" I'll say. Then she'll point out how many hours I spent watching the second round action at the Waste Management Phoenix Open. We all have our hobbies.

For a brief stretch during our wedding planning, Heine took a sabbatical from her app-based waitressing job to focus her energy solely on the registry. Her addiction became so severe that, if Registers Anonymous had existed, she'd have been the first to register. At any hour of the day I'd find her researching brands, scouring user reviews, and stressing over whether the coffee maker should be the 31st or 32nd item on our priority gift list.

The order of the list became the primary concern of her life. At the time, we were engaged in an adorable project together. Every night, I would read aloud to her from her favorite book, Stephen King's *The Stand*. That's 800-plus pages of grown up story time. One night, I took a stand of my own, refusing to begin until she closed her computer and called it a day. While describing Stu Redmond's post-apocalyptic journey, I turned and found my fiancée with her back to me, huddled over her phone, immersed in side-by-side thread count comparisons of two bedsheet brands.

Thus ended that night's reading.

I didn't contribute much to the registry, but I gave opinions when called upon and did experience a moment of inspiration, adding one of the best items on the list.[90] Luggage. The hard-case, 4-wheeled suitcase for overhead compartments is a must for the registry. Don't just take my word for it; after I pointed it out, we discovered that "don't forget luggage" was one of the 177 registry-building tips on the website.

On the whole, I couldn't get behind the idea of adding all the unnecessary crap. The opportunity cost overwhelmed the value of all the nice things we didn't need. Wouldn't we be better off getting something we actually needed? Like cash?

Never fear! Any gift purchased online can be exchanged for its cash value and put towards another item on the site. So if I could convince Heine that we didn't need $700 worth of bud vases, we could put that money towards one of the more expensive items that nobody bought. It's a good system, since I'd have been happier with the cash in nine out of 10 instances.

Here are some highlights from the registry experience:

We received one of the seven Dining Essentials we asked for. We're still alive and dining on nutrient-rich meals, so they don't seem quite as essential as advertised.

I now keep my whisky in a crystal brandy decanter instead of the bottle it comes in. The decanter lives in a cabinet, out of sight.

I persuaded Alex to remove the grill press from the list, which I regret, as I'd rather have that than the three new baking sheets we received (half-inch, full-inch, one-and-a-quarter inch).

New steel tongs, perfect for picking up the totally functional steel tongs they replaced.

A new bathroom trash can that, if purchased, would be a great place to throw away the old bathroom trash can.

Alex loves cake stands. If she bakes cookies, they wind up under a glass case, resting on the cake stand, emitting their siren's scent. We got a new crystal cake stand off the registry. We now have three fucking cake stands.

I removed the cocktailing kit. Enough of our cabinet real estate is zoned for cocktailing gear as it is. I used to tend bar, and I don't find time to use this stuff. Does anybody?

Alex denied my request to add a round of golf with Sugar Ray Leonard to the registry. I can't recall the exact price, but $36,000 feels about right.

Having been born in 1988, I feel I'm just old enough to have experienced a pre-Internet world. Those of you born in 1984 may Think Different.[91] I can recall the days prior to smartphones; heck, prior to PrimeCo phones, back when my parents were unreachable if they went out to dinner. Back when I had to memorize the number of a friend's landline to schedule a playdate. Back when we didn't even have MapQuest printouts, let alone GPS.[92] Back when the doors of my mom's minivan needed to be closed manually, and god help you if you were parked on an uphill slope.

Back then, website ownership was reserved for Trekkies and whoever invented Hamster Dance. If there are two things nine-year-old Sam wouldn't have believed, it's that Mark McGwire was cheating and that little Sam would have his very own wedding website.

Companies like Zola and the Knot make wedding websites easy. Their cookie cutter designs get the job done and can be a useful tool for making key details available to guests who don't like reading physical invitations. Addresses, directions, start time, dress code, hotel blocks, and the registry, all in one place. Wedding websites are a good thing. But, they have the word "wedding" in them, so by law they must be overcomplicated.

We need to add photo albums. We need to suggest site-seeing itineraries. We need to list Austin's top eight BBQ restaurants from Yelp. We need to share "Our Story."

I ranted a bit on this concept during the proposal chapter, demonstrating my distaste for oversharing for the sake of superficial approval in the form of filled-in hearts and cartoon thumbs. When Alex assigned me the responsibility for writing "Our Story" for the wedding website, I let loose a groan so demonstratively exasperated it woke the dog up.[93] I couldn't tell her I didn't want to write it and I couldn't tell her I was secretly working on this book. Instead, I scribbled a quick summary of the plot of *Titanic*, changing a few names and dates to match our relationship's timeline. I figured if it could set box office records and net a boatload of Oscars, it'd be good enough for our little wedding website. Heine didn't find it amusing. In the end, we settled on this compromise:

CHRISTMAS EVE, 2017
She approached the deck with short, hesitant steps. *What is he up to out here?* she thought as her loyal, well-behaved Springer Spaniel matched her strides pace for pace, fighting her animal instinct to dive headfirst into the tall grass beside the pond.

As she rounded her father's Camaro she noticed a faint glow emanating from the deck overlooking the water. *Oh! About time!* she thought, picturing the ring she'd designed in her head, and with their jeweler, countless times in the preceding months.

She saw him standing on the deck, surrounded by strings of Christmas lights that shone against the vast emptiness of an overcast Texas sky. He had both feet planted firmly in the center of a repurposed Christmas tree skirt that served as a red carpet to the premiere of the rest of their lives.

He wore his favorite jacket, the one his mother purchased for him at TJ Maxx a decade prior, and a Santa hat. She'd never forget how handsome he looked, despite his annual tradition of growing out a scraggly holiday beard.

Once she climbed down the steps and joined

him amidst the lights, he shared his prepared remarks, though nerves had rendered both of them unable to make sense of what he said. He dropped to his knee and opened the box.

"It's too dark, I can't see," she said.

"Mona, get down," he replied, swatting the curious canine's forepaws, protecting the precious moment. Theirs was a love so pure that no words of assent were necessary for him to know she'd marry him. But she said yes anyway.

An hour earlier they'd been at *Star Wars: Episode 8: The Last Jedi*. An hour later they'd be making celebratory hamburgers.

Hope to see y'all in Texas!

YOU ARE CORDIALLY INVITED TO READ THIS CHAPTER

I should apologize. I've done you a disservice. My description of Brad's legs hasn't done them justice. The extraterrestrial's extra extremities call for poetry, not puns. You know the grace and beauty a four-legged creature displays at a full gallop? Whether it's a gazelle running for its life in the Sahara or a Springer Spaniel chasing a tennis ball down my hallway, the fluidity of quadrupedal animal bodies captivates the human eye. There's more of that in Brad's movement than I've let on. But he doesn't have hindlegs and forelegs, just four legs.

His physiology is almost benthic, better suited for the seafloor than my hardwood floors. Brad's gait is as close to a scuttle as oyster is to a color. He moves like an amputee crab on stilts. Again, I fall short of accuracy. I can't compare him to any of Earth's creatures because he isn't one of Earth's creatures. *Mechanical* may be the best term, considering the machinelike rotation of the extra feet. His knees churn like gears, driving his ankles like pistons in a four-cylinder engine.

These are the thoughts that filled my head as I sat, one leg crossed over its sole contemporary, waiting for Brad to complete his assessment of our wedding invitation. We mailed them that morning and Brad held one of the extras we'd ordered in case of a late addition to the guest list. This was back before Alex's dress established squatting rights in the guest room, and Brad had assumed one of his favorite positions, lounging on the guest bed with his oyster legs fanned out across the seafoam-tinted duvet.

"You send these to your family?" Brad asked, scrutinizing the high quality paper stock from all angles.

"Yes."

"And your friends?"

"Yes."

"Do they serve as tickets? To be handed in upon entry? To prove the person in possession of the paper belongs at the wedding?" He picked up his eyes and turned my way.

"No, Brad. They're just invitations."

"Surely there's some encoded message?"

"Nope. And don't call me Shirley." His pause reminded me that Brad's planet didn't have VHS copies of *Airplane!*[94] "Forget it," I said. "Why can't you wrap your head around this?"

Brad's hand rose to his bowl cut and orbited his skull, a fleshy satellite on the edge of his cranial atmosphere. "Wrap my head?"

I could spend a lifetime explaining English expressions to this sometimes omnipotent, sometimes clueless know-nothing know it all.

"What are you trying to say?" I asked.

"I already know that your family and friends have all of this information. They know where the wedding is. They know when it is. Why do you bother handing them these documents?"

There's a lot to color in when you start with a blank easel. I gave Brad a breakdown of the postal system, which led to a discussion on the impact of email on global communication, which led to an explanation of why society would frown upon a Paperless Post invitation to such a formal event.

Brad's right, we don't *need* fancy wedding invitations. But it's a nice touch. And one that I thought we'd take care of, easy-peasy.[95]

Around the time Alex completed her eighth "final" prioritization of the registry gifts, we realized that we hadn't confirmed who'd be purchasing all those adorable towels and baking sheets. To get wedding gifts, we needed wedding guests, and to get wedding guests, we needed wedding invitations.

How hard could it be to send wedding invitations? I've been mailing letters for years. Not quite as long as I've mastered towels, but still, I knew my way around an envelope. But an invitation to a 10th birthday slumber party isn't the same as a wedding invitation. They're like oregano and pot. They may look the same, but one shouldn't be handled by children.

As usual, my lovely fiancée took the lead.

The forecast for Sunday, April 29, 2018 called for temperatures in the 60s and clear skies. A few days earlier I sat at my office, holding back a tear of joy as weather.com's "sun" icon made its first appearance since the previous October. Golf season had arrived.

A friend booked the tee time and I texted Heine the good news: "I'm making golf plans for Sunday."

Several hours later she replied: "Just made appt for invitations consultation for Sunday at 11."

To be fair, I only waited all winter to get back on the golf course, and she'd been waiting her whole life for the chance to consult with someone at a stationery shop. A lot went right that weekend. For one, we switched the consultation to Saturday, so my golf plans held up. Plus, we made an impulse decision to eat at McDonald's before we went into the stationery shop, so I knew I wouldn't get bored or sleepy since my body would be in fight or flight mode, pumping adrenaline through my veins to combat the threat of a fast-acting fast-food bathroom emergency.

I'd had a good chat with Brad earlier that week about fast food. He didn't understand why humanity chooses to eat food that consistently produces both acute and chronic health problems. Then again, he doesn't have taste buds and has never been a stoned teenager with a $1.09 to his name. Brad's planet does not have dollar menu-naires.

It won't be long before formal invitations give way to their budget-friendly digital successors. The taboo will fade with each generation, but for now, etiquette calls for the hard copy. Much of the advice we received from recently married couples revolved around saving money on silly formalities, like expensive paper stock and invitations, and at the time I wished we'd taken that advice. Looking back, I don't regret it. I'm glad we had nice invitations and Alex has keepsakes in her letter box that she's proud of. It's like McDonald's. As long as you eat fast food in moderation and try to keep the weddings you plan to a minimum, go ahead and treat yourself to some super-sized invitations.

The sun shone down on Logan Square, a hip, quickly gentrifying Chicago neighborhood where our quirky stationery shop welcomed us with open, tattoo-sleeved arms. My tee time was set, my fiancée was happy, and my stomach was coated with hydrogenated oils. Life was good.

Stationery shops, even those that profit off the wedding industry, can't afford prime real estate in up-and-coming neighborhoods on the revenue generated from stationery alone. That's why they sell cute crap and novelty books. *This is where I'll sell my wedding planning book,* I thought, absently dragging my index finger across the spines of similar "literary" works. Listicles, disguised as hardcovers with diminutive trim sizes, lay scattered on display tables. Baby survival guides, wedding etiquette books with "F**k" in the title, hipster cookbooks where all the recipes are named for '90s punk songs. The existence of these titles motivated me to finish writing this manuscript. If these things make it out of the slush pile, why not me? Besides, we have the same sales pitch. There's a constant flow of new pregnancies, new brides, and hipsters who need to learn basic cooking skills after they move out of their parents' homes. These are all gift giving occasions. Stop by the stationery shop, pick up a copy of Sam's book, send it to your newly engaged cousin. I make $2.00.[96]

"You must be Alex and Sam," a woman's voice called to us in a most inviting tone. I'm 99 percent sure the woman we worked with had an M in her name. She struck me as a Miranda (not in a *Sex and the City* way, more in the opposite of a *Sex and the City* way. You know, glasses, sweater, stationery store employment), but I'd be more confident in Meredith, or even Amanda. Let's call her Sara to be safe. That'll protect her identity, too.

Sara sat us down in the back of the store and asked us to tell her about the wedding. Within seconds, Alex had me turn around so they could review the color scheme of her dress samples. With my eyes closed, my other senses sharpened, and I listened with extra intensity as my fiancée provided every possible detail of the wedding she'd held in her imagination every night for months. Did Sara need to know about the salsa and guacamole bar? Could those details influence our invitation design? I'll never quite fathom how it mattered, but I couldn't fathom most of what was going on in my life at that time, so I waited patiently to be welcomed back into the conversation.

Next, we had to choose our font. When my oldest brother got married, our cousin put his calligraphy skills to use and wrote each address out by hand on the envelopes. As the youngest sibling and third in the flock to get hitched, it seemed I didn't warrant such effort.[97] Sara plopped a stack of sample invitations on the table and told us to find one we liked. I often hear arguments for abolishing the teaching of cursive in schools. Who needs penmanship when our society hardly uses pens? But if we don't teach children to write in cursive, how will future generations read wedding invitations? None of the sample fonts resonated with us, but Alex picked one and didn't fuss about it so I didn't see any reason that I should.

Having shared her vision, Alex was ready to move forward. Soon we had a basic design sketched out, with a glossy, textured likeness of the shabby-chic Addison Grove barn. We passed on the prospect of including a map to the venue, which made sense as we had dragged our feet on hotel blocks and had no idea where anybody would stay.

We opted for the RSVP postcard instead of the miniature self addressed stamped envelope. Cheaper, cleaner, an absolute no-brainer.

Speaking of absolute no-brainers, we proved to be absolutely brainless. We'd cultivated a list of 140 guests to invite. As such, we told Sara we'd need 140 invitations.

"Holy shit!" Sara said, entirely with her eyes. With

her voice, she said, "I didn't realize you were having such a big wedding. Will you have 300 people?"

Being brainless, we didn't realize that inviting a married couple only called for a single invitation. Our order quantity dropped from 140 to 80. Instant savings! Ignorance may be bliss, but stupidity is where the money's at.

I left the invitation consultation with a rare sense of satisfaction. Few planning experiences combined the joys of finding out something would cost less than anticipated, ended quicker than I expected, and left me with the rare feeling of accomplishment.

Could it be? Could an aspect of wedding planning have been easy?

No.[98]

This is why weddings are insane. In retrospect, working with the stationery shop held up as one of the simpler parts of planning a wedding. Still, I found 57 emails in my inbox between myself and the store. It's more than likely that Alex has an additional 50 that I don't know about. Remember my analogy from a few pages back about birthday party invitations and wedding invitations being akin to oregano and marijuana? Let me amend that. A normal invitation and a wedding invitation are like Oregano and my friend's cannabis compliance software startup. One of them is simple, the other requires seed money and a full-time staff.

Here's a brief rundown of the challenges I failed to anticipate:

The Invitee Spreadsheet: We had to confirm the names, spelling, and addresses of all the guests. This is easy enough when dealing with close friends and immediate family. My idiot friends seem to move all the time, but a text exchange usually returns the necessary information.

> Me: Send me your new address for wedding invite.
> Idiot: It's cool. I know the details.
> Me: Just send me your address.
> Idiot: I don't need an invitation.
> Me: I know, but Heine wants to send you one.
> Idiot: Don't worry about it, you'll save on postage.
> Me: Ok, thanks. I'll come to your new place to deliver it by hand. What's the address?
> Idiot: Oh, cool. I'm at 123 Big Idiot Avenue W. Unit 3.

It's not always so straightforward. For example, Alex's mom confirmed two different zip codes for the same person in a five minute stretch. And it's even more frustrating when Vivian describes potential recipients as "lifelong best friends" despite the fact that Alex has never heard of them. One of these people was named Jet, a nickname from his pilot days, supposedly. Vivian did not know his real name. He was not the only Jet on our list.

#TexasWedding.

The template Sara shared with us came with a full page of instructions. Married couples, individuals, people with a plus-one, unmarried couples, married couples with different last names, people with children whose names we knew, and people with children whose names we didn't know all required a different computer science degree to have their data properly entered into the form. I'd hate for someone to receive an envelope that said Mr. John Doe and Mrs. Jane Doe instead of Mr. and Mrs. John Doe. Just think of the confusion that would cause.

Wording: Together with their parents,
David Heine and Vivian Lewis
and
David Ofman and Barbara Ofman
Alexandria Leigh Heine
and
Samuel Benjamin Ofman
Request the pleasure of your company
At the celebration of their wedding on
Sunday, November Fourth, Two Thousand Eighteen
At half-past four o'clock in the afternoon
The Addison Grove - 11903
Fitzhugh Road - Austin, TX

Dinner and revelry to follow

Copying the text above into this book could very well be the first time I actually read my wedding invitation. Pretty solid, I'd say. You know it's a monumental occasion because we spelled out all the dates and times. My Google Calendar doesn't send me a pop up notification saying "Give dog heartworm pill At Tuesday, April First, at half-past nine in the morning."

Only the big stuff gets spelled out in letters. In reality, my Google Calendar alert reads: Mona cream cheese bomb AT ALL DAY on 4/1/18.

I don't recall choosing the phrases "together with their parents" or "request the pleasure of your company," and can't imagine Heine or I suggested we include the word "revelry," but I'm certain I would have made no objections in the interest of moving things along.

Mainly, I stressed over our parents' names. Both sets of parents divorced while Alex and I were in junior high. While none remarried, there are significant others in their lives, who have been a significant part of our lives. Would my mom want her partner's name on the invitation? Would he want his name on the invitation? If they asked for it, would that force us to include Vivian's partner? What about my dad's girlfriend, they'd been together for a few years, would he feel slighted if she didn't make the cut?

I'm so grateful none of them cared. You never know what people will be sensitive about, and that one could have gone either way.

Additional Materials: There's more to stationery shops than invitations, dummy! Duh! They provide a service for weddings, so of course they find a way to squeeze a little more of the budget out of unsuspecting, lovesick couples. Sara didn't have to bother with an upsell or a sales pitch. We came prepared with our own ideas.

Crosswords: I love crossword puzzles. I've become quite good at solving them over the years and I've even constructed a few full-fledged 15x15 grids of my own.[99] Alex and I thought it would be cute to have a crossword puzzle at every place setting as a party favor. I took to the task with my trademark, tremendous talent[100] and set to it with total tenacity.[101] I didn't want our crossword to be some dinky puzzle like the ones grade schoolers solve as vocabulary homework. I wanted a 10x10 grid mini-puzzle that followed all the *New York Times* rules for building a crossword. I had months to work on it, and littered the desk at my office with half-finished drafts. All of the answers and clues would be on theme. It would be glorious. In the end, I used a website to build a dinky vocab homework puzzle. Still, it turned out great, with answers like "Love," "Bride," and "Tacos." Congrats to Emily for being the first person to solve it.

Pencils: You can't solve a crossword without a pencil. What a great opportunity for another party favor! This will shock you, but in addition to crossword puzzles, I also love golf. Sara had connections in the personalization game who could hook up a deal on customized golf pencils. We didn't end up using Sara's contact as they had a minimum quantity of more than 1,000. We found someone, probably on Etsy, with a minimum quantity of 16. We could order in increments of 16 at a steep cost, or get one thousand for a steal. In the end we ordered 128 for the same cost as 1,000. I have no use for 850 extra golf pencils.

Before we placed the order we had to decide on our personalized message. We didn't waste time coming up with puns. "Alex ♥ Sam 11.4.2018" did the job. Luckily, I'm writing this book so I get to use the pun I thought of after the fact. "Alex ♥ Sam FOREver."

We made a special trip to the shop to confirm that the pencils conformed with Sara's vision for attaching them to the crossword. They didn't, but I loved the idea of bringing a variety of golf pencils to a wedding planning consultation. In the end, we had to figure it out ourselves, and since we needed to pack the crosswords in our checked luggage, we couldn't risk the pencils coming unstuck in transit. More evidence that weddings are insane: Two days before my wedding I bought sticky circle dots to put the finishing touches on a party favor that had been in the works for months, adhering pencils to crossword puzzles. No wonder Brad deems us worthy of study. Our species must be unique in all the cosmos for this type of behavior.

Ceremony Card: I asked Heine the day I drafted this section, "1-10, how useful was I during the wedding planning process?" I guessed she'd give me a seven. She replied, "Probably a six or a seven."
    I did a good job. A great job? Probably not. She did a great job, which was more than enough. I complained, but only in the superficial, miserly way that Alex would laugh off, as I'd eventually come around. Never in the oppositional, truly malignant way. Except when it came time for the ceremony card.
    I didn't care about the ceremony card. I still don't see what purpose it serves. Most guests know the folks standing at the wedding, and any guests who don't know the wedding party don't find much value in a Playbill. "Oh, that bridesmaid is named Mary. And the next one is named Molly. What a handy resource!" In my experience, these cards are best-utilized for cooling one's pits during an outdoor summer ceremony.
    Few aspects of our wedding struck me as more superfluous than the ceremony card, and I protested when Alex asked me to confirm the spelling of a grandparent's name, or offer my thoughts on the order of the groomsmen. My attitude did not go over well on the homefront. It was the first, and only time I can remember Heine getting angry with my wedding planning effort.

    "All of your guests receive an invitation?" Brad asked.
    "Yep," I said, leaning forward in my chair to snatch the invite from his hand. "They'll arrive in the mail in

the next few days, then we just sit back and let the replies roll in."

Earlier that afternoon, Alex and I parked our beloved Subaru in front of the post office. We sat in the car and moved all 80-odd invitations through an assembly line of envelope-stuffing, flap-licking, and stamp-sticking. We worked in silence as NPR informed us of Donald Trump's new family separation policy at the Mexican border. It was one of those moments I'll never forget.

I returned the extra invitation to its box and noticed Brad pacing. His head smacked the angled ceiling, but not hard enough to knock a tight-lipped scowl off his face.

"Everything ok?" I asked.

His legs whirled around with their customarily wide turning radius, and he finished two more laps, complete with two more echoing *doongs*, before responding. "If all of your friends and family receive an invitation," he came to a sudden halt and hid his face in sadness, "why didn't you ask for my address?"

When it was all said and done, I thought the invitations were some of the least personal, least intensive components of the entire wedding experience. A picture of the venue, the date, the time, an RSVP postcard. Done. When I asked Heine about this months later she confirmed my suspicion that she had, in fact, spent hours agonizing over these quick easy decisions without my knowledge. Somehow, I remained oblivious to the stamp selection process.

I didn't think much of them, but people raved about our invitations.

"They're so beautiful!"

"They're so YOU!"

Another job well done by Alex Heine.

To recap: Making wedding invitations was one of the easiest parts of this process, and it involved months of email correspondence, hours of outreach, data entry, in-person consultations, ego management, a fight over ceremony cards, and some tedious manual labor in a parking lot.[102]

It cost us about $1,000 to *invite* people to our wedding. What a crazy concept. Meanwhile, the same results could have been achieved with a BCC email.

This seems like a good time to point out that I love my wife. Heine, I love you, and I wouldn't change a thing about our invitations.

SUBMITTED FOR YOUR APPROVAL

"Something called *Country Living* has 66 ideas to help plan a bridal shower," Brad said. He sat cross-legged—what we called 'Indian style' back in my not-so-woke childhood—though with the extra legs he looked more contortionist than indigenous. He wasn't cross-legged so much as pound sign-legged. He hashtagged the floor. "And something called Martha Stewart has an additional 24 tips for a memorable bridal shower." My laptop perched amidst his nest of limbs. I watched him from above the top of the screen as he uploaded everything the Web had to offer to his alien harddrive. "Which does Alex require," he asked, "tips, or ideas?"

"I think you need to get off the Internet."

"I just want to help," he flipped the monitor down and Mona crept across the room to flop down beside him, burrowing her head between his feet. "Just when I thought I understood the registry and the guest list, all of a sudden you have a separate party for high-priority females to bestow gifts. Can you explain?"

I felt my mouth open, but the words never came. Yet again, Brad raised a good point. Why do we have bridal showers?

Yet again, the answer is rooted in antiquated traditions that hold no weight in today's America. Back in the day, probably around the time *The Twilight Zone* debuted or we landed on the moon,[103] when a woman's family couldn't afford a dowry or a bride's father disapproved of the marriage, a bridal shower functioned as a fundraiser to pay for the expense of hosting the wedding.

These days, it's hard to justify the ongoing existence of the bridal shower. The baby shower? Now that makes sense. An expectant mother needs provisions in advance. Cribs must be built and car seats installed before the baby arrives. But does the bride need a pie cutter two months before the wedding?

Perhaps it's unfair to deride the bridal shower for it's Hallmark Holiday *raison d'etre*. *Country Living's* 66 ideas feed into the wedding industry's campaign to normalize spending money on wedding adjacent events. But just because I say it isn't necessary doesn't mean it isn't valuable.

Bridal showers, like almost everything surrounding a wedding, are both superfluous *and* valuable.

It's a good thing for people to get together to celebrate happy occasions.

It's a good thing for more friends and family to feel involved in the wedding experience.

It's a good thing for brides to feel special.

Most of all, it's a good thing grooms don't have to attend. That is, until the infamous end-of-shower pop-in.

Having been born in 1988, the first two decades of my life didn't present many opportunities to watch *The Twilight Zone*. Growing up, I knew about the show the way Millennials knew about the moon landing. It was something that adults watched in black and white before we were born, and it blew their minds. My dad routinely discussed the show, though he'd bring up the same episode each time as if he'd never mentioned it before. Remember the one with a group of surgeons huddled over an operating table, remarking for the entire program on the grotesque appearance of their patient?

"Then at the end, they cut to a shot of the patient,

and it's this beautiful woman!" my dad would say, one hand on the steering wheel, the other resting on the carphone in his stick shift Acura Legend. "After that, the doctors took off their masks, and they were monsters. Pig-faced monsters!"

And of course I knew about the episode where the nerd breaks his glasses after finally attaining the peace and quiet required to read his books. I can only assume I have a *Simpsons* reference to thank for that.[104]

I didn't get around to actually watching an episode of *The Twilight Zone* until I noticed it on Netflix in my mid-twenties. I didn't give it the full binge, but I consumed enough to understand the underlying aesthetic. Somebody wakes up and the entire world is different but nobody else notices. Repeat.

Why do I bring this up? I'll tell you why. For thirty minutes in August of 2018, I entered the *Twilight Zone*. What else can you call a bridal shower if not a fifth dimension beyond that which is known to man?

The entire weekend felt like a mash up of *Twilight Zone* plots.

My mother-in-law stayed in our apartment, as though I woke up and suddenly Alex had aged 40 years, but nobody else noticed.

The weekend coincided with a battle between me and AT&T, so we didn't have Internet or television. That's the closest humans can get to time travel without slipping into science fiction.

I was teaching an alien about the wedding industrial complex. I can see that as a late season plotline, once the original writers moved on.

It was the weekend of the Air and Water Show. I fell asleep in peacetime, but I woke to roadblocks and fighter jets all over the city.[105]

But none of this stuff comes close to the *Twilight Zone* effect of entering your fiancée's bridal shower. It was, without a doubt, one of the strangest moments of my life. I still feel chills when I think about it.

Imagine, you walk into a room and find 25 miscellaneous women from various phases of your life. To your left, you have a friend of yours from high school, the girl whose parents let you get high in their garage. She's on the couch talking to your brother's mother-in-law. *That's odd*, you think, as your eyes scan to the next grouping. What's this? Your father's girlfriend engaged in a discussion with your mom's cousin, the one you haven't seen in five years. *They shouldn't know each other*, you think. *What is this place?*

Further along you notice your good friend's wife conversing with your aunt. These impossible combinations are all around you, each more preposterous than the last. Suddenly, perhaps due to some hormonal shift caused by the abrupt arrival of your testerone, the chatter ceases and all these women turn to you. Their faces are eager, anticipation burning in their eyes. You realize that they were talking about you. Every single one of them.

They expect you to speak.

Panicked, you search for a lifeline, finding the same knowing gleam in each set of eyes, as though everyone believes they, and they alone, understand how you're feeling.

This is the moment you realize you have crossed over. You are in a dream state. How else would such an absurd collection of women be possible?

Only after you kiss your fiancée on the cheek and

receive a cascade of approving "awww"s from the flock does your heart resume beating. *A joke*, you remember, *I should tell a joke. Something witty.* Your fight-or-flight nervous system response has kicked in, and you say something.

Before long you're served a heaping plate of food. Lukewarm salmon, salad with dried fruit in it, some sort of mediterranean grains. You explain you aren't hungry, but this crowd doesn't seem able or willing to process that fact. So you eat, slowly, and nod when appropriate. Somebody mentions an Instapot. Someone shows you a box of dinner plates. A food processor. An ice cream maker. A variety of baking sheets in negligibly different sizes. A utensil that is probably used to cut a specific style of cheese. Something asymmetrical and vintagey with empty space. You're confused. *We don't need any of this*, you think. But you are wise enough not to say anything of the sort.

You thank every woman you have ever met, smile until your face hurts, and exit through a freight elevator with a handcart loaded with gifts you didn't expect to receive until months later.

You wake up, and nobody else notices that the entire world has changed.

A PICTURE'S WORTH A THOUSAND WORDS (AND DOLLARS)

Today, in our post-wedding, back to real life existence, Alex converted a corner of our living room into a wedding shrine. The flowers from Alex's bouquet, dried and preserved in an apothecary jar, rest beside a crystal-framed 8 x 10 photograph of the bride and groom. In this standalone shot, I pose with my hands in my pockets looking backwards at Alex, who rests her head on my shoulder. Amber grasses glow beneath the setting sun of a Texas sky.

Nearby, atop a bookshelf, we display the photographs of our grandparents, the same ones we'd had out at the wedding, in matching white frames with looping gold detailing around the trim. Above those, an arrangement of charcoal gray frames house seven carefully curated wedding photos.

The wedding party leans against a low stone wall.

Alex and I stand at a distance, facing the camera in front of the shabby chic barn.

A tree trunk, growing at a slight angle, wrapped in flowers.

An overhead shot of our various paper goods: invitation, crossword puzzle, the contentious ceremony card.

The bride and groom, facing one another during the ceremony as our officiant gives his spiel.

Alex and I, forehead to forehead with our backs to the camera, the setting sun smiling down on us through the trees in the background.

At the center of it all, Alex and I stroll hand-in-hand

through the tall grass of the golden field.

Months later, my face still aches from the endless smiling.

The entire arrangement occupies about 25 square feet of wall space. I imagine it will retain ownership of that space until we have baby pictures that outrank it. Until then, Alex will take great pride in these photos. Our houseguests, at least those inclined toward the whole wedding aesthetic, gush over our shrine. Alex put serious thought into it, ordering frames well in advance, poring over the photographs, and enlisting my help to make sure each facet of the exhibit was just right.

This is as close as I'll get to discussing the research and hiring of a wedding photographer. Alex wouldn't trust me with something as important as that. For a woman who keeps boxes—I don't mean old shoeboxes, I mean "let's stop at the Joanne's Fabrics to see if they have any cute boxes"—of old birthday cards, high school secret note correspondences, and old wedding invitations, the posterity of wedding memories is a serious concern. She found our photographer herself and tasked me with hiring a photo booth, the kids' table equivalent of a photographer. We'll get to that in a moment.

My role came after the fact, when it came time to comb through the digital album and select which shots we deemed worthy of printing. Again, something that was mostly up to Alex's discretion. My job involved tedious clicking, uploading 300-odd digital images to whichever online photo printing service we used. Most files were marked for economy grade 4x6, but the cream of the crop earned premium quality, glossy, upgraded status. These were the lucky photographs destined for the shrine. The others would live for eternity in the shadows of our multiple new photo albums. Obviously, these albums rest on the bookshelf below the shrine.

It doesn't end when you take the photos.

It doesn't end when you look at the photos.

For me, it didn't even end when I finished my tedious clicking chore, sentencing 300 photos to life in a maximum security album. After all the clicking practice, I forgot to click save.

It ended after I repeated the 300 clicks.

LIGHTS, CAMERA, DISTRACTION

The official definition of a Millennial is someone born between 1981 and 1996, but an equally accurate description would be anybody who had a photo booth at their wedding. It wasn't all that long ago that weddings didn't have photo booths. I imagine it won't be all that long until weddings no longer have photo booths. Boomers had camcorders, Gen Xers had digital cameras, and God only knows what today's 15-year-olds will use to capture the brave new world of their Zoomer nuptials. But for now, we live in an age where photo booths are very much a thing at weddings.

Like most things at weddings, there are too many vendors looking to provide photo booths. And like most things at weddings, all of these vendors are pretty much the same. "All the same" was a popular response for me when Alex needed input in the months leading up to the big day. Which of these bands sounds best? Which of these photographers? Caterers? invitation fonts? bow ties? All the same. Still, none of them came close to being as all the same as photo booths.

On the surface, as a photo booth user I've found them interchangeable. The same props, negligible differences in user interface, and ultimately uniform results.

Once I got into the research weeds, I found even more similarities. Prices? All the same. Set up time? Staffing? Upgrades? Incompetent customer service? All. The. Same.

I narrowed it down to two options. I could hire one of the nine similar vendors in the Austin area, or I could ask MQ. MQ is Mike Quattrochi, a friend of mine who worked for a photo booth company at the time of the wedding. MQ could provide the same product as the others, but could give me a substantial discount if I drove the equipment from Chicago to Texas and had him set it up during the cocktail hour. A nice offer, if not for the fact that we were flying, not driving, to Texas. MQ was out, though his contribution to the photo booth saga had just begun.

Seeing as they were all the same, my criteria for selecting a vendor had nothing to do with quality or price. I went with the one with the most generic, standardized platform. Fake Name Entertainment[106] didn't just do photo booths, they did DJs, lighting, photographers, you name it. Their website read like a menu at the Cheesecake Factory. I thought a company with the ability to expand to this many avenues within the industry, in multiple cities, must be doing something right.[107]

Plus, at the bottom of the quote they provided, I saw multiple Wedding Wire Couples' Choice Awards, back-to-back Best of Weddings commendations from the Knot, and a ribbon boasting the company's inclusion in The Knot's Best of Weddings Hall of Fame.

The first sign of the impending disaster would have to be the six separate confirmation emails I found in my inbox. I'm all for double checking to ensure accuracy, but I lose faith when each confirmation comes from a different person. They must handle each customer by committee. I got the distinct feeling that the company was run by 23-year-olds. Maybe I'm biased, since MQ's CEO was 23 when he started a photo booth company.

The second sign of the impending disaster was when the photo booth wasn't working during our wedding reception. Though to be fair, by this point the disaster was no longer impending.

The third sign that we were in the midst of a disaster was when the printer stopped working.

The props all looked great. I'll give them that.

The on-site operator, on the other hand, did not look great. He looked extremely sweaty and incompetent. Luckily, MQ was there to stand over his shoulder, shaking his head in disapproval, transforming the disaster into a hilarious memory.

A second employee arrived later in the evening. He couldn't fix anything, either.

We liked Fake Name Entertainment because they offered duplicate prints. We planned for guests to keep one print and paste another in the guest book beside little notes like "We love you! Congrats! - Cousin so-and-so." That plan didn't work out, on account of the busted printer. But of all things that can go wrong at a wedding, I'm ok with this being ours. Nobody got food poisoning, it didn't rain, and I never raced to the VIP bathroom. I can live without the goofy photo of Heine's dad's friend in oversized novelty glasses and a top hat.

Besides, I got to write a strongly worded email that resulted in a full refund. Any time you can use the phrase "good deal of stress and embarrassment for the bride" you know you're getting all the money back. Now THAT is a highlight of my wedding weekend.

A strongly worded email:

Hello,

We hired a photo booth for our wedding last night and the equipment did not work. The attendant couldn't fix it, and I believe I saw an additional employee on site trying to work out the problem without much success. I don't know if there was ever a time during our event that your photo booth functioned properly. The camera itself had problems, and the printer didn't work. This was an enormous disappointment and caused a good deal of stress and embarrassment for the bride and me.

As you can see in the history of this email thread, we opted for Fake Name as our photo booth vendor because of your quick and reliable printing capabilities. We planned to have our guests incorporate their photos into our guestbook as a way to relive the excitement of the evening through informal and fun photos. I'm worried now that our guestbook will serve as a reminder of the botched photo booth experience that stood out as a major flaw in the evening.[108]

At the end of the night we received a packet of printed photos. Almost all of them are so poorly lit that I can't determine which of my guests are in them. I'm sitting here with a pile of unusable photo strips and an empty guestbook,[109] meanwhile, my guests don't have a souvenir of the wedding, which for more than half was an out of town experience in a new city.

I would call Fake Name's performance last night a complete failure. We paid for a working photo booth, a competent employee to manage it, and a functioning printer from 7:30-10:30. We didn't get any of that. I expect a full refund.

I am happy to give you the benefit of the doubt and assume this is not the norm for your company. Please make this right.[110]

A GROOM WITH A VIEW

Historic, matchless, iconic, inspired, momentous, storied. These are only some of the adjectives you'll find on the landing page of The Driskill's website. A landmark hotel in downtown Austin, Alex grew up certain she'd stay at the Driskill on her wedding night. She even took me to their famous lobby bar for a cocktail during my first visit to the great nation of Texas. That was long before marriage was on our minds, back when a block of rooms meant Lego houses, not wedding bells.

Who doesn't love a good hotel? Whether they're filling with blood during *The Shining*, lining the coasts of exotic beaches, or scattered amongst pewter tokens in a disheveled Monopoly box, hotels are all around us.

Alex delivered room service at a five-star hotel back in her college years, waiting on some of America's most respected celebrities. Ted Turner complained about the price of his orange juice, Bill Nye opened the door in nothing but a towel to receive his lox and bagels, and Ice Cube invited her in to fix the thermostat. With her insider insights, booking The Driskill would be easy like Sunday morning.[111]

Things don't always go as planned. Remember when Alex called her dream venue, the Montesino Ranch, just days after I proposed? That call didn't go as planned. Neither did the one she made to The Driskill a few months later during our venue scouting trip.

"You need the special sales manager, but she's on leave, so the group sales coordinator can help, but she only works weekdays...Can I help? No, I only handle non-wedding events. But I can direct you to someone's voicemail." It's as if these people have never dealt with a customer before. They react to every question as though we're the first couple to ask how wedding blocks work at the most popular hotel in the city. People are the worst. If only every business in America were run by my Type A friend who organizes bachelor parties. We'd have colonies on the moon, and they'd all be well stocked with Coors Light and have a system in place for when guests call about wedding blocks.

Having never booked a block of rooms at a classy establishment before, we were unaware of the attrition clause. Apparently, hotels don't like holding reservations that don't end up filled. The Driskill offered to reserve a block of 20 rooms at a competitive (read: outrageous) rate, but should any of those rooms go unbooked, we'd be on the hook for 80 percent of that competitive rate.

My interest in staying at the Driskill dropped by 80 percent.

Staying at a luxury hotel isn't for everyone. Scratch that. Of course it's for everyone. Paying competitive rates to stay at a luxury hotel isn't for everyone. Alex and I knew we wouldn't fill all 20 rooms. Our friends wouldn't stay there, they'd book a party house on Airbnb for a fraction of the cost. Most of our family members wouldn't stay there. They'd book a family house on VRBO for a fraction of the cost. We'd reserve 20 rooms for the doctors and lawyers we invited, plus any guest who won the Mega Millions between receiving their invitation and booking their accommodations. That number wasn't likely to break single digits. Even if we won the battle and got the hotel booked quickly, we'd lose the war of attrition clauses.[112]

But it wasn't up to me. It was up to Heine, and her main concern in booking a hotel had nothing to do with our out of town guests. She needed a suite with enough space for a team of beauticians to transform my lovely bride into a lovely bride.[113]

The Driskell's suites boasted very strong Texas names, but they lacked the most important Texas quality: size. The Lyndon B. Johnson suite offered enough space for Heine to contemplate escalating the war effort in Vietnam, and the Cattle Baron suite sounded like a good place for 100 head of cows to graze, but would either fit the bill for a saccharine of bridesmaids to have their hair and makeup done? We'd never find out, as some actual cattle barons rustled up a booking before we could say giddy-up.

The Yellow Rose suite was our best option, but Alex didn't like the layout. Isn't it amazing how three clicks of a virtual tour can wipe away twenty years of girlhood visualization?

Like any respectable Type A person, Alex had a Plan B: The Van Zandt. If The Driskill screamed oil money East Egg, The Van Zandt echoed tech startup West Egg. What it lacked in historic, iconic, storied, landmark, etc., it made up for in sleek modern Austin hipness. And it had the room rates to match.

We sleuthed through the website, admired the rooftop pool, and sent an exploratory email.[114] Eventually, somebody got back to us, apologized for the delay, and informed us of the competitive (read: outrageous) base-level room rates, two night minimums, and 90 percent attrition policy.

Bring on Plan C.

Alex and I took a step back. Something seemed off.

We were on top of things, asking for availability more than six months in advance, leaving voicemails for special group sales coordinators all over town, only to find an alarming scarcity of accommodations. The rooms we could find, even the single bed, lowest level rooms, had jacked-up rates. As Vivan would say, we didn't fall off the turnip truck yesterday. Something was up. But what?

We took care to avoid conflicts when selecting our wedding date. We consulted the calendar to make sure there were no music festivals or holidays, but neglected a key component of Texas culture. Nobody checked the University of Texas football schedule. Sure enough, the Longhorns had a home game during our wedding weekend. Supply and demand gored a hole in our hotel budget.[115] Wherever we stayed, so long as it was in the city of Austin, it was going to be expensive.[116]

Alex explored options at smaller hotels while I kept at it with the modern goliaths. My next venture took me to the South Congress neighborhood, accurately described by Google as a "vibrant stretch of hip boutiques, trendy lodging options, and Austin-original eateries." If you've read this far, you know "hip, trendy, and vibrant" fit me like a 36 short suit.

Some of y'all probably hear "South Congress" and think of the bats. The underside of the Congress Ave Bridge has crevices that serve as a perfect hangout for bats. Today, a colony of bats live underneath the bridge, between the rumbling of Congress Avenue traffic and the rushing waters of the Colorado River. Every night, just before sundown, the bats are said to take flight, I assume to feed or, considering they've been there since the '80s, complain about all the transplants ruining their city. Tourists line up along the bridge to watch this miracle of nature. I was once one of them. I stood on the bridge, suffering the slings and arrows of outrageous souvenir hawkers, and waited for the bats. And waited. And waited. It was peak season for bat viewing, I was told. And yet, like a pitcher in the American league, I didn't pick up a single bat. Since then I've visited Austin a number of times and am still yet to see one.

Bats or no bats, my journey took me south of the bridge to the South Congress Hotel. First cousin to the Van Zandt and disappointing step-child of The Driskill, it checks all the boxes on the fancy hotel prerequisite list, though it checks them using a Crayola instead of a Mont Blanc.

No attrition, plenty of rooms, and a suite large enough for two diminutive people like Alex and me to get lost in. We booked it, and we spent far too much money doing so. I'll give you a brief rundown of our time there, but I'll try to remember this is a book about wedding planning, not a yelp review.

The South Congress Hotel: ★ ★ ☆ ☆ ☆

In my inbox you'll find 42 emails between me and one of the hotel's sales reps, let's call her Julie, spanning from March to October.[117] That's a lot of emails, as I honestly can't remember if Alex or I was Julie's point person. Julie's email signature features links to the hotel's inclusion on a "Hot List" and an "It List." I doubt they'll add a link to this book's Amazon page.

The pricing chart Julie gave us showed the premier suite, the Milton Suite, listed at "around $1,000." I guess when you're paying that much for a room, you don't really need to know exactly what it costs. We stayed in the Milton Suite. As you can imagine, I will experience buyer's remorse for the rest of my God given time on this earth.

Perhaps the price tag wouldn't be so terrible had the room been less terrible. Duct tape held the couch cushion together, small mounds rose out of the area rug, and the general design of the room rendered most of the furniture unusable, downgrading it to clunky decor. It wasn't all bad, though. It was still a very nice hotel room, but for paycheck-per-night prices, do they really need to upcharge for M&Ms? I didn't bill them for labor after reapplying adhesive tape to the couch.

Prior to our stay, I inquired about parking. Julie graciously informed me of the $32/night parking fee. I graciously reminded her that I was paying "around $1,000" a night to stay in her hotel, and suggested that perhaps, as a show of good faith, that fee could be waived. I understand how they may assume that a guest who can afford to spend "around $1,000" on a hotel room wouldn't balk at the cost of parking. On the other hand, let's call it the right hand,[118] I wasn't about to pay more to park my car than I did to rent it.

I'm not accustomed to staying in the most expensive suite at a nice hotel. I thought I'd be treated like the most valuable customer, seeing as I generated the most value of all their customers. I didn't expect a red carpet, but I did expect some modicum of preferential customer service.

The South Congress, much like our nation's Congress, didn't quite meet the lofty expectations they'd promised. For example, Alex and I confirmed our plans with Julie to ensure the lobby bar would be open for a small, informal afterparty. We'd brought this up on several occasions in the months leading up to our stay. Each time, we received assurances. I imagine a beaming smile on Julie's face as she agreed, time and again, that we could place a food order the day of the afterparty to have some late night snacks ready upon the arrival of our friends.

You can imagine my frustration when, two weeks before the wedding, evidence indicated that Julie had not been in touch with the lobby bar at all, and we needed to convince them to stay open late on a Sunday. You can imagine my greater frustration when, two goddamn weeks before the wedding, our hotel asked that we sign a food and beverage commitment contract.

"There's no way I'm signing any more contracts for this wedding," Alex said. We just couldn't do it. No more contracts, no more commitments, no more menus. We'd had enough. I shouldn't have to remind staff of things we'd already arranged. I shouldn't have to wait 10 minutes for the lobby bar manager. I'm the most valuable guest in the hotel. Is it too much to ask that they read my emails?

They were cool with it in the end, but after 10 months of dealing with caterers, venues, photo booths, bands, photographers, liquor packages, shuttles, and parking attendants, having someone ask you to sign a french fry and chicken wing minimum order agreement is a tough pill to swallow. However, that pill went down a little easier when I noticed that they neglected to add the food order to our bill.

If I sound like a snob, good, I should. I was paying snob-level money for slob-level service. After we'd checked out, the few guests of ours who'd booked rooms at the hotel complained about unhelpful staff members and cramped conditions. Needless to say, I regret staying at the South Congress, and I think Alex would agree that if we could do it all over we'd rent an Airbnb for a fraction of the cost. "Discounted" rooms ran our guests $300 or more per night, and in the end they'd have been happier in an Embassy Suites.

A hotel block should be a blessing. If the bride and groom's family and friends stay there together it can add to the overall experience, transforming the wedding from a one night affair into a shared weekend-long celebration. When guests mingle at the lobby coffee shop and relax together by the pool, they forge a sense of community that feeds into the spirit of the wedding. Instead of finding a hotel that suited everybody and brought us closer to our loved ones, we wound up isolated. It was the top room, but the saying is true: it's lonely at the top.

Let me amend that star rating.

My updated review: ★ ☆ ☆☆ ☆ Maybe try The Driskill?

SHUTTLES, NOT SPACE SHUTTLES

"Do you always look this way?" I asked. It occured to me that Brad's human form could be a costume. Maybe he's a shapeshifter. Maybe his true alien body was an amorphous cloud of gas, or something reptilian and skinless. He stood in the center of the living room, shuffling Mona's tennis ball between his four legs like a game of Hungry Hungry Hippos. For someone with two left feet, he put on quite a show of coordination. Granted, he had two right feet to go with them. He glanced up at me, shrugged, and continued teasing Mona.

Even in the form he's in, I thought, does his body work like mine? Does he have a skeleton, muscle tissue, vestigial organs? If his species didn't evolve on Earth, what are the odds he'd look so much like an Earthling? What are the odds he had a spleen?

"Why the sudden interest in my bodily form?" he asked, perhaps reading my thoughts. Mona sat and released a high-pitched whine. She'd evolved to whine rather than think. That's what domestication did to dogs. A wolf would fight. Mona whines. It worked, too. Brad rolled the ball her way and she clamped her jaws on it the way her feral ancestors would clamp onto their dinner.

Brad joined me on the couch. "It's just a body."

"Tell that to the bodies I need to transport to our venue."

"Happy to. Where are these bodies?"

"Christ, Brad," I sighed, shook my head, and continued. "We've got 100 people coming to Austin for our wedding, right? Well, they'll be staying all over the city, but we need them all to get to the venue. To make sure they get there on time we need to provide transportation."

Brad's eyes opened to the size of dinner plates.

"Whatever you're thinking," I held up a hand to silence him, "please don't offer to help with any supernatural transportation nonsense. We're doing this the old fashioned, non-science fiction way. The last thing I need is another flash."

Brad's eyes shrunk back to their standard size.

"As always," I said to my alien friend, "your usefulness is out of this world."

The previous night, Alex looked up at me over her backgammon app and asked how many seats we'd need to provide for our shuttle service.[119]

"I don't know. It's hard to forecast."

This diplomatic sidestepping of a firm answer didn't satisfy her.

"There's no way to know," I continued, "Some of the Texans may drive. Some of the out-of-town guests may take Ubers. Some guests will rent cars at the airport; maybe they'll drive, too."

She scrunched up her face and shrugged, which meant that answer wouldn't cut it, either.

"If we're going to supply transportation, I think we need to assume most of the guests will use it and make sure we have enough seats for everyone."

She placed her digital opponent screen-down on the bedsheet and turned her unscrunched, beautiful face towards me. "Or they can just figure it out on their own. How about you take charge of the shuttles?"

Oh, goodie.

Decisiveness, not indecisiveness, creates much of the frustration and drama for wedding planners. The sheer volume of choices Alex and I (mainly Alex) had to make never let up. Each one impacts several others, and each of the people waiting on our choice feels that their question is the most pressing. One of the most challenging, if not the most challenging part of wedding planning, for me, was deciding whether or not to make a decision.

Decisions are a catch-22. Alex demanded that I make more decisions on my own, but I can't make a decision about her wedding without her feedback, unless I want to risk making the wrong decision. I've noted this observation before, but it's important for any would-be-groom to heed this advice. Do the legwork, organize the research, anticipate questions, and be ready to move on all options before you present them to the boss.

That's what I did with the shuttles.

The transportation racket runs a pretty good swindle. They know they've got me by my muffler and there's nothing I can do about it. Not only do they know that guests need to get from A to B, but they also know that guests need to get back from B to A seven hours later. They offer somewhat reasonable hourly rates because they know the driver will spend seven of the nine paid hours sitting in a parking lot playing Words With Friends. Trust me, I wasn't the first customer who thought I could beat the system by booking two separate one-way rides. Each one way trip runs to about a four-hour rate.

When you finally concede that there's no alternative, that's when the real scams come into play.

Miscellaneous administrative fee? Why not?

Meal for the driver? Hey, it's a party.

20 percent built-in gratuity? Makes sense, after all, the driver will be working for 20 percent of the time I'm paying him for.

To receive a quote from the shuttle companies, I had to fill out their online questionnaires. Apparently, to provide an accurate estimate they need my standard personal information, my pick-up address, drop-off address, pick-up time, drop-off time, date of booking, number of passengers, type of vehicle, home address, garage code, home security password, mother's maiden name, the story of how I lost my virginity, my exact weight, shoe size, net worth (pre- and post-booking of the shuttle), contact info for my most recent landlord, the last four digits of my social security number, and the first five digits of my social security number. Only then will you hear from a sales agent.

After filling out these wildly elaborate online forms, I received emails from the two shuttle companies I'd identified as the best options. Both of the sales agents thanked me for my interest and asked if I could provide details about my upcoming booking. Even with the pick-up times, locations, date, previous year's tax return, cheek swab DNA sample, third grade report card, and the detailed explanation of what services I would need in the "additional comments" section, they still needed more. They don't actually read the online form. They use it as a tool to separate serious customers from window shoppers. Only truly determined clients would go through with the ACT practice test and still have the patience to provide all the same information in a follow up email. Anybody who replies to Doug is a guaranteed sale.

Doug was the first to get back to me. He asked for

all the information I had filled out in the online form. I replied with something along the lines of, "All of that information is in the online form. The information also appears to have automatically generated in the body of the email you just sent."

I never heard from him again.

Instead, I booked with Lance. Lance did a great job of stopping me from beating the system and ensured I booked everything at full price. However, he did waive the 20 percent included gratuity and warned me that paying with a credit card would include additional processing fees. Lance called me with great news on the morning of the wedding. They'd managed to wrangle some SUVs to replace the shuttle bus that had suffered unexpected mechanical issues that morning. Well, at least the mechanical issues were unexpected, as I'd never hear the end of it if I had booked a shuttle for the date it was due to break down.

I should open a wedding transportation company. I'll advertise top-of-the-line shuttle buses. Anytime customers book a shuttle, I'll order a handful of Uber Black Cars and apologize for the unexpected mechanical issues. Online reviews will praise my customer service and resourcefulness, and I'll pocket enormous savings because I'll be charging wedding vendor prices without any employees, vehicles, or office space. All I need is Wi-Fi and a couple of rideshare apps. Hell, I'd probably get discounts for using the apps so much.

Lance got it done, and I heard from guests that they had a blast getting rowdy on the way from A to B, and even more fun staying rowdy on the way from B to A. But I wasn't on the party shuttle. Instead, Alex arranged for us to enjoy a private ride home.

After booking the shuttles, I told Alex about my exchange with Doug. I railed about his incompetence and insisted that a company so inept at reading comprehension and communication didn't deserve our business. Alex then told me that she'd also been in touch with Doug, and had, in fact, given him more than $500 of our business.

Doug: 1

Sam: 0

In exchange for that outrageous price, we'd enjoy a 25-minute ride from the venue back to the hotel in the backseat of a 1949 Plymouth.

Yep.

$500.

25-minute car ride.

0 seatbelts.

1 very expensive photo op.

I love my wife.

CHA CHA REAL SMOOTH

I'm speaking to you now as a married man.[120] I hadn't even proposed yet when I started jotting down notes in this Google Drive document. Now I'm married, and still jotting down notes in this Google Drive document. Alex is my wife and I'm fully committed to her no matter what, even when she says things like, "This is one of my favorite songs" as a TV advertisement fills our home with the sweet sounds of DJ Casper's Cha Cha Slide.

She made this surprising remark a few days ago, and it got me thinking about the music at our wedding. Alex, despite her affinity for the Cha Cha Slide, has an ear for music and loves to hijack the bluetooth connection at parties. "DJ Heine spins the hits," she often says, as she picks both crowd-pleasers and more eclectic selections from her Spotify account. Get a few Pimms cups in her and she'll put together an unforgettable playlist.

I like the Cha Cha Slide, too. I've been Cha Cha-ing real smooth with the same steps and enthusiasm since my bar mitzvah days. When I was single, the Cha Cha Slide was pretty much the only song I felt comfortable dancing to. It's not that I don't like dancing. I love dancing. I just never felt comfortable dancing at a bar or a nightclub. Dancing as a means of seduction wasn't my style. If there's a sexual component, awkwardness prevails. But at weddings, when I'm bumping my tush with great aunt Florence and kicking off my Sunday shoes with eight-year-olds, I can really cut a rug.

Regrettably, we didn't slide to the left, reverse reverse, take it back now y'all, or Charlie Brown in our shabby chic barn. But we did need to pick a song for our first dance. And we had to pick an entrance song, a father-daughter song, a mother-son song, and make the critical decision between hiring a band or a DJ.

Hands on your knees.
Get funky with it.
Everybody clap your hands.

Unless you have a cash bar, few aspects of a wedding reception can mar the evening worse than bad music. A rubbery chicken breast only sits on the plate until it's eaten or cleared; a cringe-inducing speech, however long, eventually ends; but an obnoxious emcee with a lackluster band or DJ lasts the entire reception. Music is the lifeblood of the party, and the person with their finger on the pulse of the tunes defines how guests will remember the celebration. With this attitude in mind, we set out to find a band.

Finding a wedding band in Austin, Texas, is like finding a screenwriter in West Hollywood. Your barista is in a band. Your hairdresser is in a band. Your Old Texan Diamond Guy is in a band. You can't two-step in that town without tripping over a musical act. But we weren't in that town, and finding a wedding band in Austin gets a lot tougher when you're not in Austin.

I'm reasonably comfortable with the following blanket statements:

There's nothing wrong with hiring a DJ for a wedding reception.

Bands are way better than DJs.

You get what you pay for. Rather than make the obvious comparison to steak and hamburgers, I'll make a more personal analogy and bring this discussion of wedding bands into the golf realm.

Bands are country clubs, and DJs are municipal public golf courses. Either way, you're getting 18 holes out of it and it's important to remember, whether dancing or golfing, that it's all in the hips. The Country Club will cost you, but you know you're going to have finely manicured conditions and the amenities will be top notch, like how an expensive band can usually be counted on to provide top-level instrumentation and a professional front man to emcee the event.

The municipal course still provides hours of entertainment, but you aren't totally sure what you're in for as you step up to the first tee. Most municipals have a few patchy stretches, and some DJs have a tendency to rely a little too heavily on the Black Eyed Peas.

Of course, there are exceptions. Municipal courses are often incredible values and a DJ can do an excellent job and save you a bundle of cash. Bands have off nights, too. Even the most exclusive private courses need to aerate their greens.[121]

Back in the day, I suspect searching for a wedding band meant consulting the Yellow Pages, setting up auditions, or maybe even attending shows to see the group in action at a local bar. That sounds like a lot of work. Luckily, we have the Internet.

According to the World Wide Web, there are 500,000 wedding bands in Austin. Some of them have self-produced videos on YouTube as marketing tools. Many of these videos convey the band's style and skill, while others are so unjustifiably terrible that us viewers are left with no choice but to assume they're jokes. If this book were a longform article, I'd link to a few good ones here. Unfortunately, this book is an old-fashioned, Yellow Pages–era throwback to print media. Imagine the level of quality that comes with using someone's basement as a set. Imagine the level of quality that doesn't fully disguise the washer and dryer in the background.[122]

We made our selection based almost entirely on strangers' online reviews. This is true of just about every decision in life, so why would our wedding band be any different? The B Sharps[123] received high marks for their musical performances, but like an outbreak of acne on my brother's teenaged upper back, 1-star reviews popped up among the otherwise smooth expanse of the band's web presence.

Anyone who's ever been on Yelp knows there's nothing to gain from reading positive reviews. If you want the truth, if you want to get real value out of the site, look for any post that begins, "I'd give them a 0 if I could." That's where you'll get the straight dope. All of the negative reviews for the B Sharps cited the poor responsiveness of the band's management team. Hell hath no fury like a bride scorned by lackluster communication from a band manager. However, even the most scathing reviews qualified their 1-star rating with a hefty dose of praise for the quality of the band. "The band was amazing! Manager took a long time to confirm details." One star. I put more weight into the first half of that review, Alex agreed, and we hired them.

Just like that, we were all done. Easy.[124]

Would we require a four-piece band? A five-to-six-piece band? Perhaps their seven-to-twelve- piece option?[125]

Will the group perform during the ceremony, or just

the reception?

Are we interested in a separate string quartet for the cocktail hour?

Does the venue have its own sound equipment? Will we need microphones for the ceremony? Lighting effects for the reception? How much set up time does the venue allow?

Ah, the details. What sort of wedding task would it be if it didn't demand we relay a series of questions to various other vendors and venues, aggregate their responses, and hope nothing gets lost in translation?

How did we ever make these decisions and hammer out these logistics? Don't ask me; I'm just a guy writing about planning his wedding. Alex is the one who planned it. Somehow, she got it all sorted out, all the while doing her best to shield me from the outrageous scams to come. But what sort of miserly groom would I be if I didn't sniff out a scam from a mile away?

"The B Sharps would be happy to emcee the reception for an additional fee."

I wasn't ready for that one. "Next, we'll hear from the Maid of Honor...that'll be $200, please." Emceeing the reception involved approximately five sentences. In terms of absolute costs, it's a pretty minor scam, but in terms of the dollars per effort ratio, dem was fightin' words.

"The B Sharps take special requests. Our trained professionals are capable of learning new songs for your event for an additional fee."

I wasn't ready for this one, either. It's not like the band is taking requests from patrons at a bar. They are hired professionals. Sure, it'd make the job a little harder, but that's life. Sometimes you have more challenging days at work. The shuttle driver doesn't charge more if it rains. He tightens his grip on the wheel, works a little harder, and does the job.

"The B Sharps will play 45-minute sets, separated by 30-minute breaks."

That's almost as much rest per hour as the shuttle driver gets. We'd have them for four sets of 45 minutes, with a 30 minute break between each. That comes out to being on break for one third of their work day. Typical Millennials.

"The B Sharps will provide a three percent discount if you pay in BitCoin."

Typical Millennials.

Alex served as the metaphorical roadie, doing most of the heavy lifting when it came to our interaction with the band. She curated the Spotify lists to play between sets, facilitated communication between the manager and our friend Aaron, who provided the music for our ceremony, and made sure we had our deposit in on time. All I needed to do was contact my mom and have her select a song for our mother-son dance.

The father-daughter and mother-son dances are brutal wedding traditions. At most, they are enjoyed by two individuals, and in some cases only one. The bride and groom spend the entire day in the spotlight, and after reciting their vows and surviving the nerve-racking ceremony, they want nothing more than to get off their feet and have a drink. The rest of the guests couldn't care less about watching these awkward slow jams. That leaves the father and the mother.

The mother is guaranteed to love this moment. Her little boy is all grown up. He doesn't need her anymore, but she's still got him until the end of the song. She relishes having one last moment to remind all in attendance, "Look what I did! This is my boy! I made this!" She deserves every ounce of recognition.

The fathers, well, I've seen a few who just want it to end. I don't doubt they're happy for their little girl, but every now and then Pops doesn't have the moves or the motivation. I've come across one or two scowling dads doing their best Reverend Shaw impression.[126] Still, the tradition lives on, taking up 10 minutes of everybody's time at weddings throughout the world.

I had one job. Text my mom and find out what song she wants to dance to. I could handle that. Days went by, then weeks, until one day Heine alerted me that the band needed all the songs submitted within the next 48 hours.

"Perfect," I said. "I need to call my mom anyway. It's her birthday."

Whenever I call my mom, I think about J.K. Simmons's Oscar acceptance speech. He stood on stage and counseled the world to call their mothers more often, and once they had Mom on the phone, to let her talk until she's finished. I can't tell you how many hours that advice has cost me.

After wishing her a happy birthday and receiving a thorough synopsis of what new species of wildlife she suspected were creeping around the house (coyotes? Feral cats? Wild turkeys? Empty space?) I told her I needed the song. She promised she'd let me know the next morning.

I don't remember what song she danced to with my brother Rick, but I'll never forget the mother-son dance between my mom and my brother Andy. I can see Andy reading this right now, mentally denying any memory of this story. I'll give you the short version. While Andy and Mom danced to the Beatles' *In My Life*, Andy's new bride turned to the wedding party and said, "Does anybody else see his hand on her butt?"

I'm guessing my mom had *In My Life* picked out for years, knowing that eventually one of her four sons would ask her to dance on his wedding day. It's less likely that she had a backup song ready to go for Rick, and nearly impossible that she'd come up with a third option for me within 48 hours.

As I said a few pages back: luckily, we have the Internet.

Let's do an experiment. I'll Google "Songs for Mother Son Wedding Dance" and we'll check where her selection ranks on the list...(these ellipses are a time machine, taking you back to when I drafted this paragraph and stopped to do some Googling)...

Results: inconclusive.

Van Morrison's *Days Like This* didn't appear on a top 40 list, but ranked eighth on a top 60 list. All that time travel and we're right back where we started. The point is, she came up with the song on time, and I'm almost certain the band didn't charge us to learn the chords.[127]

A short story:

"Sam," Alex said, standing over the stove in heels and a lacy slip. "Before you take the car to golf today, I'd love to get your input on what song we should pick for our first dance." She slid the omelet from pan to plate and placed it on the table in front of me. "Enjoy!"

Believe it or not, this story is fiction. Here's how I know:

The omelet: Heine loves to cook, but isn't a breakfast person.

The outfit: Heine loves to be comfortable, and is rarely seen around the house in anything but sweatpants or Gap Body pajama shirts.

The car: If I'm golfing, there's a pretty good chance she's going to some sort of gardening supercenter, so if this were real life, I wouldn't get to take the Subaru.

If none of those gave it away, you must have figured it out when she asked for my opinion on music. Don't misunderstand me, I'm not insinuating that Alex wouldn't be gracious and welcoming of my insights. It's just that she knows my taste in music. I don't have bad taste, nor do I have an acquired taste, or even an eclectic taste. I have no taste.

I'm that idiot that doesn't know what to say when asked what kind of music he likes.

For my entire childhood and early teen years, my favorite song was Billy Joel's *We Didn't Start the Fire*. You should have seen my misplaced pride when warned by the karaoke emcee on Rick's 21st birthday that I may struggle to keep up. The Wednesday night crowd at Champaign, Illinois's White Horse Inn never saw me coming.

Alex asking me what song we should dance to would be the equivalent of me asking her what club to hit on a golf course. She knows the names of the clubs, and that they're used for golf, but matching the club to the distance; hell, even judging the yardage to the green would be a total crapshoot.

Thankfully, my beautiful and kind future wife never put me on the spot. I was spared the agony of throwing up a musical prayer and hoping it wouldn't be laughed at. "Radiohead, are they still a thing?"

Alex bought a tennis racquet a few months ago. Like

most athletic equipment bought on impulse, the racquet spends most of its life in storage. Recently it saw the light of day, as we hit a few balls at a local park. I joked that her patented power slam earned her the on-court nickname of the Texas Twister.[128] She insisted on changing it to the Texas Tornado. Why? Do you really have to ask? Aren't you familiar with Tracy Lawrence's 1994 smash Country hit?

Neither was I. But Heine made sure I'd never forget it by playing it on repeat throughout the day. "Why didn't we dance to this at our wedding?" I asked.

"I liked our song better."

It was only then, nearly a year after we tied the knot, that I thought to ask how long ago she'd picked out the song for our first dance. I half expected she'd say she'd known it since girlhood.

"I think I settled on it about the time we started dating," She said. Wow. How romantic. Something about our relationship must have inspired the choice. She knew I was the one!

Nope. This turned out to be a coincidence.

I guess that's enough suspense. We danced to Patsy Cline singing *You Belong to Me*. We even bought the record and framed the cover. If you're looking for a thoughtful gift for your spouse, go steal that idea right away.

NO PASTOR IN OUR PASTURE

Cows on Parade.

Perhaps you're familiar with this public art phenomenon. Fact-checker, you may want to look into this, but I believe Chicago was the first United States city to hold a Cows on Parade exhibition.[129] Life-size fiberglass cows popped up all over the city, in parks, at train stations, outside of museums and stadiums, maybe even at Mrs O'Leary's. Local artists submitted proposals and those selected painted their cow in a specific style or theme. This all happened around the same time that Blue Man Group premiered in Chicago. Apparently, I haven't been attuned to high culture since I was nine, as I can't think of anything else that's happened in my hometown since then.

I'll always remember the cows because my friend Scott's mother was one of the artists selected by the cow committee.[130] I was udderly mooved by the small canvases on which she'd sketched her three designs, and I remember the unpainted albino hide of the full-size cow in their garage before she got to work on it. Hers was the cow with tiger stripes, though I don't recall where it prowled on Chicago's streets.

Alex, too, has ties to the cows. Every year for Christmas her dad gives her a scale model of one of the bohemian bovine beauties. At time of writing, they're grazing atop our kitchen cabinets. As it happens, Scott, the cow artist's son, is one of the two friends I credit with introducing Heine and me,[131] making him the natural choice to officiate our ceremony. All we had to do was ask him.

Alex and I aren't religious. She doesn't subscribe to Christianity, just Christmas, and I haven't attended a high holiday service since before the first time I got high.[132] We weren't about to have some priest talk to us about Jesus or some rabbi get sidetracked for thirty minutes talking about ostrich burgers and *The Matrix*. Sadly, these are actual examples from my brother's bar mitzvah weekend. The idea of having a priest or rabbi pronounce us husband and wife in the presence of some higher power made about as much sense as Creationism. We made a more natural selection, choosing someone meaningful to perform the ceremony.

Scotty fit the bill like spots on a cow. Not only is he one of my closest childhood friends, but he had developed a friendship with Alex totally independent of me while they were in college. He understood us both as individuals, and as a couple. We knew from day one that he'd be the man for the job.

Conveniently, Scott was in town from D.C. for, of all things, the opening of his mom's new art gallery. What better place to blindside him with our request than a crowded room filled with his relatives and family friends?

I have some experience in this scenario, having acted as the officiant for two weddings. I really can't picture a situation in which the person asked to do it isn't caught off guard. The routine plays out the same way across the world.

"Who, me? Really?" they say, blushing a bit, sincerely incredulous.

"Are you sure?" they continue, offering a self-deprecating quip to mask their true emotions as they realize the magnitude of the compliment they've been paid.

"Of course I will. I'm honored," they conclude. At least, they conclude with the speaking portion. Meanwhile, inside their head it dawns on them, *Holy shit, this is their wedding, I can't fuck this up.* Then, while the rush of panic rises within them and they reflexively clink their coup glasses, staring mindlessly at a painting curated by their mom,[133] another thought calms their nerves. *If it were that important, they wouldn't have asked me to do it. I'll be fine.*

More often than not, you can expect a lame joke to follow this exchange, usually an impression of the priest from *The Princess Bride*. Scott was no exception, performing the Vulcan Salute and practicing his opening line, "Shalom, please be seated."

Wedding ceremonies, like humans, share 99.9 percent of their genetic makeup. However, like humans, they come in all shapes and sizes. Our ceremony would take place beside a Texas ranch. The wedding I officiated two years earlier was held in a suburban brewery. Weddings can be fat, skinny, composed, neurotic, long, short, loud, and, if you're sitting in the back of the church when the air conditioner's busted and the oscillating fan hums in your ear, far too quiet to follow.

I'd love to tell you that no matter their differences, all ceremonies are perfect just the way they are. But this isn't kindergarten. There are wrong answers when planning your ceremony. This may come across harsh, but I'm speaking on behalf of every average guy sitting in the sun, waiting for the damn thing to be over.

Keys to Planning a Wedding Ceremony:

- Nobody cares about your favorite poem. I

- understand that you feel obligated to bring up your best friend who didn't make the cut as a bridesmaid, but Lord Byron is dead, let's not have him crash as a plus-one.
- Unity candles are super lame. We get it, two flames become one. How about we skip to the part where I'm at the bar and gin and soda become one?
- We're all very impressed that your sister learned a new song on her acoustic guitar. It's lovely. It'd be even more lovely to listen to her stilted rendition while holding that gin and soda during the cocktail hour.
- Freedom of religion is all well and good, but in the interest of time, let's keep the cultural demonstrations to one per family. We're all just trying to house some hors d'oeuvres as soon as possible.
- Mom, Dad, we'll sit through whatever speeches you've got lined up, but please don't open your mouth until mine has three hors d'oeuvres in it.

As you can see, time is of the essence. No matter what, the bride and groom will look back and say, "It all happened so fast!" so they may as well plan for the ceremony to happen so fast. That's exactly what we did.

No outside speakers. No time-sucking symbolic rituals. Scotty would talk about how great we are, we'd recite our vows, stomp on the glass, and clock the whole thing under 15 minutes. Ba-da-bing, got-a-ring.

Show's over, and at the end of the day, it is a show.

Wedding ceremonies may as well be done in community theaters. It's a performance designed to elicit an emotional response from its live audience. With Scott locked in, we'd finished casting our ceremony. Flower girls, ring girls, an indifference of groomsmen, a saccharine of bridesmaids, two weepy mothers, and a pair of proud papas. The players were set, and Heine, our director and creative muse, had given the cast very specific notes for costumes and props (*Asymmetrical? Empty space?*).

We'd established the setting, done our best to ensure proper lighting, and scored the show with a one-man acoustic orchestra. One rehearsal would be enough to memorize the choreography and blocking, and we'd handle that the day before the curtain rose for our debut.

The only thing left to do was write the dialogue.

Pat, I'd like to buy a Vow

Heine froze, spoon in hand, the chicken tikka masala dripping from its suspended position halfway to her mouth. At first, I thought something unusually scandalous had occurred between the typically amicable cast of *Bachelor in Paradise*, but as globs of rice continued to sputter into Alex's homemade pottery class bowl, I realized there were other forces at work.

"What now?" I called from the living room, leaning forward to finish off the remaining morsels from her spoon.

"Come here, quick!"

I swung my weight forward and released the premature grunt of a much older, fatter man with more serious back problems. "This better be good. The worst thing on TV is on."

"Hurry, before I forget the line," he called from the guest room.

Knowing that Brad doesn't have the capacity to forget anything, I stopped at the sink to refill my water glass before joining him. I found him sitting at the desk beside my laptop, sweat-drenched, saturated strands of his bowl cut clinging to his domed skull.

"What the hell is going on in here?" I asked, wondering if someone had finally made use of that jump rope I bought on Amazon a few years earlier.

"You complete me," Brad said.

"You're dripping in sweat!"

"You complete me!" He echoed, rising to his four feet. "It's perfect!"

Glancing at the monitor, I caught the end credits of *Jerry Maguire* scrolling by. "Oh, ok. You want me to steal Tom Cruise's line. Got it. But why are you so sweaty?"

"It was emotional. My tear ducts are similar to your human sweat glands."

"It's a good line," I said. "But I think Heine's seen the movie."[134] Brad gave a "that makes sense" nod and sat down, wicking sweat from his forehead with the back of his hand, ready to rack his unparalleled brain for the right words to express my love. Even for hyper-intelligent fictional literary devices, writing vows presents a challenge.

I wrote the first draft of my vows in February, about eight and a half months before I'd have to recite them. Heine and I, along with a few friends, took a ski trip to Keystone, Colorado, where she could relive her college days on the slopes and I could attempt to ski for the first time in my life.[135] After the trip we split up at the airport, as Alex flew directly to a work trip and I headed home. I breezed through the Sunday crossword I had printed in advance, and with hours left and the benefit of 37,000 feet of perspective, I flipped the paper over and let my heart speak through my pen.

Brad and I reviewed the first draft of my vows the night before he sweated out Rod Tidwell's contract negotiations. Once he grasped the objective, he eagerly took to offering his unsolicited assistance.

Here's a fun exercise: tell me about some vows you remember hearing at a wedding.

I'm guessing this exercise is going about as well as most other attempts at exercise, i.e., you're lying down while your recently purchased jump rope gathers dust in the guest room.

Somehow, we've all agreed on the expectation that our vows should be beautifully written expressions of true love, which is an admirable goal, if not an attainable one. Think about it, finding the right words to express love is the ultimate aim of the greatest artists in history. Why do we expect that your buddy from Accounts Payable can achieve what only Shakespeare, Cameron Crowe, and a handful of other rom com screenwriters have been able to achieve in the entire history of the written word? Somewhere between *Romeo and Juliet* and *Jerry Maguire*, the bar was set a little too high for us amateur auteurs.

Vows are forgettable, derivative clichés. That doesn't mean they're bad. They're supposed to sound the same. How many ways can you tell someone you love them and you want to spend the rest of your life with them?[136] It's okay to forget vows, as long as you don't forget to uphold them. I memorized my vows and I can barely remember them. That doesn't mean I've forgotten that I love Heine and want to spend the rest of my life with her. That's why we all say "I love you and I want to spend the rest of my life with you." Why fix what's not broken?

Still, we struggle to find the perfect words. And it is a struggle. I thought writing vows would be easy.[137] Of everyone on the planet, Alex is the person I'm most comfortable sharing my feelings with, so why would it be hard to share my feelings with her?

Here's what I wrote on the plane. Try to imagine this scribbled in the print of a serial killer, utilizing capital letters at random so my declaration of love and fidelity reads like a ransom note from the Joker.

Heine,

I wrote these vows on the back of a crossword puzzle during my flight home from our ski trip in February. I had never skied before, but that didn't stop you from bringing me to the precipice of a double black diamond at 10 am on my first day. The ensuing 45 minutes featured a whirlwind of physically and emotionally draining moments for both of us...but mainly me. I was upset, and felt an unfamiliar fear settle over me as I fell from mogul to mogul. But soon, that fear gave way to exhilaration, and the anger quickly transformed into a feeling of trust. Although I tumbled uncontrollably for 50 feet, I never worried that I'd be hurt. I remember looking up and watching you glide down to my long lost left ski. Later, you'd tell me that around that time, a good 20 minutes into the ordeal, you were finally able to stop laughing behind your facemask. For those who haven't caught on, this story is a metaphor. That day, I learned that with you by my side there's nothing I can't overcome. You took me beyond my comfort zone, and by trusting in you I emerged stronger and more in love with you than ever. And for the record, I would fall down that mountain everyday if I knew it'd make you laugh. We don't live on a mountain, we live in a shoebox apartment in Roscoe Village, and that's where we built our life together. Everyday you amaze me with your intelligence, affection, and dedication to finding the optimal arrangement of 4x6 framed photos on our wall. Most of all, I'm amazed that you chose me, and continue to choose me despite my melodramatic response to ankle injuries, inability to pass up a pun, and seemingly endless stomachache. Not a day goes by without me thinking of how lucky I am to have you. I vow never to forget that. Over the years I've fallen in love with you bit by bit. It began with little things, the enthusiasm with which you told me you were always down for backgammon, the passion you put into your karaoke performances of "Beast of Burden," the way you'd call waitresses 'darling,' and the confidence you showed when accusing Ruderman of cheating at Settlers of Caton. You've proven again and again that you are capable of accomplishing anything in your life through your intelligence, work ethic, and charm. The little things I love about you kept building, and one day I realized that nothing mattered to me as much as your happiness, and knowing that you felt loved. Without you being happy I can't be content. Without you feeling loved I would never feel fulfilled. Without you I'd probably still be stuck on that mountain.

Not bad. Certainly not good, but for a first draft, I had some workable material. A little long at 467 words, but again, we're talking raw material. Some of this survived to the final draft, but substantial chunks were discarded on the grounds that "it was just the elevation talking."

Between the time I jotted down the long-winded

story about my inferior skiing and our wedding day, I added various notes and ideas to a document on Google Drive titled "Super Secret Vows."

Super Secret Vows Notes

When did I first know I loved Heine?
- This is a vows staple. It's reliable, relatable, and presents an opportunity to share intimate idiosyncrasies, bringing guests never-before-published insights on a relationship they thought they knew.
- Plus, I already came up with some on the plane.

Alex's word count restrictions
- The bride didn't want me to ramble on too long, and I wanted to zing her for meddling with my vows.
- *Hey stupid, don't say anything negative about the bride in your vows.* This joke got cut. As did the joke about how frequently she rearranges the framed 4x6 photos on our wall.

Something about "core memories" like Pixar's *Inside Out*
- I realized a shift took place in my mind after we'd been together for a few years. The biggest moments in my life now featured Heine, whereas they used to feature my family or friends.
- This premise allows me to explain how she hasn't replaced these groups, but rather become the heart of them, a touching sentiment sure to elicit a tear from the weepier guests.
- Ex. Waking up at sunrise the morning after we moved in together. No curtains, mattress on the floor. Will never forget that feeling.

- Illustrates how our journey has already begun, and can elaborate on the memories we look forward to sharing in the future.

Magnitude of the moment
- If it takes me three weeks to commit to a haircut, this must be a pretty big deal.
- Probably best not to make any references to hesitation or past commitment issues.

Weddings are parties and it's easy to make promises
- It's hard to keep promises when the party ends.
- I can combine a joke about how, a week from now, we'll be on the couch with Mona watching the *Last Airbender* cartoons, but the vow isn't to be there during the cartoons, it's to be there when things aren't easy.
- Footnote: nothing is easy.

The Laundry Anecdote
- All serious couples pass through a series of ubiquitous phases. There's the "we haven't said 'I love you' yet" phase where it's really awkward to watch characters in romantic comedies talk about not having said "I love you" yet, and there's the "we both know we'll get married but haven't talked about marriage yet" phase. While in the latter phase, during a laundry folding session, Alex said something about "the guy" she'd marry. I stopped her and said, "what guy? I'm the guy."
- This is a cute story about laundry, so obviously I'd use it as my opening.

Forget "Til Death to us Part"
- What a downer.

- Why not say it as "every single day that we live" instead of "until we die"?
- I probably thought of this one while high, or in that half-sleep zone where all the ideas seem profound.

Joke about how I'll always be the right man for her, since I'm already an old man
- Will you still love me when I become an old man, a curmudgeon who complains about small aches and pains, has severe if undiagnosed digestive problems, whose idea of a wild Saturday involves a crossword puzzle and the Golf Channel?
- This joke, while hilarious, takes a lot of time and puts the focus on me, instead of her.

Alex combines Texas charm, Boulder chill, and an Illinois driver's license
- Solid line, showcases different aspects of her life, will get a laugh.

Cinco de Mayo Empanada Party
- A nice memory of a time I felt really in love that never had a chance of making it into the final vows. One benefit of brainstorming for your vows (and writing this book) is that your mind begins to associate more and more memories like these.
- Alex sat outside with her future bridesmaid, Jenny, as I sat inside with our future ceremony guitarist, Aaron. He strummed away while I watched her tell a story through the window. I couldn't hear her, but I knew she was very happy in that moment, wearing an Astros hat, drinking a White Claw on Cinco de Mayo.

Another story
- One day between engagement and wedding, Alex

and I enjoyed some Saturday afternoon Wii *Mario Kart* racing.[138] In the middle of a race I turned to her and said, "Holy shit, we're going to spend the rest of our lives together." She kept her focus on the race and said, "Yeah, I know."

Some of that made the cut; some of it, thankfully, did not. In the end, I adhered to the word count limitations and abstained from joking about the word count limitations. In truth, the content doesn't matter nearly as much as the length and the delivery. Nobody remembers the words, but they will remember the effect.

If it's said with confidence and you've practiced enough to control the cadence, then you'll do fine.

These are the last 394 words I spoke to my fiancée before she became my wife:

A few years ago, while folding laundry, we talked about weddings. You said "When I get married, I want *the guy* to help with the planning." I said, "What guy? I'm your guy." That was the exact moment I realized something that, in the back of my mind, I'd known for a long time: that we'd always be together. I wasn't scared, and I wasn't nervous; instead, I was overcome by a sense of purpose. That night I realized that you make my life meaningful.

I've fallen in love with you again and again. I fell in love when we first started dating and you texted me that you were "always down for backgammon." I fell in love as you performed "Beast of Burden" at karaoke, when you drew hearts on all my golf balls, and every time you've called a waitress "darling." I fell in love watching you walk down the aisle, and I can't wait to keep falling in love with you for the rest of our lives.

Your combination of Texas charm, Boulder chill, and an Illinois driver's license gets me every time. Every day you amaze me with your intelligence and affection. I admire how you love your family, and how you've embraced being a part of mine. Most of all, I'm amazed by your patience with me. No matter how melodramatic my minor injuries or how bad my puns get, you always love me for who I am, and I will never take that for granted. I understand how lucky I am spending each day with you as my friend and partner, finding inspiration in your example, and finding new ways to laugh with you.

It's easy to imagine returning to our life after today, sitting in our apartment explaining to Mona how the family dynamic has changed now that we're husband and wife. It's harder to visualize the unknown challenges we'll encounter in 10 years, or 30 years. I vow to keep you smiling through all of it.

I still skip a beat when you enter the room. You've redefined what friendship and family mean to me, and I promise that I will always be there to make you feel safe, happy, and loved. I meant it when I said it over laundry, and today we make it official. Heine, I am, and vow to always be, your guy.

I spoke these words slowly and clearly. They went over well. I'm sure nobody remembered any of them by the end of the week.

Alex's vows, which clocked in at more than 700 words (but who's counting?), also mentioned laundry. We'll wash, dry, fold, and love each other forever.[139]

BUT WAIT, THERE'S MORE!

Welcome back, folks. *Applause.* We're here today to introduce the all new Magic Wedding 3000. Now, before the break we showed you how the Magic Wedding can eliminate even your most grueling, time-consuming wedding planning tasks with just the press of a button. Just wed it, and forget it! *Astonished gasps, disbelieving laughter, applause.*

That's right, Gary, it really is that easy!

Oh my goodness! Folks, how about a big round of applause for your author, Sam Ofman. Sam, come on out here. *Crickets.*

Thanks, Gar. Now folks, earlier in the program you watched as I experienced some difficult times.

I'll say! *Laughter.*

Oh, Gary. I know we had some laughs, but there's no joking about how valuable the Magic Wedding 3000 will be when it comes time for you to plan that special day. You see folks, I didn't have a Magic Wedding when I planned my wedding. *Incredulous gasps, hurried whispers.* It's true, folks. And boy, was it tough. So take it from me, the Magic Wedding 3000 is worth all four payments of $59.99.

Shipping and handling included!

That's right, Gar! The Magic Wedding 3000 is the one thing that won't put you over budget. Call in the next 20 minutes and you'll receive, as a special bonus exclusive, a stainless steel engagement ring set, complete with Jeweler-to-Layman dictionary. That's in addition to the fully accessorized Magic Wedding 3000, which includes:

- A foolproof proposal script. We guarantee she'll say "yes!" (Guarantee is not a binding contract, individual results may vary)
- One dream venue (Bicoastal couples subject to additional charges)
- Catering (No substitutions, special requests for allergies will be ignored)
- A five-piece band (Song-learning surcharge may apply)
- Invitations (Choose from more than 40 fonts!)
- A one-size-fits-all suit (Suit not guaranteed to fit, individual body sizes may vary. If suit does not fit consult your physician immediately)
- One wedding dress (Machine washable, as though you'll ever wear it again)
- Four (4) groomsmen and four (4) bridesmaids (Bachelor and bachelorette parties not covered by our insurance)
- Two sets of personalized vows (Complete the enclosed MadLib and submit along with a self-addressed stamped envelope. Materials must be received six months prior to ceremony to ensure receipt of vows by event date)
- One fully adjustable officiant (Settings include Rambling Rabbi, Unintelligible Priest, and Nervous Half-Drunk Friend)
- Transportation, flowers, accommodations, registry, wedding website, and more!

Wow, Sam. Talk about a value! The Magic Wedding 3000 really does provide everything you need for a wedding.

You'd think so, Gary. But wait. There's more!

That's enough of that. But seriously, there is more.

While juggling all of these elements, most of which relate directly to the engagement, reception, or ceremony, Alex and I also dealt with a slew of auxiliary projects that coincided with the wedding.

After an endless back-and-forth to get Alex the perfect engagement ring, I had to return to the Old Jewish Diamond Guy's office to start the process over again for our wedding bands.

Before the Big Day, there's the day before the Big Day. Hosting a rehearsal dinner meant planning an entirely new event.

In the midst of planning the most important day of our lives, we made time to plan the most complex vacation of our lives.

As though that isn't enough, just wait.[140]

Honeymoon

You just read my vows, so you'll remember the line about how married life would be easy one week after the wedding. At first, we'd radiate post-wedding joy, showering our officemates and tertiary friends with photos of the amazing event they weren't invited to. Wedding radiation has a much shorter half-life than regular radiation, and before long our glow would wear off. Eventually, I'd do or say something insensitive without realizing it, Alex would give me the silent treatment, and for the duration of time it takes for me to realize how what I'd said or done was insensitive, we'd engage in our first marital spat.

The cliché reads: honeymoon's over.

A lot of attention gets paid to the reality check associated with the conclusion of the figurative honeymoon, as if couples are routinely blindsided by short-term bliss coming to an end. This is a fallacy. Alex and I, and I presume most intelligent couples, understand that the Just Married mobile will run out of gas.[141] We all come down from the newlywed high, and that's okay. Instead of focusing so intently on proclaiming the demise of the metaphorical honeymoon, let's examine the creation of the literal one.

I won't dwell on this too long, but I think it's important for anyone planning a wedding to remain mindful of the additional time, energy, and expense of honeymoon planning. Here's a novel idea: let's use my personal experience planning a honeymoon to illustrate the challenges of coordinating the trip of a lifetime.

Some newlyweds depart for their honeymoon the morning after their wedding reception. Kudos to them. It takes some serious chutzpah to walk down the aisle on Saturday and take an aisle seat on Sunday. I don't know how the immediate honeymooners do it, transitioning from a weekend full of constant nerves and adrenaline directly into all the anxiety of travelling abroad. Alex and I tied the knot 1,000 miles from our front door, so getting her dress home in one piece on a routine Tuesday-morning flight provided enough stress. There's work to be done, gifts to be packed, photo booth operators to have fired. Loose ends that can't be tied while untying your shoes at a TSA checkpoint. The whole experience leaves you sapped of energy.

To mitigate the additional exhaustion, we postponed our honeymoon until a few months after the wedding, allowing us to get out of Chicago in February. Those of you from a warm-weather climate may not fully comprehend how big a deal that is. Consider this: the wind chill on the night we left for our honeymoon dipped to minus-57 degrees.

NEGATIVE FIFTY SEVEN.[142]

I wore ski goggles to walk Mona that morning. When we landed at our destination, it felt 137 degrees warmer than when we boarded.

We found a compromise to stave off the post-wedding return to reality. Rather than rush into a big trip or return to normal life right away, we took two days off, rented a cabin in the woods, and took our dog on what's now popularly referred to as a "minimoon." Our minimoon gave us a chance to decompress in a private outdoor hot tub, where we set up a laptop to watch *Frasier* reruns and developed brutal head colds.

Romantic, right?

Planning our minimoon took about half an hour. I've spent longer scrolling through Netflix. Planning the full-scale honeymoon better equates to watching all eleven seasons of *Frasier* on Netflix. You open your laptop and spend 23 minutes looking at the same thing over and over again. Whether it's 263 episodes of physical comedy and lowbrow innuendo dressed up with pretension and affected accents or 263 beachfront hotels, travel blog reviews, and wildlife tour seasonal pricing charts, there's plenty of content in which to lose oneself. Zoom in on a resort island off the coast of Thailand and you'll get an idea of the limitless choices.[143]

Wedding and honeymoon planning share a similar cadence. In the same vein that you can't book the caterer until you have the head count, you can't always book a hotel in Chiang Mai until you know when your flight out of Bangkok takes off. All of the components need to come together before you can move forward with any of them. But with honeymoon planning, you also enjoy the language barrier, time difference, and currency conversion.

Alex and I honeymooned in Thailand. Southeast Asia today is a lot like *Frasier* in the late '90s, rapidly growing in popularity among white people. The best advice I have for anyone planning a trip to Thailand is not to tell anybody that you're planning a trip to Thailand. If you tell people you are travelling to Italy, they'll say, "You'll love it." If you're headed to Mexico, "What fun!" Thailand? "Here's the itinerary from my second cousin's ex girlfriend's trip two summers ago, you'll need this."

You don't need their itineraries. You can do it all by yourself. Pick a few destinations, book hotels, book activities. It'll be a blast. You're travelling internationally with your soulmate. Try not to make it a chore. Besides, you don't need any more chores. Remember, this is all happening in the free time left over from spending all of your free time planning a wedding.

Exterior Exterior Stones

After our Texas proposal we drove home in a Subaru filled with furniture, clothes, and general Texacana. Somewhere between Alex's three pairs of cowboy boots[144] and her grandmother's yellow chair, we squeezed in a box labeled "fragile." It housed an antique crystal chandelier with transatlantic origins that, I believe, stretch back five generations. It's one hell of a fixture, but it needed fixing.

Once home, our landlord suggested we take it to a long-running specialty store for repairs. "I can't wait to hear what they say about it," he added.

Our expressions gave away our confusion.

"These guys are tough to impress. They've seen it all."

We have a strange dude for a landlord, so it was easy to ignore the impulse to ask questions regarding his history with the lamp store owners, how they earned their discriminating reputation, and why he could possibly have such enthusiasm for their opinion of our little chandelier. Regardless, I was eager to bring it in and see if it warranted a reaction.

We took it in and discovered a hoarder's attic of antique lighting fixtures. We could barely navigate the aisles without brushing against a dangling bulb or getting clotheslined by a permanently extended cuckoo clock. Every item piled up in that store had as much sentimental value, and probably as many years under its belt, as the Heine family chandelier. Like so many ailing bulbs around us, my hopes of impressing the strangers behind the counter dimmed.

We watched as the people ahead of us in line presented their lamps, smiling the naive smile of someone who thinks they're special. They had not been warned of the proprietor's high standards.

A desk lamp shaped like a wood cabin? Meh, use it for firewood.

Something that made me think of pop art and the 1960s? It lacked pop.

Our chandelier? Wait, did his eyebrow just twitch? The proprietor asked about its origins. He was intrigued! How intrigued? Not very. But we moved the needle. Remarkable? No. but remarked upon? You bet.

I wish more people we encountered during the wedding planning process, people who see multiple engagement rings every week as part of their job, possessed the same discerning attitude as the lamp shop proprietor. Just once, I'd have liked a venue representative to have stopped the tour to ask to see Alex's engagement ring, only to skip the empty "Oh, it's gorgeous!" in favor of something like, "Oh, one of those. Okay."

Unfortunately, or fortunately, Alex's engagement ring is like our chandelier. It's truly one-of-a-kind. When people admire it—for its design, if not its size—I wholeheartedly buy into their sincerity. It doesn't look like something you see advertised by Kay Jewelers. Jared, the galleria/IKEA of jewelry, doesn't promote yellow diamonds with raised, vintagey, asymmetrical elements. Nine out of ten rings look the same to the untrained eye. Alex's is the 10th.

Designing a unique engagement ring wasn't easy, but that didn't stop me from thinking that designing a wedding band would be.[145] I mean, how hard could a simple wedding band be?

Once again I found myself acting as a translator between Old Jewish Diamond Guy and Heine. One spoke fluent Jewelry, which I didn't understand, and the other spoke pidgin Jewelry, which I didn't understand. OJDG would draw a line on a sheet of paper and ask if I was still with him. I'd be completely lost, but I had to lie because what self respecting man could admit to succumbing to utter confusion when looking at a straight line? Is it the ring seen from above? Is it an axis of some sort? Should I be focused on the empty space?

It couldn't have been much easier for him to make heads or tails of my drawings. I'd email him a sketch explaining what Alex envisioned, using terms like "support poles," only to apologize in the following sentence for using the term "support poles." The language barrier explains, in part, why more than five months passed between sending a "let's get the ball rolling on the wedding bands" email and stopping by the office to pick up the finished products.

The unique aspects of Alex's engagement ring (raised? asymmetrical?) muddled the design process for the wedding bands. No, Reader, that's not a typo. We're talking plural nouns. Bands, as in more than one wedding band. Alex's engagement ring would be flanked on both sides. After all, good things come in threes, and a star only shines as bright as its supporting cast. Fat Tony has Legs and Louie. A Thanksgiving turkey has mashed potatoes and stuffing. Alex has Mona and me.

We presented a new challenge for OJDG from the outset. The raised element of the engagement ring didn't allow for the wedding bands to line up flat against the middle band on her finger. Those darn support poles got in the way.

I went in to talk it over.

We exchanged emails.

I went in to talk it over.

We exchanged emails.

What began as Alex's dream ring had become my recurring nightmare.

I left OJDG's office following another Jewelry as a Second Language course without knowing with any certainty what the rings would look like, how much they'd cost, or when he'd have them made. Whatever questions I had for him went unspoken, as I didn't know what they were, only that I needed to ask them. Another standard appointment.

Weeks passed without contact until I ran into OJDG on the Brown Line. Once we'd made sufficient eye contact so as to eliminate the plausibility of pretending not to have seen each other, he assured me that everything was on track and suggested I stop by the office.

Countless emails, a few trips downtown, and five months later we'd found a way to bend the exterior rings around the base of the engagement ring. Diamonds cover the circumference of one, rubies encircle the other.

Alex now has three pieces of jewelry that are completely unique in all of world history.[146] She also has the luxury of mixing and matching these symbols of eternal love based on her mood and outfit, and since all three rings feature asymmetrical designs, she enjoys more mix-and-match options than a fully accessorized Mr. Potato Head. I took a stab at the math and failed. I think she has more than 30 combinations at her fingertips.

Jewelry, I've learned, helps the wearer express him or herself. A stylish ring makes a statement about who you are, how you perceive yourself, and how you want others to perceive you. Alex's rings make those statements. They say, "I am an artist. I am a complex individual who values beauty and originality."

On the other hand—my hand—you'll find a much simpler token of our commitment.

By now you've become acquainted with me. You know I'm not an artistic-minded soulful expressionist. I'm a sarcastic, miserly, entitled white guy. What do I know about wearing a wedding band?

To find out, I looked to my role models. I thought back to my father and announced to Heine that I'd go with a simple gold band like the one he wore. Later, when I asked him about it, he informed me that he's never worn a wedding ring.

Next, I turned to my best man, who I knew wore a

ring because I'd watched him struggle to remove it at the start of all of our rec league basketball games. I often remark that I am the smallest player in that league by 20 pounds, and the next-smallest guy is my brother. I keep my weight a secret. I joke about how skinny I am, and I think people generally assume I'm exaggerating. Here's a good example to prove it. My brother, who is a relatively small man himself, wears a ring that I could easily slide onto my thumb. He wasn't much help for size. But the color looked about right. I'd go with something silver.

I returned to OJDG's office to pick out a band. No design sketches. No drawings. No language barrier. Just me trying on a few options and saying, in the universal language of finger pointing, "That one." My ring, like the finger it rests on and the body the finger connects with, is remarkably thin.

It turns out silver isn't a common material for wedding bands. When you see a silver ring, there's a good chance it's made out of white gold or platinum. How can you tell the difference between the two? Hold out your hand and have an Old Jewish Diamond Guy drop a ring made of white gold into it. Then have him drop a ring made of platinum into it. That's how I learned. It's the difference between having me dropped on you compared to having my brother dropped on you. Neither weighs too much, but there's an obvious discrepancy.

As expected, the heavy one costs more. As expected, I got the lighter one. It looks great. It fits. You'd never know it wasn't platinum, but you'd probably guess it's made of silver.

But Wait! There's Still More!

License and Registration

Every day on my morning commute I pass the Village Discount Outlet, a thrift store that, somehow, hasn't been forced out of business by rising rents and property taxes in a largely gentrified neighborhood. Hell, they even own a permanently deserted parking lot across the street. How they survive by selling used clock radios and secondhand jeans for $3 a pop is beyond my comprehension of economics. To be fair, after passing the AP Econ tests in high school, I haven't spent much time studying the supply and demand curves for pre-owned footwear.

Examining the items in the display window of the Village Discount Outlet is one of my simple joys. For me, there's no need to check a calendar or consult the weather forecast. I follow the changing seasons based on the rotating items hanging on the other side of the glass.

Ugly Christmas sweaters in December.

Red dresses for Valentine's Day.

Novelty T-shirts for St. Patrick's.

Cubs gear in the spring.

Workout clothes for those beach bod days of summer.

XXXL Bears jerseys—running the full spectrum of regrettable quarterbacks—means it's fall.

And, finally, Halloween costumes in October.

I often feel the urge to stop in on the way home to pick up a Joakim Noah shirt for my brother or an adorable children's outfit for my niece, only to remember that these are used items, and while my nieces wouldn't mind, their parents may prefer gifts with less experience on their resumes. About a month before the wedding, a new piece captivated me on my walk home. This was an exceptional, spooktacular garment, and after three weeks of waffling I finally caved and became the proud owner of an orange jack-o'-lantern sweatshirt.

It didn't have Mona's face on it,[147] but I gave it to Alex as a pre-wedding present anyway.

No, she didn't wear this ludicrous piece of clothing during the wedding. It wasn't suitable attire for a symbolic ceremony, though it was more than formal enough for the moment we took our first official step toward legally becoming husband and wife. At the Travis County Clerk's office, I filed the paperwork to wed the Great Pumpkin.

If you're fortunate enough not to have taken a recent excursion to the DMV or waited on hold with the IRS customer service line, you may have forgotten the unfathomable inanity of government bureaucracy. Rest assured, if you ever need a marriage license, you'll be reminded.

Travis County enforces a three day waiting period between receipt of a marriage license and the ceremony. The only explanation I can think of for this policy, which forced Alex and me to fly to Texas a day earlier than we originally planned, is quite brief. In a word: bureaucracy. But be careful, as the license expires after 90 days. All licenses must be signed by a qualifying officiant and returned to the Clerk's office within 30 days, regardless of how many days remain in that original 87-day sweet spot.

Remember, this is all because Alex and I agreed that we love each other and want to be together. Why can't Uncle Sam take our word for it?

The 72-hour rule doesn't apply to those who volunteer to attend (and pay for) a premarital education course. Those who graduate from the course have marriages that last, on average, three days longer than those who skipped class. They also allow special exemptions for military members on active duty and the staff of the Department of Defense. There's nothing on the website regarding the Department of Education, but I assume they created the premarital education curriculum and could be exempt from the waiting period with a special waiver from the president.

To receive our license, Alex and I made the trek to the County Clerk with all the required documents in hand. This process must be done in person, with both parties present, in possession of approved forms of identification. We drove into the lot four days before the wedding with passports in one hand and bean and cheese burritos in the other. I was ready to prove who I was, and make a big stink if they demanded a second form of ID.[148] This is a government office we're talking about, so despite the fact that it was a quiet Wednesday morning, we still had to wait in line in the entryway for at least a few minutes. Visiting the County Clerk without waiting in line would be like eating a bean and cheese burrito without the accompanying flatulence, or hiring a wedding vendor without being up-charged. Waiting in line is unpleasant, but it's an essential component to having an authentic experience.

Having successfully waited in line, Window Drone 1 offered her sincere, federally approved, non-denominational, gender-neutral congratulatory message and directed us through the glass doors into the main office space. The fluorescent hum, muted blue wallpaper, and lingering scent of hand sanitizer gave the room a clinical aura. A state-run mental asylum would look and feel the exact same. But I wasn't there to commit myself, I was there to commit myself to Alex, and before the wait time could drive us insane we were waved up by Reception Desk Drone 2. Reception Desk Drone 1's absence caused longer-than-usual wait times. I don't know what function Window Drone 1 serves, but it must be redundant because Reception Desk Drone 2 asked for all the same information and documentation. Then she asked for $81.

In Travis County, $81 can get you a bean and cheese burrito every day for a month or a legal partner for the rest of your life. Of course, that figure is subject to reduction should you complete the premarital education course, have a hard copy of the certificate proving you completed the course, and be sure the hard copy is dated and signed to indicate you've completed the course in the last year. You'd think active military members would get a break on the license fee, too. After all, they're exempt from the waiting period, and surviving basic training ought to earn the same perks as passing Marriage 101. You'd be right. Sort of. Active military members don't have to pay the marriage license fee if they are, and this is a copy and paste moment, "preparing to be deployed to serve in a hostile fire zone as designated by the United States Secretary of Defense." How many men out there have made a joke about their wives being a hostile fire zone? Am I right, fellas?

Call me a coward, but I'd happily fork over $81 to avoid hostile fire.

And how many wives avoid hostile fire by having their husbands spend $81 on a marriage license instead of 30 bean and cheese burritos?[149]

Credit card swiped, Reception Desk Drone 2 shuffled us over to Cubicle Drone 4, a portly, jovial drone, who beckoned us towards his cubicle with a grin as wide as the one on Alex's jack-o'-lantern sweatshirt. Cubicle Drone 4 had too much charm to be a drone. He put us at ease with a disarming smile, cracked an inside joke with Cubicle Drone 3, and exuded a *joie de vivre* that had no place in a County Clerk's office.

How did this guy end up here? I thought.

Then he started working.

Oh. I see.

Cubicle Drone 4 didn't have all his fluorescents humming, if you know what I mean. The one thing you expect from a drone is mastery of the repetitive drone tasks they face each day. You expect the grocery bagger to have a certain familiarity with bagging groceries. There's not a ton of variance from task to task. I had similar expectations for Cubicle Drone 4, which, sadly, were not met, forcing me to take action.

"Excuse me, but you spelled that name wrong."

"Hold on, that's not the address we gave you."

"September is the ninth month, not the seventh."

"That's still not how you spell my last name."

Would you let your grocery bagger put the eggs under the milk? Twice? Cubicle Drone 4 displayed his trademark happy-go-lucky attitude, playing it off as though inputting a series of incorrect data points wouldn't be a big deal. I know, it's astonishing, but a government office had a lackadaisical attitude towards clerical errors. I wasn't about to find out what hoops the County Clerk would have me jump through to correct a license after the fact. What if it impacted my three day waiting period eligibility? Could I get my $81 refunded without being deployed to a hostile fire zone? Better to speak up and get it right the first time.

With the form filled out and adequately fact-checked, Cubicle Drone 4 bid us a hearty farewell, sending Alex and me to our final destination, Print Station Drone. Print Station Drone has a great gig. Not only does he have the pleasant task of handing happy couples a freshly minted marriage license, but he also takes a photo of the couple holding the license. In typical bureaucratic fashion, these photos get instantaneously uploaded to Print Station Drone's computer, where he proudly turns the monitor to show you the result within seconds. It's all very impressive.

Then he informs you that you can access the photo on the County Clerk's website. Great! This sounds too good to be true.

Then he tells you that it should be available to view online in four to six weeks. Ours didn't appear online for three months. It's probably still there if you want to look up what Heine's jack-o-lantern sweatshirt looks like.

The Day-of Gift

I love tacky novelty gifts. It is a personality flaw that I have accepted as a part of my identity. Owning this part of myself does wonders for my emotional wellbeing, but it doesn't bode well for the quality of the gifts I buy for Alex.

The first time I had to buy Alex a present was Christmas of 2015. We'd been together long enough that I couldn't do something thoughtless or skate by on just taking her out for dinner. In the end, I stayed true to myself and had a personalized Rubik's Cube made, featuring a different picture of Mona on each of its six sides. It was adorable. It went over well.

About a year later I gave her a coffee mug, with six pictures of Mona arranged in a playful collage around the exterior of the ceramics. Well, It went over.

When I discovered that there's such a thing as a "day-of gift" in the made-up world of modern wedding commerce traditions, it shouldn't surprise you that my instincts guided me to gifts with our dog's face on them.

The day-of gift, which Heine explained was not optional, would have driven me over the edge had I not been desensitized to the outflow of cash in the preceding months. Do we really need to buy each other *another* present? According to an article on WeddingShoppeInc.com, yes we do. And they have 23 ideas! I only bring them up because the opening line of the piece reads, "You thought you were done, didn't you?" which happens to be the theme of this entire book.

The day-of gift serves one of three purposes. First, there's the nerve tonic gift, something to warm up cold feet and put your partner's mind at ease before the ceremony. This ranges from a funny T-shirt to a risque photograph. Other times, the day of gift acts as a sentimental memento. A secret note placed in the bride's shoe, or stitching your initials and the date into a hidden section of the wedding dress. Last, there's the first official use of the new last name or the abbreviation "Mrs." WeddingShoppeInc.com displays a mug with the word "wifey" on it in gold lettering.

I opted for the second option, as a momento gave me the best opportunity to include Mona's face.

Mona would not be at the ceremony. If you've ever attended a wedding in which the couple's dog participates, you'll agree that, while it's a cute idea in theory, in practice it's a total pain in the bustle. Somebody gets assigned to full-time dog-sitting. Dogs get dirty. They bark at inappropriate times. They poop in inappropriate places. They scare my aunt. As if that weren't reason enough, for us to have Mona at the wedding would have meant driving instead of flying, and a two-day road trip fueled by fast food meant I too would be at risk for inappropriate pooping on our wedding day. Better to leave the dog behind.

As a compromise, I thought it'd be cute to have a tiny picture of Mona mounted onto a solid base for Alex to carry in her bouquet. Doesn't that sound like a nice day-of gift?

I felt pretty good about it until Alex asked what I had in mind.

"I feel pretty good about it," I said, not wanting to give away the surprise.

"It better not have Mona's face on it," she replied.

"It does."

"Then cancel it."

Bummer. I knew the idea was better than what she imagined, but I couldn't risk giving her something with Mona's face on it after she'd expressly told me not to. So I did what any wise married man would do. I folded instantly.

I told her my idea and she loved it. We followed through on it with a pair of mini Mona magnets, and our sweet dog found her way to be, not just at the wedding, but in her favorite place, smack dab in between the two of us as we stood at the altar. Now that very same Mona magnet lives on our fridge.

Done. Easy.[150]

That day-of surprise was no longer a surprise. By Alex's count, I still owed her a day-of gift. Having come up with one idea I'd exhausted my cache of ideas. It's a good thing I had Alex to help me come up with another one.

For round two I went for option three. Hours before Alexandria Leigh Heine became Alexandria Leigh Ofman, she'd get the monogrammed stationery to prove it. A simple gift, and one that she'll make use of for years. I picked the design with tiny cacti and succulents on the border. Women love succulents. That's probably the best advice I have for any gift-giving man. Succulents, throw blankets, and diamonds.

With Alex's day-of gifts purchased, all I had to do was show up to my own wedding and I'd find out what cute little gift she'd lined up for me. The magnets and stationery totalled approximately $40, a mere drop in the ocean of wedding expenses. There are a lot of great gifts out there for $40. I could always use a pair of 50-percent-off Gap jeans. Or would I be the proud owner of a wallet-sized risque photograph?

Silly Sam, this is a wedding expense. If you can do it for $40, then it can be done for $400. Alex gave me, as a day-of gift, a $300 gift card to my favorite golf course. Oh, and she wrapped it in a new tri-fold leather wallet. Meanwhile, I got her a $3 picture of Mona and some stationery off Etsy that she told me to get. I lost the gift-buying contest, but I won the gift-receiving contest.

A day-of gift should make you feel comfortable about marrying the person who gives it to you. Alex felt comfortable knowing I can follow directions and do cute things with our dog's face, and I felt good knowing that my wife-to-be would let me go golfing after we got married. Sometimes, everybody wins.

Here's a Tip: Lie to Yourself

Humans have an amazing ability to justify their behaviors. Whether everyone's doing it or someone else started it, we find a way to warrant our actions. It's easier to change our beliefs to accommodate our actions than to alter behavior to match our beliefs. It helps us avoid cognitive dissonance, if I recall my Psych 101 rote memorization. Examples:

I believe that I am somewhat "green," living an environmentally conscious lifestyle. I justify this view of myself by minimizing paper towel usage, often ripping one sheet into quarters. Meanwhile, I produce a ton of trash, have no idea how composting works, buy almond milk, and generally stomp around the globe leaving behind carbon footprints visible from Brad's home planet.

I believe that I'm a kindhearted person because I do nice things for Alex sometimes. Meanwhile, I ignore the pleas of the homeless people I pass on the street and said horrible things about my friend Henry earlier in this book.

I believe I'm humane because I love and care for my dog. I also eat meat and refuse to watch those chicken farm documentaries.

It's easier to focus on the parts of our lives that reinforce our positive self image. I've discovered that this type of self-serving white lie is essential for staying on budget when planning a wedding. You're going to go over budget. It's inevitable. Rather than fight about money or make sacrifices in your spending, you can just lie to yourself. It's great!

Those flights to Texas we bought to plan the wedding don't have to count towards the wedding budget. Those were family visits. New wicker baskets for the flower girls to carry? They'll use those next Easter. See how easy that was? I just cleared hundreds, maybe more than $1,000 in the budget. Like juking the stats in *The Wire*, a little creativity in the bookkeeping makes all the difference.

When Alex would say we're staying under budget, I don't think she counted the cost of her engagement ring as a wedding expense. Doesn't that sound good? Having your ring and wearing it, too.

Three days before the wedding Alex and I audited our vendor spreadsheet to make sure we'd remitted payment when necessary and wouldn't run into any issues over the weekend. We were over budget when we started. Imagine how we felt when we realized we still needed to tip these people.

The day-of-coordinator, for her one day of ambiguous helping out, receives a tip. The hair and makeup people get tipped. The shuttle driver who sits in his car for 80 percent of his workday, oh, you better believe he gets tipped. The band, the caterer, the photographer, the florist. I spent a year shopping around, negotiating, and reluctantly emptying my pockets to countless vendors. Then, on the day I'm finally going to receive the services we shelled out for, I find them all waiting, shoulder-to-shoulder with upturned palms stretched out in front of them, expecting more.

When travelling abroad, the local tipping customs vary from culture to culture. To sidestep any faux pas, travellers research online what, if anything, they should provide in gratuity. This holds true for bellhops, waiters, cab drivers, you name it.

Weddings aren't all that different from foreign countries. People dress differently, perform unusual rituals, and often hesitate to taste strange-looking foods. So even though we held our wedding in America, we turned to the Internet for guidance on the tipping culture of the wedding world. This may be difficult to believe, but WeddingWire, a website that exists solely to increase the amount of commerce surrounding American wedding culture, suggests you tip everybody. $200 for the coat check attendant? What an industry! They even want me to tip the parking attendant. Remember him?[151]

Two days before the wedding, Alex and I drove our insured rental car to the local Chase bank. We withdrew $1,500 and set most of it aside for tips. The rest would go toward incidentals of the wedding weekend and our minimoon. We then lied to ourselves about the bulk of the allocation and said it didn't count toward the budget. I slept like a baby thinking I'd somehow made money on the transaction.

Isn't that better than actually staying under budget?

TEXAS WEDDING!

I woke up the day before the wedding at Dave Heine's new house in Boerne, Texas. Alex stood beside the bed, looming motionless above me. She stared at her abandoned pillow, hovering in her Gap Body sleepy shirt. I turned over the key in my mental ignition until the sputtering gave way to the soft purr of my thought engine.[152] She wasn't transfixed by the impending comfort of the linens or paralyzed by the sight of a spider. She was frozen. Brad followed me to Texas.

I sat up on the edge of the bed, rubbed my eyes with the base of my palms, and walked out to the living room. The new house had a lot in common with the old house. The same photos from old hunting trips, class pictures of Alex and her siblings from their elementary school days, and the typical Texas tropes: a toy tractor, well-worn cowboy hat resting on a well-worn easy chair, old signage from the Independent Cattlemen's Association on the wall. You can take Brave Dave out of Heine Farms, but you can't take Heine Farms out of Brave Dave. His Texas flag, triangularly folded in its display case, had been flown outside the Capitol before being presented to him a few years earlier. I forget why; perhaps because he's such a Texan that the governor felt the need to sign a certificate stating the fact.[153]

Brad sat at the kitchen counter inspecting Dave's collection of rattlesnake tails, which live in a ceramic bowl on the counter. *Ah, the decor of a bachelor.* "I wouldn't eat those," I cautioned as I slid my boxer briefs on the neighboring stool. The cool metal of the stool strummed my hamstrings.

"I don't eat anything," he said, pushing them aside and rotating his celestial orb of a head away from me. "And I guess I don't mean anything to you either. When were you going to bring me back into this book? It's been chapters since you utilized me as a device to demonstrate how crazy weddings have become in American society."

Brad was right, but I wasn't about to join him in breaking the fourth wall. As the author, I decided to move on like nothing had happened.

"I'm glad you made it," I said. "Are you excited for tonight?"

"Tonight? I'm certain the wedding is tomorrow. The invitation clearly states, in full lettering, 'Sunday, November Fourth, Two Thousand Eighteen at half-past four o'clock in the afternoon.'"

"That's correct. The wedding is tomorrow," I sighed, rose, and took a glass from the drying rack next to the sink. "The rehearsal dinner is tonight."

"Rehearsal dinner..." he mumbled to himself. I filled my glass with filtered water straight from the fridge, a perk of modernity that Dave had to adjust to in his modern kitchen. I waited across the island from Brad as he struggled to make sense of the term. "I can't even guess," he said. "You rehearse the act of eating dinner? Or you eat dinner while rehearsing for a performance? Both sound absurd."

"The rehearsal dinner is pretty much a smaller, more informal wedding reception that takes place the night before the real wedding."

"Why does it exist?"

"I don't know."

"Who attends?"

"Too many people."

"What happens?"

"Everyone congratulates the bride and groom and gives speeches and gets drunk. It's the same as the wedding but without dancing."

"I see. And why does it exist?"

I'm sure many couples host modest, entirely satisfactory rehearsal dinners. They probably limit the guest list to the wedding party and immediate family with a handful of out-of-town guests. And I'll bet they find a small private room at a local haunt.

Our rehearsal wasn't like that. Ours could easily have replaced the actual wedding reception and nobody would have been any the wiser. Including me. How could I tell the difference after seeing the back-and-forth email exchanges between Alex and the potential venues, arguing about the size of the guest list, selecting bar packages and catering menus, picturing the new outfit Alex bought for the occasion, and answering endless questions from friends and family regarding logistics, dress codes, and all the other nonsense that accompanies wedding planning?

Traditionally, the groom's parents host the dinner, which meant my lovely mother would take charge of all the above headaches. But my lovely mother lives in an isolated corner of Southwestern Michigan, which doesn't make her an expert on downtown Austin BBQ joints. Alex and I stepped in to help with the planning, calling famous Texas BBQ hotspots like Stubbs[154] and Franklin Barbeque, only to find they'd been booked months earlier. The UT Longhorns had a home game that night, we were told time and again.

We booked the upstairs room at Lamberts Downtown BBQ. Great. All done. Easy, right?[155] Surely my lovely mother could take the reins now that we had our venue. My mother is—and I'll borrow a favorite phrase of hers—one sharp cookie. She knows, much like I know, that it's safer to confirm every detail with the bride than to make a decision and hope the bride approves after the fact. My mother—to borrow a favorite phrase from my mother-in-law—bless her heart, called us to confirm every decision surrounding the event.

Most of these decisions couldn't be made without a firm headcount. So who gets invited to a rehearsal dinner? The wedding party and their plus-ones brings our tally to 14. Add the immediate family and we're up to almost 30. Then there's the question of the out-of-town guests, which in our case meant nearly everybody. The parents, who demanded a handful of personal invites to extend for the wedding itself, insisted that those same invites serve as weekend passes. Aunts, uncles, cousins, and friends from Chicago would feel left out, so let's bring them into the mix. In the end, we had 76 of 100 wedding guests on our rehearsal invite list.

An exclusive, intimate affair.

Seventy-six also happened to be the maximum occupancy of the upstairs private room at Lamberts. This figure caused my lovely mother a great deal of stress, and no amount of "it'll be fine" could put her at ease.[156]

Our numbers outgrew the limit for table seating, which meant we'd have a buffet and one fewer decision to make. From there all we had to do was hold my lovely mother's hand as she asked about every item on the catering menu.

"Yes, brisket sounds great."

"Yes, mac and cheese sounds great."

"Yes, Mom, they all sound great."
"For the love of God just pick one."
She did. And it was fine.

PRACTICE MAKES PERFECT FOR EACH OTHER

All of life's most significant events require preparation. If you have a career-defining presentation at work, you run through the PowerPoint slides at home with your dog standing in for the Board of Directors. When the championship match approaches, you focus on the fundamentals and study game film all week. Every year, when the *Jeopardy!* online test registration email pops up in my inbox, I make sure to run through the practice questions. Whether it's work, school, athletics, or even game show qualifying exams, we take practice seriously. But a job is what you do, not who you are, sports are just a game, and I'm not smart enough for *Jeopardy!* When it comes to the most meaningful moments in life, none of these stack up against a wedding ceremony.

Despite this, I've never participated in a ceremony rehearsal that didn't feel like the last 10 minutes of class before summer vacation. Nobody pays attention, the teacher has totally checked out, and any portion of the lesson plan a student may accidentally absorb disappears the moment the bell rings.

It's strange, but with all the planning that goes into hiring a photo booth and picking out cutlery, we hardly practice at all for the part that's truly important. Perhaps that's due to the jovial attitude and overall conviviality of the wedding weekend. We're all here to have fun and celebrate, not to buckle down and learn our choreography.

There's not much to it, really. It's mostly a question of walking. Who walks, who they walk with, when they walk, how fast they walk, and where they should stand when they're done walking. Still, the rehearsal is as reliable a shit show as me eating at Chipotle. Returning to the last-day-of-class analogy, this comes down to the role of the teacher. In my experience, it's not often clear who runs the show during a rehearsal. The bride and groom look to the day-of planner, who looks to the venue coordinator, who looks to the DJ, who looks to the officiant, who, in our case, looked back at the bride and groom.

Imagine my surprise when, as the officiant for a buddy's wedding, I was met with a classroom full of wedding party members, pencils at the ready, waiting for my lecture to begin.

Luckily, it isn't rocket science. It isn't even pseudoscience. It's just knowing when to walk, where to stand, when to talk, and when to be quiet. It's an easy A, and there isn't even a final exam. There are exceptions to the standard lackadaisical atmosphere. You can do what my friend Al did and hire Nurse Ratched to plan your wedding and run the rehearsal.[157] Al's wedding planner took on 100 percent of the material in this book, and she took her job seriously. I've been in rehearsals that start with a party bus, hers started with a syllabus.

The good news is that none of it ends up making a difference. If the first bridesmaid and groomsman pairing walks too fast, and the third set starts down the aisle too quickly after the second, few guests will notice and none will care. When the flower girl misses her cue and goes the wrong way, it'll be a hit. Take a look at how the groomsmen and bridesmaids flank the happy couple the next time you attend a wedding. There's no chance they get the spacing right. The indifference of groomsmen will go shoulder-to-shoulder with no overlap at a 40 degree angle while the saccharine of bridesmaids stagger in front of one another, perfectly in line with the bride and groom. Half of the groomsman will stand with their hands behind their backs, one will have them in his pockets, one clasped in front like he needs to pee, and the rest will keep them at their sides holding invisible suitcases.

Bridesmaids, I've found, have an instinct for when to move the train and where to hold their bouquets. Of course, they can't practice those parts because the rehearsal isn't a dress rehearsal; they just know the drill by heart. That, or they have common sense and demonstrate an innate understanding of how to help one another.

You don't see a lot of that across the aisle, where any behavior can be forgiven so long as the best man hasn't lost the rings.

Mother Nature, like most mothers, can't help but cry at weddings. In our case, she was so overwhelmed by emotion that she cried her eyes out for the two weeks leading up to our wedding day. Her tears showered down on Austin in record-breaking precipitation. The deluge caused flooding at water treatment centers, which forced area health authorities to issue a boil notice. Locals were encouraged to boil tap water prior to consumption, and they only lifted the notice a day before we arrived. Thankfully, by the morning of our rehearsal, Mother Nature had dabbed her eyes dry, and we had nothing but sunshine all weekend.

Unlike most rehearsals, which take place in the evening immediately preceding the rehearsal dinner, we held ours earlier in the day. We wanted to use the actual ceremony site rather than run through the order of operations in a hotel conference room. It helps to orient yourself against landmarks at the site. Knowing that you'll stand one step to the left of a tree ensures you'll be in the right spot during the actual performance. We held the rehearsal early in the day because the Addison Grove had another wedding the night before ours. They warned us that it was imperative that we not disturb the bride of the day. God forbid we spoil the illusion that our weddings are any more special than diners at a restaurant, watched closely by the hostess who needs to turn tables in time for the next reservation.

Predictably, our rehearsal was a bit of a shit show. Nobody took charge, the flower girls pinballed between their parents' knees, amped up on their breakfast sugars, and when the time came to actually rehearse by running through the ceremony from the top, all those in attendance gave a collective, "Nah, we've got it."

Our friend Aaron, who we'd enlisted as our ceremony musician, didn't bring his guitar and had less-than-reassuring updates on whether he'd have all the audio equipment he'd need by the next day.

Both of my parents gave Oscar-worthy performances pretending not to have been told, several times, what role they'd play in the ceremony.[158]

One of the groomsmen stood with his back to the altar.

As the chaos unfolded and all hope for getting hitched without a hitch seemed lost, a sudden stillness settled in the air. Our nieces' ceased their giggling and the sunlight, which a moment prior had danced through the canopy of branches, stopped dancing, almost as though it shone down on Beaumont instead of

Austin.[159]

"So this is the spot?" Brad's voice carried down from the heavens. I looked skyward to find his four legs dangling from a limb of the live oak, the very tree beneath which I'd say "I do" the following evening.

"This is it," I smiled up at him. "What do you think?"

"I think you need more practice."

"Nah, we've got it."

"How can you be so calm?" He pointed to my groomsmen, the ones huddled in conversation instead of lined up silently, at just the right angle, with identical posture and hand positioning. "That one looks to be backwards."

I looked out at the tableau in front of me. Parents, siblings, friends, all smiling, all celebrating Alex and me.

"This is it, Brad." I finally figured it out. "This is what it's all about. The wedding is tomorrow, and we're all here now. We're done with worrying. Look around. They're all smiling. They'll keep smiling whether they walk when they're supposed to or not. They'll keep smiling if the chips are stale. They'll keep smiling if the band sucks, if the shuttles are late, and they'll keep smiling if the parking attendant hassles them about outside alcohol. They'll keep smiling because they're here. They're here for us. And we'll keep smiling, too."

I'll Speak Now, then Forever Hold My Peace

This isn't a book about my wedding. This is a book about planning my wedding.

We've reached the point of celebration, where we're no longer concerned with planning and ready to experience the wedding. I didn't set out to write about the wedding, but if you've made it this far it'd be a shame to deny you the satisfaction of an ending. God forbid my little tale of buying an engagement ring and falling asleep at a place that rents tablecloths doesn't tie up all the loose ends.

Should I end it like *The Sopranos* and cut you off now without any closure? Or do I borrow the cloying storyline of *Friends* and demand to know if Alex got off the plane in Austin? Nah, those aren't my style. Instead, I'll follow the *Seinfeld* template.

For those of you unfamiliar with the late 1990s television milestone, *Seinfeld* wrapped up with a two-part episode featuring the four lead characters on trial for breaking a small town's Good Samaritan Law. The prosecution called an ensemble cast of witnesses to speak to all the horrible acts the defendants committed during the previous 170 episodes. The sitcom treated viewers to a highlight reel of their favorite characters reprising their memorable catchphrases and Seinfeldisms.

Fans and critics felt the *Seinfeld* finale fell flat, but I liked it. It's nostalgic and it doesn't take itself too seriously. I want to say the same thing when I look back on this book. So while I walk you down the aisle of my memories, I'll try my best to trot out an ensemble cast of my own. My apologies to the red-faced dope of a Nordstrom salesman who thought he was done getting zinged.

What's the deal with weddings?

Our rehearsal dinner got off to a great start. At least, I assume it did since everyone was having a good time when we showed up 30 minutes late. My soon-to-be father in-law gave us a ride in his Camaro, but only after the final whistle of the Longhorns game.

While squeezing into the Camaro, I joked to Dave, "Aren't you glad your daughter found the one man in the country who can fit in the back of this car?" He laughed, so I suggested he borrow that line for his speech, promising I wouldn't take credit for the joke.[160]

The afternoon leading up to the rehearsal dinner was a strange time for me. Alex ran an errand, abandoning me in our overpriced and underwhelming hotel suite. The idea was for me to relax before the wedding weekend whirlwind. I tried to read, but couldn't focus. I tried to nap, but the only place I've napped in my adult life is the loveseat of the rental showroom. I was alone with my thoughts. Thoughts of public speaking. Thoughts of lifelong commitments. Thoughts of social anxiety.

My stomach picked up on these thoughts and intuited their portent. My stomach doesn't respond well to stress. In this case, it saw fit to fight fire with fire, matching the calm before the storm with a storm of its own. Well versed in this brand of intestinal insubordination, my brain anticipated the rogue, self-sabotaging behavior of its undersized and overactive organ and prepared for the situation by reminding me to pack 11 name-brand antidiarrheals. Once the acute effects kicked in, I could operate with the confidence of a healthy human being who doesn't live in fear that his body will commit BBQ betrayal.

With a layer of loperamide coating my stomach lining, and buoyed by the peace of mind it generates, I stood in front of the bathroom mirror ready to attack the day. I ran through my vows by memory, focusing on pacing, enunciation, and eye contact. For the better part of two months I'd mumbled these lines aloud while walking to and from the train, and the man in the mirror clearly knew them cold. Stress gave way to confidence.

That good feeling evaporated as I searched my toiletries bag[161] for shaving cream and came up empty. *Thanks a lot, Brain*, I thought at myself, turning the bag inside-out to no avail. *Did you think I could shave with Imodium?*

I don't have a thick beard. Give me two weeks and a natural chinstrap sprouts up, dark on the outsides with a tangerine-tinged blond goatee. A friend of mine likes to offer me the use of his credit card for shaving purposes. I don't totally understand the joke, but I get the gist of it. Even with a thin beard, taking four blades to my face without the aid of aloe-enriched lubricant is a prickly prospect. Add the fact that I was 24 hours away from the one time in my life I couldn't afford to show cuts and irritation, and the lack of shaving cream became a serious problem.

Most hotel patrons staying in the premier suite would think to call the front desk and have them run up a can of Barbasol. If you recall my experience with the South Congress, you'll understand why I put that thought out of my head. I opted for lathering up my cheeks with hand soap. A risky move, no doubt, but I got away with it.

I ran through the vows once more in the shower, and by the time I toweled off Alex had returned and Dave was on his way up to catch the fourth quarter. Dave's love for UT football wasn't the only passion of his to rekindle in the months leading up to the wedding. The anxiety and depression that plagued him for so long had lifted, revealing the badass cowboy accountant we'd all missed so dearly. He'd been physically present when I proposed at Heine Farms—standing by his trout pond on a Walmart Christmas tree skirt—and he'd be fully himself to give his daughter away. When I look back on my wedding, I won't just think of it as the day I got married, but also as the day of Dave's recovery, which makes the memory all the sweeter.

The rehearsal dinner was the first time we saw our guests in one place. That is, outside of the meticulously curated spreadsheet we filled out for the stationery shop. The collective group is easy to contain when they're represented as names typed out in 11-point font, neatly aligned in spreadsheet cells. Seeing them in the flesh delivered a bit of a shock, and one made worse by the fact that it was also the first time our guests got to see us, as they all wanted to see us right away.

Alex and I entered the upstairs private room of Lamberts BBQ unprepared for the celebrity status bestowed on the bride and groom. We were spared the paparazzi flashbulbs, but got a taste of Beatlemania as a sea of smiling faces and outstretched arms tried to pull us in for a hug, pat our backs, or shake our hands.

Women swooped in on Alex, their lips already forming the word "gorgeous" before she had a chance to show off her ring. I regretted not inviting my Old Jewish Diamond Guy. Thirty emails and two trips to his office later he'd have probably declined.

My brain, still bitter from my earlier Imodium/shaving cream zinger, refused to process the swarm of approaching stimuli and wouldn't communicate orders to my body. I responded to the throng of adoring guests by raising my arms in front of my face like a boxer on the defensive, pantomiming my bowling stance, staring down the lane over an imaginary 12-pound ball. This wasn't effective, as I felt someone awkwardly squeeze an elbow in greeting. Another hand landed on my shoulder from behind. I turned to the right to see whose body it connected with, but I'd been duped. A classic gag. As I swiveled left the culprit slid a cold bottle of Lone Star into my hand.

It was my friend Andy, who I'd known since the 2nd grade and had been a roommate of mine for four years before I moved in with Heine. A familiar face. A thoughtful gesture. I dropped the bowling ball, lowered my defenses, and calmly greeted my guests. Sometimes all you need to settle your nerves is two Imodium and a good friend to hand you a bad beer.[162]

"Thanks so much for coming," I shook hands with the first guest.

"Thanks so much for coming," I embraced the next.

"Thanks so much for coming," I said to everybody for the next 48 hours. It got to the point where I couldn't stop saying, "Thanks so much for coming." The flight attendant on the trip home didn't know what to make of it.

The rehearsal dinner never provides more value than the moment the unsolicited speeches begin. It's worth inviting more people to the rehearsal solely to give them a chance to tap the microphone and slur their way through an improvised toast. This way they can't justify doing it again at the reception.

There's no middle ground for the unscripted rehearsal dinner toast. It will either be a unanimous success or instantly forgettable, but almost always a disaster. To be clear, this statement doesn't include the planned rehearsal dinner speeches. When my non-best man brothers went up, they'd thought through their remarks. When Alex's mom took the stage, she clearly hadn't. Don't ask me how she got there, but her speech included a warning about the perils of spending a night in a Texas jail. She cemented her speech in the Unanimous Success column with this gem: "That top bunk is a real sunnuva bitch."

Last second inspiration struck Alex's brother, too. He took the stage without having taken notes. We'll certainly never forget his blessing on our marriage: "You guys have good heads on your shoulders. You'll probably last a lot of years."

Andy, my friend with the Lone Star, later confided that he planned to speak, but his opportunity was usurped by another buddy of ours. This friend is perhaps the king of unrehearsed off-the-cuff speeches.[163] I gave a speech at his rehearsal dinner, opening with a joke about how he would wing it if we swapped places. Boy oh boy, did he wing it. Whenever a speech veers into the childhood bullying committed by the best man, there's a good chance a line will be crossed. Here's a line that crossed the line: "I've known Sam since his brother Rick would hold us down and fart in our faces. Bare ass!"

The memory of his mother's face as he delivered that line never fails to elicit a smile.

These speeches can't be made at a wedding. They require an informal setting. And quite frankly, it's nice to give people a chance to hold the microphone, even when it's your uncle who wants to tell a very long story about his own wedding. Better here than the shabby chic barn.

While the cavalcade of unexpected orators stumbled through their half-baked anecdotes of Alex's and my childhoods, those halcyon days played out on the adjacent wall, projected in a slideshow of baby pictures and early '90s Halloween costumes. My dear, sweet mother is a sucker for slideshows. Nothing in her life has brought her more joy than her four sons, with the exception of narrating her four sons' bar mitzvah slideshows. So when she asked Alex to provide childhood photos for the rehearsal, I got on the phone immediately to make sure she understood the difference between running a slideshow of pictures on a loop in the background and gathering all in attendance to listen to her recite a series of corny captions. Once in a lifetime was embarrassing enough. She's such a mom.

After my friend had adequately warmed up the crowd I took the microphone and invited my groomsmen to join me for the presentation of their groomsman gifts. The bride and groom aren't merely required to purchase day-of gifts for one another, but also, the wedding industry demands we purchase gifts for the wedding party. My brother Andy gifted his groomsmen a golf club. My brother Rick gifted his groomsmen a bag of golf tees. Much like engagement diamonds, there are heuristics for setting a budget for these gifts based on one's salary.

I purchased my gifts months in advance, ordering them from an artisan in Western Australia. In the spirit of bringing together Alex's and my cultural backgrounds, I presented my indifference of groomsmen with Star of David bolo ties.

The crowd went meshuga.

Gift rating: ✡ ✡ ✡ ✡ ✡

The rest of the night passed in a series of anonymous schmoozing and "thanks so much for coming." Did I have to pretend to recognize a few guests? Sure. Did everybody's clothes reek of BBQ for the rest of the weekend? You bet. Did the rehearsal prepare me for the real thing? I'd find out soon enough.

Tradition dictates that the bride and groom not see each other on their wedding day prior to the ceremony. I know couples who, while not strictly adhering to this antiquated practice, still pay homage to it by sleeping in separate rooms on the eve of their big day. The tradition must predate photography. In the age of capturing the moment, tight schedules often call for the bride and groom to spend an hour saying "cheese" before they say "I do."

I had no intention of finding alternative lodging after the rehearsal dinner. For what we paid for our suite, you better believe I'd be sleeping in it. How long Alex permitted me to stay in our room after waking up is another story. By the time I finished serenading her with a wedding-day parody of "This is Halloween" from *The Nightmare Before Christmas*, I had mere minutes to grab my suit and clear out. Alex's bridesmaids were on their way for a full slate of beautification treatments as foreign to me as they were to Brad.

At 9:00 am on my wedding day I walked up South Congress Ave. in a white undershirt and flip flops, a 36 short suit slung over my shoulder, on my way to watch cartoons with my nieces. I spent the next hour nursing a short Starbucks coffee—my jittering hand caused about half its contents to dribble onto my shirt—and learning about grey whales and sea snakes from the *Octonauts* crew. My family took me out to breakfast to calm my nerves, only to seat me in the corner and treat me as though I had a perfect game going through 7 innings. Isolated against the wall and pinned on both sides by 4-year-olds, I had no outlet for stress relief other than incessantly folding and unfolding a plastic straw. If only the fidget spinner craze had held on another year.

I ate nothing.

I said nothing.

I thought about the fragile state of my psyche and how it mirrored the fragility of a beached sea snake.[164]

"Are you nervous?" My brother Dan asked from the driver's side captain's seat of our minivan Uber. As the youngest of four brothers my childhood car trips were spent in the back row of a Nissan Quest. Seniority prevailed, and the captain's seat was a rare treat for lil' Sam. On the way to my wedding, upgrading to the middle row of our Uber, I took my first baby step out of childhood toward sitting shotgun in the adult life that awaited me as a married man.

"Huh?" I said, huddled over my phone to check on early Sunday action for my fantasy football roster.[165]

"Are you nervous?" He repeated.

"Not really," I said. And it's true, I wasn't nervous. By hosting an enormous rehearsal dinner I'd escaped most of the wedding-day jitters. I'd already thanked everyone so much for coming. I'd already survived public speaking. I'd already taken Imodium and successfully shaved with hand soap. I'd already realized that I could get away with anything because everyone was so deeply entrenched on my side.

We arrived at the venue with a few hours to kill until show time. I played a few games of cornhole and sat around watching football with my brothers. I even cracked a beer. If the groom's room had an in-unit washer and dryer, it would have been indistinguishable from a routine Sunday. The Vista West Bunkhouse probably had a laundry room, but we made do with the Addison Grove accommodations.

The photographer stopped in to snap candid shots of our fraternal rituals and gave me a 30-minute warning for the "first look." I'd finally lay eyes on Heine's wedding dress. But first I had to dress myself. I donned the infamous 36 short. It fit perfectly. I may not have struck a silhouette as traditional as what Rueben had envisioned with his 36 regular, but I thought I looked damn good. I felt ready, so I dispatched my best man to the bridal cottage to see if Alex did, too.

My wedding day was much more stressful for Rick than it was for me. He travelled to Texas with a five-month-old infant in tow, and if that didn't create enough challenges, all that parenting ate into the time he needed to write and rehearse his best man's speech. He spent most of the weekend pleading with me to ghostwrite his material. To make matters worse, he had no choice but to suffer through direct interactions with my friends' parents, the very same friends who'd returned from playdates at our house 20 years earlier complaining about how Sam's brother had farted in their faces.[166]

Rick returned from the fact finding mission at the bridal cottage shaken, a glossy look in his eyes.

"Are they ready for me?" I asked.

"My bowtie isn't good enough," Rick said. He scanned the faces in the room. "She wants all of the bowties to look better than mine."

I didn't send my groomsmen to Men's Warehouse to rent matching suits. Having suffered through that ordeal myself,[167] I knew they'd appreciate a more relaxed dress code. I told them that my suit would be dark grey and that they could wear any grey suit in a lighter shade than mine. I even sent them a picture of my suit for reference. My best man demonstrated the trademark indifference of a groomsman, ignoring the instructions and showing up with a suit several shades darker than my own. A sloppy bowtie knot may not look good, but at least it drew Heine's attention away from the rest of his wardrobe.

The wedding gods aren't without a sense of humor. For hours they lured me into a false state of comfort, allowing me to believe that, finally, on my wedding day, with nothing to do but watch football and drink beer, things would be easy.[168] Somehow, among the entire wedding party, I, the man with no sense of style whatsoever, had the most experience and skill with bowties. Tying a bowtie, something I'd practiced with the aid of Youtube videos and a mirror in the preceding months, is tricky enough when the tie is wrapped around my own neck. The task became a true test of dexterity and focus when performing it face-to-face with a squirming adult who'd just polished off his third IPA.

No longer tied up with bowties, I left the groom's room and found our photographer, who posed me in the grass with my back to the bride's cottage. I stood in the shade with my hands clasped behind my back, waiting for Heine to tap me on the shoulder. These moments of anticipation lend themselves to panic. While standing on the Christmas tree skirt at Heine Farms, my mind raced with thoughts of rejection. Here, my thought engine revved anew with imaginary worst-case scenarios. *What if I hate the dress? What if, in the first look photos, it's obvious that I'm faking my surprise and amazement? I'd immortalize my disapproval and insincerity. I could "accidentally" turn away from the camera so there'd be no visual evidence of my reaction. I could pretend to sneeze right as—*

Alex's finger on my shoulder brought me back to reality.

I turned towards the camera. It's a good thing I did.

I had never seen a wedding dress like Alex's before in my life. I doubt I ever will again. Like her engagement ring, her dress is fundamentally different from 95 percent of wedding dresses.

It's blue. Not dusk or rain or oyster blue. Just normal, light blue.

Five months earlier, when Vivan remarked at the rental showroom that a certain piece of glassware matched Alex's dress, I assumed she meant there was a shared textural element. I was wrong. I never would have guessed she meant the color. Most grooms turn around and find their brides in a white dress. They say, "Wow. You look beautiful," because they're supposed to and probably because they mean it. My first look reaction is best captured by Bugs Bunny. My eyes transformed into thumping hearts and my jaw fell three feet. Unfortunately, I lack the intrinsic knowledge to accurately describe the look and material of a wedding dress. The good news is my wife has this memorized and I have great access to her.

"The dress had three layers. The first was 100 percent silk double face satin. Then 100 percent silk hand-painted organza. Then a layer of tulle."

"Got it. And the top?"

"The top was A-line cut, exposed back, silk with lace topper."

"Got it. And was it beige or oyster?"

"It was ivory." I rolled my eyes. "Fine. It was white."

Once the once-over was over, Alex returned to the cottage and I retreated to the groom's room. I ran through my vows one last time to make sure I still had them down. My memory was a steel trap. I made the final unmarried bathroom run of my life for a last-minute nervous urination and discovered that, thanks to Imodium, my memory wasn't the only steel trap in town.

The guests arrived. Some came in a shuttle, the rest in Uber Black Cars that cost me the same price as a shuttle. Somehow, without any made-to-order custom signage, they all found their way to the ceremony area to take their seats. That was my cue to join Heine, the parents, and the wedding party in the bridal cottage, where we milled about with nervous energy until the guests settled in. I distinctly remember shaking my arms to release the tension. The day-of coordinator lined us up at the door, in pairs, and asked if we remembered where to walk, when to walk, how fast to walk, and when to stop walking.

If only we'd rehearsed this.

The indistinct chatter of our closest friends and family (and Henry) wafted our way from the ceremony site, our friend strummed away at his acoustic guitar, and Alex's brother-in-law took Vivian by the arm and started down the path. Just like that, what started with Alex showing me Regina's jewelry website had evolved into this moment. Our wedding was off and running.

The walk from the cottage to the altar measured about 100 yards. This distance allowed my father ample time to make light of the formality of weddings. "Look at those cows, Sam," he said, walking on my right. "Do you remember your cousin's college essay about cows. How did it go? He wanted to be a cow? Or his professor was a cow?"

"Hey Dad," I said. "I've got Mom crying on my other arm right now. Can we talk about it later?"

We made our way up the aisle amidst the smiling faces of our carefully curated guest list. The book club ladies dabbed at weepy eyes. The impossible combination of women from the bridal shower suddenly all made sense. The bachelor party attendees each looked on with a clean conscience, as my status as a Not Strip Club Guy left us with no post-debauchery shame. Somehow, my cousin got a hold of a Jewish star bolo tie and wore it to the ceremony.

I bid farewell to my parents when we reached the altar and embraced Scott, who, in the months between accepting the role of officiant and standing at the end of the aisle, eventually came to terms with the fact that we chose him, of all people, to be a part of the ceremony.[169]

Two-by-two, the wedding party strolled down the path and took up their posts. As adults, they proved competent and reliable at walking at the right speed to the right place at the right time. The flower girls were not adults, which means they are far less reliable but infinitely cuter. If we wanted flower petals laid out in uniform patterns and straight lines, we'd have assigned the task to my cousin, the one who wanted a cow as a roommate at Yale. I'm glad we picked the little girls, who were far more adorable than cousin Brian and didn't throw any petals into the grass, though we'd already established that petals don't contribute to a $500 confetti fee.

Once the grandparents corralled the flower girls, the guests' collective attention turned toward the bridal cottage. The music changed. The guests rose to their feet. And there she was, escorted by Brave Dave, not just the bride of the day but the bride of my life. That twentysomething bespectacled short-haired girl who drank Wild Turkey 101 and refused to lose at Mario Kart. The girl who thought Abigail Adams designed the U.S. flag. The girl whose ring is unlike any other in the world. The girl in a blue wedding dress.

She carried a Texas-sized bouquet, and the thistle looked nothing like the Night King's army of the dead. Tucked securely between the protea and the peonies was a gift with Mona's face on it. There was no pink, but there may have been some pink that wasn't so pink that it was pink.

Scott gave his spiel. I remember almost none of it. Alex read her vows, in which she praised my laundry skills. She handed me the mic and I ad libbed a joke about how my vows would seem inappropriately heavy on the jokes after hearing her vows. I then delivered my joke-heavy vows. Later, Alex told me that I looked insane, staring at her with murderous intensity as I focused too hard on pacing and enunciating from memory.

She slid a white gold wedding band onto my finger.

I slid one of her three asymmetrical, possibly raised, vintagey wedding rings onto her finger.

I do. I do. We did.

We kissed. They cheered. I stomped on the glass.

Man and wife.

Easy.

DINNER AND REVELRY TO FOLLOW

While the guests made their way to the cocktail area for signature drinks and guacamole, Alex and I enjoyed a restful photoshoot. The day-of-planner shuffled relatives along the conveyor belt, sliding them into frame just long enough to snap a keepsake that they'd likely never see before ushering them off as the next set took their place.

"Now just Alex's parents." The photographer said, not bothering to take her eye from the aperture.

"Now Alex's parents with just Alex."

"Now Alex's parents with just Sam."

"Now Alex's parents with Sam's uncles."

"Now all we need is Sam's uncles with Alex's nieces and we're all done!"

Two photo albums later, we'd captured all the possible combinations of our big crazy family. Meanwhile, back at the cocktail hour, a glob of queso got snagged by a member of my other big crazy family's ZZ Top beard. I'm pleased to report that Tiffany tittered her way to the kitchen and successfully communicated Heine's demand for a new queso recipe.

I'm also pleased to report that the parking attendant performed a duty beyond his job description of narcing on outside booze and changing light bulbs. While our guests lined up beside the fence to take selfies with the longhorns, the parking attendant dropped off a bag of feed pellets. Was it worth $400? Who knows? It may have been premium quality feed.

Alex and I performed a quick round of "thanks so much for coming" at the cocktail hour before guests were herded away from the cattle and into the shabby chic barn. The day-of coordinator then whisked us toward the front door, where we'd wait to make our grand entrance and go straight into our first dance.

We planned to walk in with Chuck Berry's "You Never Can Tell" playing. Despite our combined age of 59 years the moment we stormed the barn, we could both pass as teenagers and we wanted the old folks to wish us well. Unfortunately, the song didn't play, and throughout the evening we'd corroborate the online reviews of the B Sharps. The band sounded great, but whoever managed them, and the iPod hook up, was consistently out of tune.

After our dance, I thanked everyone so much for coming. I then thanked Alex for planning our wedding. Somehow, she'd manage to make all of it a reality without the aid of a Magic Wedding 3000.

It's a good thing we had the crossword puzzles at every place setting. I don't know what else our guests would have done to amuse themselves during the mother-son and father-daughter dances.

By the time Alex and I sat down our guests couldn't wait to stand up and Cha Cha Slide onto the dancefloor. Unfortunately, they had speeches to endure.

My father has four sons. One of them got married, at which point he had four sons and a daughter-in-law. A few years later, another of his sons tied the knot. He gave a speech that night, proclaiming, "I'm so glad to finally have a daughter." This was a "welcome to the family" moment for his existing daughter-in-law. With such a proud history of exemplary oration, we steeled ourselves as my father took the microphone. He spoke for about 10 minutes and miraculously kept his feet out of his mouth. I remember two components of his speech. First, he falsely credited one of my friends for introducing Alex and me, claiming his friendship with Heine during their college years at Boulder was the reason we were all in attendance that night. The friend in question went to college in Illinois. Second, he listed the opponents from the classic NES video boxing game *Mike Tyson's Punch Out*, a game I'm not sure I've ever played.[170]

Brave Dave Heine was next to take the stage. He made a killer joke about me fitting in the back of his Camaro, went extra heavy on the Texas accent, used the term "head of cattle" to amuse the Northerners, and handed off the mic in fewer than 60 seconds without putting a hoof in his mouth.

Allison, the maid of honor, wept through her prepared remarks and cleared the way for Rick to stumble through his unprepared remarks. My brother must have skipped the chapter from *The Best Man's Duties* on brevity, as he did his papa proud, clocking in at 11:26. Maybe it's genetic.

A member of the catering staff delivered dinner to Alex and me while her colleagues set up the taco buffet. Much like the tasting at the caterer's kitchen five months earlier, we had far too much food in front of us. Unlike our tasting session, I didn't try to finish it. The adrenaline flowing through me masked my appetite, but I have it on good authority from some guest gourmets that the Way too Much Pork was a better selection than the Greasy Beef for Fifteen.

The band never played the Cha Cha Slide, but that didn't stop everyone from tearing it up on the dance floor. Alex and I moved in and out of the mob. Wherever we went people lit up with excitement, blessed by our presence. We moved from table to table, accepting praise for throwing such a swell party. We passed the entryway table, where the arrangement of family photos and bud vases matched the practice-arrangement Alex made on Allison's kitchen table two days earlier.

Beside the photos, on another piece of rented furniture, next to the vase of river rocks and Heine's bouquet, our guestbook lay open to a half-signed page. Beside it, I noticed the new, $30 scotch tape dispenser Alex purchased for guests to adhere their photo booth prints alongside their notes. *What a steal*, I thought, demonstrating how numb I'd become to the excess spending required to get the details just right. Our guests had signed the book and composed brief notes of gratitude and best wishes, but something was missing. Where were the photo booth pics?

Our victory lap around the venue entered the final furlong, and there we discovered a profusely sweating photo booth operator fumbling with a piece of hardware. MQ stood over his shoulder, shaking his head in comic condescension. MQ would continue to casually stroll by the inept photo booth operator to cast disapproving glares and provide status reports. These actions made the worst part of the evening into a hilarious memory for Alex and me. We may not have any quality photo booth pics in our guestbook, but we have mental images of Mike standing behind a flustered employee with his arms crossed over his chest, emanating disapproval to entertain his friends.

The wedding flew by, as time tends to do when fun's being had. One moment Aaron, the ceremony guitarist, had coaxed his way onto the stage to step in as lead guitar and vocals for a tune,[171] the next minute Fetty Wop's "Trap Queen" brought an exhausted crowd back to its feet for a much-needed second wind. We'd all need our energy for the hora.

I grew up in a largely Jewish community. As such, as a 13-year-old, I attended a bar or bat mitzvah most weekends. By the end of that year, my friends and I could dance the hora in our sleep. Circle left, circle right, arms up to the middle, arms down to the outside, repeat. Dancing the hora, I've found, is not like riding a bike. These days, though I dance the hora with largely the same group of people, we do so far less frequently and with far less fluency. It's like when an old TV show has a reboot. The same actors return to the same sets to play the same characters, but it's hard to not focus on how everyone looks older. It just isn't the same. Throw in a few Texans who have no idea why the Jews tried to reinvent line dancing, and you've got our wedding hora.

When the emcee calls for "a few strong young men" to perform the heavy lifting in the hora, he often means it. I've hoisted a chair leg and struggled to bear the weight of a hefty groom or two in my day. For Alex and I, one strong young man per chair would do the trick. It was an easy day at the office for those enlisted to raise us up and down. Me sitting in the hora chair is like a bald man sitting in the barber's chair.

Safely returned to terra firma, Alex and I clutched at our stomachs. Was it nausea? The hora is the carnival ride of Jewish traditions[172], so a little queasiness is understandable. No, it was hunger. It was high time for pie time.

When I asked Alex what she remembers most about

our wedding reception, she said, "The pies." I've attended cake weddings, and I've attended donut weddings. They're all well and good, if you're into that sort of thing. If you're reading this book as part of your own wedding planning experience, I hope it's not too late to cut the cake and embrace the joy of hosting a pie wedding. Remember, memory is closely tied to smell. The scent of 16 fresh-baked pies isn't easily forgotten.

It was cruel, but we teased our guests with the promise of pie. A line of eager guests followed their noses, lured by the olfactory siren of the pie table. The vultures circled patiently as Alex and I performed the traditional four-handed slice of matrimonial dessert. They bit their tongues behind closed-mouth smiles as Alex force fed me a forkful of fruity filling and flaky crust. We set down our plates and stepped back, clearing space for the feeding frenzy to begin. But it didn't. The pies disappeared back to the kitchen for the catering staff to cut into single servings. This was, for the congregation of pie lovers, a devastating moment. I can still picture the look of dejection and disillusionment on cousin Brian's face.

Not long after dessert, the bartenders announced last call, the band finished their final set, and all that remained was for Alex and I to make our grand exit. Our contract required the entire venue to be cleared of trash, broken photo booth hardware, photo arrangements, rental furniture, and humans in one hour's time. But there's always time for one last photo op.

Much like the preceding hundreds of minutes, the final minute of our wedding would not be left to chance. Simply walking out of the venue whilst showered in cheers from our loved ones sounds like a once-in-a-lifetime moment to me, but I'm a simple boy from the Midwest. In Texas, you learn to think big. Alex thought big, and to this day I have a box of leftover sparklers to prove it.

Our friends and family, lit sparklers in hand, waved us into our future as we strolled toward the infamous 1949 Plymouth and the lifetime of bliss waiting at the other end of a 45-minute Texas drive. The costumed chauffeur opened the rear door and we climbed in. We slouched on the single bench and drew a deep breath.

I never wanted to get married. I wanted to be married. Sitting in the Packard with Alex's hand in mine, I had everything I wanted, and I knew that I always would.

HAPPILY EVER AFTERWORD

I pressed my key card against the sensor and the indicator on the lock flashed green. "I went a little nuts," I called into the Milton Suite. Ice cubes clattered in the plastic cups of cold brew I clutched between my ribcage and forearm. In my other hand I grasped a paper bag, weighed down by 4,000 calories of breakfast tacos, its base weakened by a metastasizing stain of leaking grease. I shouldered my way in, kicked the door shut with the back of my heel, evaded the bump in the carpet, and deposited our post-wedding breakfast onto the coffee table. "I spent as much on tacos for two this morning as we did on tacos for 100 last night," I said over my shoulder. No answer came from the bedroom.

Normally, when Torchy's Tacos are involved, Heine comes-a-runnin'.

"Heine?" I called through a mouthful of migas.

From the bathroom, a voice entirely different than my wife's replied, "What am I looking at?"

Brad! I raced to the bathroom and found my alien pupil standing at the counter, head down in deep concentration. He beckoned me with a wave, not bothering to turn from what captivated his attention. In the mirror, his dark hair fell over the bulbous northern hemisphere of his skull, blocking my view of his face.

"There are so many," he said. I glanced down and chuckled.

"67, to be exact."

"What are they?"

"Hairpins. They are called hairpins. Alex wore them in her hair to keep every follicle in place."

Brad ran his fingers through his bowl cut. "Does that mean my follicles are out of place?"

I slung my arm around Brad's shoulder and led him away from the bathroom. "Why don't we sit down for a taco and I'll try to explain."

Back at the coffee table, Brad told me how he'd made use of his vaguely defined omnipresence to attend the wedding. I answered his questions as best I could, trying not to lose my cool when he inquired about the purpose of the parking attendant. I told him how Alex and I excused ourselves from the lobby bar in the wee hours of the morning and called it a night. Never one for clichés, Alex didn't insist that I carry her over the threshold to the bedroom, preferring I follow her to the bathroom to remove 67 pins from her hair.

"And that's all there is to it," I said. The look of disbelief on Brad's face told me he was better off not knowing about thank you notes, name changes, or IRS joint filing. "Are you satisfied with your lesson on human marriage and wedding traditions?"

"Wow." He said, propping all four legs onto the coffee table and leaning back against the duct-taped cushion. "Yes. Very satisfied. I never could have sorted through all of the required steps necessary for humans to wed. It is a remarkable evolutionary condition that falling in love triggers an instinct to perform such detailed practices."

"I wouldn't say that."

"You don't find it remarkable?"

"No, it is. But it's not exactly required."

"What do you mean? What isn't required?"

"Any of it, really."

"But when you fall in love, you have a wedding and

get married and have children. This is the way of humanity."

"Yes, but you can have children without being married, you can get married without having a wedding, and you can fall in love and choose not to get married. None of it is required."

Brad opened his mouth, put his feet down, and leaned forward, dumbstruck.

"And weddings don't need to be elaborate," I continued. "It's all optional. It's not like we're salmon spawning up river. We choose to do it." I balled up the aluminum foil from taco number two and sipped my iced coffee. "You look confused. What's on your mind?"

"You're telling me that you and Alex could be together," he extended his arms and mimed an alligator chomping it's teeth in some misguided attempt at human gesticulating, "without photo booths and suit shopping and venue trips and diamond rings?"

"Yep."

He stared at me and shook his head. My alien friend frowned and rose to his four feet. He went out onto the balcony and stared at the frozen traffic stretching down South Congress Ave.

"I'll never understand humans," he said.

And in a flash, he was gone.

I didn't realize it at the time, but months ago, while explaining to Brad why humans keep dogs as pets, I'd stumbled upon the perfect analogy for weddings. There are a million reasons not to get a dog. They smell, they shed, they get dirty. You have to walk them. You have to board them when you go out of town. You have to feed them and train them and buy them medicine. It's a full-time job to take care of an animal, yet when my friends ask if they should get a dog, I say yes.

The reason? Having a dog is the best. You will love your dog, and your dog will love you. I'm not wise enough to say with certainty what life is about, but striving to have as much love in your life as possible strikes me as a pretty good guess. So get a dog.

There are a million reasons not to have a big wedding, too. It takes forever to plan, it costs a fortune, you have to buy a dress that you'll never wear again. You have to go behind the caterer's back to confront her boss and insist on the availability of strawberry rhubarb pie. You have to invite Henry. It's a full time job to plan a big wedding, yet when my friends ask me if they should have a big wedding, I say yes.

The reason? Having a wedding is a blast. Even if it's just for one night, their wedding will bring more love into their lives. And regardless of my advice, they're probably going to have a big wedding anyway, so why not enjoy it?

So you're going to get married and you're going to have a wedding. What next? When Alex and I first announced our engagement, I couldn't believe how often our friends and family gave us the same advice: don't worry about the details. Nobody notices, they said. You won't remember half of them, they said. Perhaps that's true for me, but Alex notices, and Alex remembers. Yesterday, I asked her if she'd change anything about the wedding. Without hesitating, she said, "I'd have bought smaller candles that would have fit in the votives and gotten a different photo booth." Trust me, she remembers.[173]

Here's my advice:

Don't write a book about planning your wedding. I

wrote this book in disjointed 20-to-30-minute sessions at 6:30 in the morning before going to work. It doesn't matter which side of the bed you wake up on when you spend the first half hour of the day thinking about stressful tasks and superfluous spending. It's hard to forget the parking attendant when you're writing about him for two years. It's bad for your blood pressure. Don't do it. Plus, my book already exists and I don't want you siphoning off my sales.

Other than that, I'm not any more qualified to give advice than the next guy. Remember, I'm not an expert on weddings. I'm not even the authority on my own wedding. I fully anticipate Alex will read the first draft of this book and tell me that I'm way off on most of the details. This next piece of advice is the best I've got.

Don't listen to people's advice. Newlywed couples warned us against almost everything. We were advised not to invite too many people, not to invite too few people, not to splurge on a band, not to rent anything unnecessary. The list goes on. At a certain point we agreed that we'd be better off ignoring everyone and making our own decisions. That meant making our own mistakes. We're okay with that. I'd rather regret having the '49 Plymouth drive me home than regret not having the '49 Plymouth drive Alex home. Making your own mistakes is the only way to truly learn from them. If 100 people tell you not to try a shot of Malört, you still have to taste it for yourself. Otherwise you aren't experiencing life.

The wedding isn't for your guests. Who cares if they remember? It's not their wedding; they aren't supposed to remember. I can't tell you about my sister-in-law's wedding dress. I don't know what the food was like at that wedding, or what color napkin I used. I don't remember and she doesn't care that I don't remember. Make decisions to please yourself, not the plus-ones.

The "it's not about the guests" mentality should remain top of mind for guests, too. Getting married made me a better wedding guest the same way working in restaurants made me a more conscientious and patient diner. For example, I will never again bother a bride or groom with questions about the dress code. My uncle texted me one week before the ceremony asking if he should wear a sport coat or a suit. If you are important enough that your outfit is of consequence, then the bride will likely have provided you instructions with more than one week's notice. If you have to ask, then you don't need to know. Wear pants and long sleeves, stand in the back, and it'll be okay.

I'm glad Alex and I[174] planned the wedding ourselves. I don't think we would have enjoyed it as much had we hired a planner to do the heavy lifting and make all the decisions. The more challenging the journey the sweeter the destination, so don't lose hope when your eyes dart back and forth between dual monitors, conducting a side-by-side comparison of identical photo booths. As long as you don't pick the one we did, all the work will pay off.

Is the wedding industrial complex a good thing? I'm not sure. Our culture glorifies weddings for the sake of its own profits, but if it makes people happy, then can it be all that bad? We romanticize weddings the same way we idolize rock stars or brand athletes as heroes. We know someone is on the other side raking in cash, but we want to feel a part of something bigger than ourselves. The danger is in the expectation, the acceptance that this is how weddings *should* be. The only thing your wedding should be is whatever you want it to be. That could mean a shabby chic barn, a backyard pizza party, or the top floor of the Empire State Building. Will I judge you if it's different from what I want? Maybe, but who cares what I think? It's not about me.

Planning a wedding is an exercise in disillusionment. Not only do you see how the sausage is made, but you see that the factory employees are churning out hundreds of sausages just like yours every day. Earlier in this book I said that your wedding isn't special. That isn't true. Your wedding may not be special to the catering staff or the day-of planner, but it is special to you. That's all that matters.

The guests don't matter.
The vendors don't matter.
Only the two of you matter.

Don't compromise on anything for anybody. Do it your way and enjoy it as much as you can.

That's all I got for you. If you need any other tips, ask my wife. She's right here on the couch, laying next to Mona, in position A, in our cozy little world *of being married.*

[1] This is the schtick. If you aren't ready for wordplay and an incredulous curmudgeon whining about how expensive everything is, you should probably stop reading. Don't return the book, though.

[2] Also, there are footnotes.

[3] I should have warned you, but about 8% of this book will be fiction.

[4] It took 20 minutes and a painful demonstration to explain the jump rope I bought on Amazon. It didn't take nearly as long to change the subject when Brad asked when I last used it.

[5] When this manuscript is finished, Apple will have unveiled the iPhone 12.

[6] The shape of a diamond.

[7] So far so good. My ring finger still has a ring despite substantial gnawing.

[8] Tuesdays and Thursdays from 2-3:20, ADV 412 - Classic Campaigns.

[9] At time of drafting, we are four days away from my first venture into Moana for Alex's 29th.

[10] In retrospect, it was Mona's birthday!

[11] Purchased by an ex-girlfriend

[12] Purchased by an ex-girlfriend

[13] She was right. They are disgusting.

[14] Empty space? Asymmetrical?

[15] Adjusting to life with a ring follows the same timetable as adjusting to life after having wisdom teeth removed. On the first day you think you'll never regain confidence chewing solid food, but after a month you're chomping into Fuji apples without a second thought. Four weeks after the wedding, the ring became a natural extension of my body.

[16] Possibly Raised? Exterior Stones?

[17] Nothing is easy.

[18] Those of you who work in finance are thinking, "They make stones that small?"

[19] A year later, eight days before the wedding, we'd win this tournament.

[20] Zing!

[21] Just like Heine!

[22] It shouldn't. It should be raised and asymmetrical with empty space.

[23] The table is the length of a diamond's top side, the size of the plateau. I will know this for the rest of my life, and Regina could only name three of the four Cs.

[24] My old roommates, childhood friends who'd grown into adulthood friends, held to their childlike love of drinking games while also developing responsible domestic behaviors. As a result, they kept an old IKEA table top on hand to use as a playing surface during alcohol-fueled tests of coordination, thus protecting the negligibly cleaner IKEA table top below. Heine and I didn't have much use for such methodology, but the point is, there's a time and place for affordable and replaceable IKEA furniture.

[25] It'd be a few years before we learned the terrifying truth behind how the Astros hit all those dingers.

[26] She still has the 3D printed model, presumably kept in the same box where she keeps old birthday cards and save the dates from other people's weddings.

[27] I'm not making this up. He actually said that.

[28] "Right in my wheelhouse" is the type of phrase I taught myself to avoid using around Brad, as "what's a wheelhouse?" is a question I'm not able to answer.

[29] With the exception of me loving Wing Bowl, the annual gathering of my friends in which we all provide buffalo wings from different restaurants throughout Chicago and gamble like degenerates on the NFL's conference championship games.

[30] No pun intended, though I think on a subconscious level all of my puns are intended.

[31] Christmas Eve, if you prefer Christianity to *Seinfeld*.

[32] Goobers.

[33] Or, if you don't have a ring handy, fall down a mountain and have a near-death experience.

[34] Sort of like how I forced this "force" pun.

[35] Nothing is easy.

[36] A couple years earlier, during a visit to Texas, I snuck out with the boys to grab some beers and shoot pool. Between games, Dave Heine admired our group and addressed Zach, Clint, and I with a paternal air. "I'm just glad to be here spending time with my son," he nodded to Zach, "my son-in-law," he nodded to Clint, "and..." he turned to me, "and what are you, and when are you going to be it?"

[37] Nothing is easy.

[38] The only difference is she knew we'd get married, and I know I'll never get to sneak out to golf on vacation.

[39] Nothing is easy.

[40] Nothing is easy.

[41] Yet another tradition Brad would struggle to comprehend.

[42] I think Groom's Quarters is a real term, though it's plausible I made it up.

[43] I hope the mayor of Wimberley reads that and adopts it as a new slogan.

[44] Yes, that's the name of the town the Simpsons move to when Homer works for Hank Scorpio.

[45] Alex likes queso, and Vivian was ready.

[46] "Gorgeous!"

[47] Nothing is easy.

[48] We attended a big high school.

[49] You probably figured this out by now.

[50] Remember when I said I couldn't pass up a bad joke?

[51] Don't worry, this isn't the start of a metaphor for "putting the pieces together."

[52] Somehow, I obliged the high school girls but insisted on his invite to my future wife.

[53] Except for Henry.

[54] Nothing is easy.

[55] One of these guys is in my book club.

[56] I joke, but this would actually be extremely useful content.

[57] Update: I crushed it.

[58] No pressure, Dan.

[59] Another homonym!

[60] Homonyms!

[61] He completed the journey, and likely still has the tan lines to prove it.

[62] Pun intended. Unnecessary word play is my strong suit.

[63] I warned you that my 45 minute jokes weren't funny.

[64] Nothing is easy.

[65] I've always coveted the billy club. Reuben keeps it in the backseat of his car, just in case.

[66] Nothing is easy.

[67] Butterflies already have dibs on this.

[68] Until the elevator button switches from B to G, it's the Basement.

[69] Nothing is easy-peasy lemon squeezy.

[70] Not all that impressive an accomplishment given my metabolism.

[71] See what I mean about the 45 minute shtick?

[72] Fasting.

[73] *The Chocolate End of the Spectrum* would be a good title for my memoir. That, or *God Bless Alex Heine*.

[74] This is a way better phrase than Montezuma's Revenge.

[75] Alex took a picture of me sleeping on that loveseat. It is my favorite picture of me.

[76] "But as for me and my house, we will serve the Lord." I wonder if my crazy new family will join me in fasting on Yom Kippur.

[77] I hope you appreciate these ZZ Top lyric jokes, as they were totally lost on Heine.

[78] It didn't.

[79] Low Bs on Southwest.

[80] First of all, I wrote this section when America was swept up in Jon Snow Fever around the time of the series finale, so forgive me if it's dated. Second, I didn't read the books, so leave me alone if this isn't totally accurate. Also, who reads books? Nerd! Third, the original idea was to match flowers to characters from *The Wire*, that way I could use one

that wasn't at the wedding, match it to Wallace, and write "Where's Wallace?"

[81] Sweet on the outside. Poison on the inside.

[82] A substantial percentage of this book was written at 6:30 am while cinched into these shorts.

[83] Nothing is easy.

[84] Nothing is easy.

[85] Do these exist? Quick Internet search says they do, and they are sweet. Think of Darth Maul's lightsaber, but if it were made a long time ago in a galaxy we live in. The type of galaxy with swords instead of lightsabers.

[86] Evidence of an amazing wedding.

[87] Nothing is easy.

[88] Badass socks with Dennis Rodman on them.

[89] Nothing is easy.

[90] The best wedding gift, by far, was the dust buster. I don't know how we ever lived without it. Our house is constantly covered in dog hair, and a handheld vacuum is a godsend.

[91] We covered Apple in ADV 412: Classic Campaigns.

[92] When JK Rowling wrote *Harry Potter and the Sorcerer's Stone*, the Marauders Map was magic; 15 years later and we all have one in our pocket.

[93] I know. You're 50,000 words into "our story" right now. I am a hypocrite. Shut up and keep reading.

[94] I remember renting *Airplane!* from Blockbuster with my friends in middle school. We watched it in Eric's basement and paused the tape during the turbulence scene when the woman streaked in front of the camera and flashed her breasts. Classic 12-year-old boy behavior.

[95] Nothing is easy-peasy.

[96] For any acquisitions editors reading this, think of the great potential for backlist sales!

[97] Don't get me wrong, I love being the youngest. The oldest may get calligraphy and a better turn out at graduations and other first in the family milestones, but that doesn't come close to the joys of being spoiled rotten for 30 years. I'll gladly tackle the Four Questions at the seder in exchange for

being the baby.

[98] Nothing is easy-peasy.

[99] I know, I'm a nerd. As such, did you catch that kickass alliteration of "eff" sounds?

[100] Trying too hard for the T sounds.

[101] Ok. I'll stop.

[102] And we got to do the whole thing all over again with thank you notes! More time, money, new addresses, new design, new spreadsheets. It never ends. It's never easy.

[103] This reference will make sense soon, I promise.

[104] I looked it up. I'm right! There are approximately 700 *Twilight Zone* parodies in *The Simpsons*.

[105] The Air and Water Show creates a lot of traffic. I wrote two other drafts of the Bridal Shower chapter but scrapped them because, upon review, they were just multiple pages of me complaining about how much time I spent in traffic that weekend.

[106] This is the best I can do to protect their identity.

[107] I was wrong.

[108] I laid it on thick, huh? Really nailed this guy.

[109] Ouch.

[110] This is the friendly way to say "Give me a refund or I won't be changing your companies name in the book."

[111] Nothing is easy like Sunday morning.

[112] Sorry. That was cringe-worthy.

[113] If, like the first editor to read through this manuscript, you're thinking, "I thought this would happen at the bridal cottage," then you have underestimated how early in the day the hair and makeup treatment begins. Alex would be hours into the process before we had access to the Addison Grove.

[114] About a month later, while watching the Golf Chanel's pre-tournament group selection coverage leading up to the 2018 Dell Technologies Match Play event in Austin, I recognized the player interviews took place by the rooftop pool at the Van Zandt. Golf! Wedding planning! Synergy!

[115] Bad pun: We had a Hook 'em Horn in our side.

[116] Worse pun: Austin, more like costin'!

[117] The exact stretch TripAdvisor identifies as optimal bat viewing season.

[118] Right, as in correct.

[119] She refuses to play me in analog backgammon these days, accusing me of cheating because I win too often. Love is never having to say, "I concede."

[120] Spoiler alert?

[121] Man oh man do I love labored golf metaphors. At least I'm past that phase where everything was about laundry.

[122] I made it about laundry!

[123] Slightly more effort went into this fake name than went into Fake Name Entertainment.

[124] Nothing is easy.

[125] In a confirmation email, they later referred to the 7-12 piece band as "impractical."

[126] The Footloose fans who picked up this book must be loving all these Footloose references.

[127] Heine and Brave Dave danced to Tom Petty's "Wildflowers."

[128] My nickname would be the Illinois Boy, and anybody who's played tennis against my dink-and-poke style would agree.

[129] My editor tells me that while Chicago was the first US city to host the cows, it was alone in breaking from the official CowParade name.

[130] I must be maturing. I didn't make a Cowmittee pun.

[131] Remember that road trip to Las Vegas when those two guys wouldn't stop cutting jokes about some girl I'd never heard of named Alex Heine? He was one of them.

[132] I was 15. We watched *Remember the Titans*.

[133] This detail may not be as universal as the rest of the scene.

[134] Not to mention I already made a joke about this movie line back in the proposal chapter.

[135] My previous experience was in Wisconsin as an adolescent. Alex assured me, as a "chillitist," that Wisconsin doesn't count as skiing.

[136] One. "I love you and I want to spend the rest of my life

with you."
[137] Nothing is easy.
[138] I'm Donkey Kong. She's Luigi.
[139] She snuck in a quote from *The Last Airbender*, too. She's the best.
[140] There's more!
[141] The Just Married mobile hasn't changed in 70 years. It's still a 1949 Plymouth.
[142] "If you're going to mention my high school back acne, can you at least credit me with dropping you off at the airport on that -57 degree night?" - My brother Dan after reading an early draft.
[143] Once, while doing this, all the hotels popped up, indicated by a tiny "H". Alex said, "Wow, look at all these hospitals!"
[144] Yet to be worn.
[145] Nothing is easy.
[146] Nothing is easy.
[147] This will make sense soon, I promise.
[148] Editor: Please don't cut this fart joke.
[149] Again, Editor, please don't cut these fart jokes!
[150] Nothing is easy.
[151] I sure as hell do.
[152] What a cool way to say "brain."
[153] Heine has since explained that the state bestowed the flag to Dave to honor Heine Farms' 100 Year Farm status.
[154] Alex isn't a fan, but the name recognition would be good for the tourists on our guestlist.
[155] No.
[156] It was fine.
[157] Al doesn't read books, but if he ever read this one, he'd say. "Holy shit, I'm glad I hired that wedding planner and didn't have to do any of this stuff."
[158] The role: walking, at the correct speed, at the correct time, to the correct place.
[159] That's another Footloose joke.
[160] Until now. Sorry, Dave.
[161] The same bag I hid the engagement ring in on the way

to Texas ten months earlier.

[162] I later realized that, since we were 30 minutes late, he must have held onto that beer for a long time. Impressive commitment.

[163] This is the friend who also ad libbed a proposal after falling down a mountain. A great candidate for speeches at a bachelor party, if not the wedding itself.

[164] *Octonauts* is a great show. You can learn a lot about marine life from this cartoon.

[165] Antonio Brown, before he lost his mind.

[166] Bare ass!

[167] Toddler socks.

[168] Nothing is easy.

[169] In retrospect, as a man who stands no more than 5'9", picking a 6'3" officiant made for some poor optics in the wedding album. He dwarfs Alex and I in photos of the ceremony.

[170] My oldest brother has two go-to party tricks. 1. He can rattle off prime numbers 2. He can rattle off *Punch Out* characters in the order you face them. Glass Joe, Von Kaiser, Piston Honda, Don Flamenco, King Hippo, Great Tiger, Bald Bull, Piston Honda 2, Soda Popinski, Bald Bull 2, Don Flamenco 2, Mr. Sandman, Super Macho Man, Mike Tyson.

[171] I hope Aaron checked with the band to make sure they knew the song, otherwise he'll have an invoice in his thank you note.

[172] Now I want to design a Jewish amusement park. Step right up, folks, be the first to ride the Seder Crusader! And there's your mother, operating the Guilt-a-Whirl. Jokes!

[173] I also asked her what advice she has for couples planning weddings. She said, "You can have it all. It's your day to be as happy as you can be, so get everything." I wrote an entire book whining about expenses and she spoke a single sentence that proves I'm wrong.

[174] Mostly Alex

ACKNOWLEDGEMENTS

This shouldn't come as much of a surprise, but I'm going to start by thanking Alex. If you haven't realized it yet, I'll use this opportunity to make sure you put this book down knowing that I am deeply in love with my wife. Alex's patience allowed me to write this book, and so did the fact that she allowed me to write this book. She never asked for her personal life to be shared like this, but she let me do it anyway. She's the best.

I'd also like to thank everyone who appears in this book. Many people and scenarios are exaggerated for effect, and I hope you'll forgive any misrepresentations. I had a lot of fun at the expense of others, but never intended to hurt feelings or damage reputations. I tried to present my experiences accurately as I remembered them.

You don't win friends with salad. You don't keep friends with memoirs. Sorry, I couldn't resist one last Simpsons joke.

Did I mention Alex? Thank you, Alex.

ABOUT THE AUTHOR

Sam Ofman

Sam Ofman is a happily married writer living in Austin, TX. He is the world's second foremost expert on the planning of his wedding. He earned an MA in Creative Writing from Northwestern University. Sam won the 2015 EyeScream Media Fiction Award for his first book, The Solutionist. Contact him at samofmanbooks-@gmail.com.

Manufactured by Amazon.ca
Bolton, ON